Classics in Semantics

CLASSICS

IN

SEMANTICS

Edited by

DONALD E. HAYDEN

and

E. PAUL ALWORTH

Philosophical Library
New York

CONTENTS

INTRODUCTION

The word "semantics" is derived from the Greek *semantikos*, meaning "significant," which is from *semainen*, to "signify or show by a sign," which in turn is from *sema*, "a sign." The word is regarded as akin to Sanskrit *dhyati*, "he thinks." It would thus appear that even in the ancient world there was thought to be a close connection between "thinking" and the use of "signs." Or, as the opening lecture in the *Ways of Mankind* series put it several years ago, "While we begin by speaking as we think, we end by thinking as we speak." More nearly to our purpose, perhaps, is C. Day Lewis's comment in *The Poet's Way of Knowledge*, "How can I tell what I mean till I see what I say?"

For many years, the word "semantics" was used to indicate the classification of changes in the signification of words. Baldwin's *Dictionary of Philosophy and Psychology*, 1901-1905, for instance, records this item under the heading of semantics: "The doctrine of historical word-meaning; the systematic discussion of the history and development of changes in the meanings of words." More recently, in the twentieth century, the meaning of the term has been extended to cover the study of the relation between signs and their referents, as well as the reaction of human beings to signs—including even the unconscious and social influences of language.

S. I. Hayakawa, editor of ETC., A Review of General Semantics, has delineated a variety of "fields" of semantics. 1. Significs. The area of logical empiricism; from Lady Welby through A. N. Whitehead, Bertrand Russell, to Rudolf Carnap and Charles Morris; 2. Pragmatism. The meanings of symbols in relation to the practical effects on human behavior; from A. B. Johnson through Charles Peirce and William James to John Dewey and George Herbert Mead; 3. Literary Criticism. The application of semantics to practical and theoretical study of literature; from I. A. Richards and C. K. Ogden to Ernst Cassirer and Susanne Langer; 4. Linguistics and Anthropology. Especially the study of American Indian languages; from Edward Sapir and Benjamin Lee Whorf and Bronislaw Malinowski to Clyde Kluckhohn and Dorothy Lee; 5. General Semantics. The area of language-thought-behavior; from Alfred Korzybski to S. I. Hayakawa and Anatol Rapoport, ETC., and the Society for General Semantics; 6. "Affiliated fields." Nondirective counseling and group dynamics—Kurt Lewin and Carl Rogers, for instance; 7. Mathematical physics and mathematical biology. The work of Nicholas Rashevsky, Anatol Rapoport, and others; 8. Cybernetics. The area of communications engineering; the work of Norbert Wiener—leading into modern "machine translators."

In the selections here, there is, of course, no attempt to be inclusive. What we have tried to do is to choose representative essays, with respect both to chronology and to theme. From Plato representing the ancient world to the contemporary writers, the selections cover a span of more than 2000 years of interest in language. They suggest both the breadth and the depth of concern about communication—about meaning—about man's most distinguishing characteristic.

ACKNOWLEDGMENTS

"Of Speech" from the book *Leviathan* by Thomas Hobbes. Everyman's Library. Reprinted by permission of E. P. Dutton and Co., Inc.

"Of Words" from the book *An Essay on Human Understanding* by John Locke. Introduction and editing, 1961, by J. M. Dent and Sons, Ltd. Everyman's Library. Reprinted by permission of E. P. Dutton and Co., Inc.

"Introduction" from the book *A New Theory of Vision and Other Writings* by George Berkeley. Everyman's Library. Reprinted by permission of E. P. Dutton and Co., Inc.

"Of the Origin of Our Ideas" from the book *A Treatise of Human Nature* by David Hume. Everyman's Library. Reprinted by permission of E. P. Dutton and Co., Inc.

"Of Definition" from *A System of Logic* by John Stuart Mill. Reprinted by permission of Longmans, Green and Co., Ltd.

"Fashions in Language" from the book *Words and Their Ways in English Speech* by J. B. Greenough and G. L. Kittrodge. Reprinted by permission of the Macmillan Company.

"The Object of Linguistics" by Ferdinand de Saussure from the book *Course in General Linguistics*. Reprinted by permission of the Philosophical Library.

"Thoughts, Words, and Things" reprinted from *The Meaning of Meaning* by C. K. Ogden and I. A. Richards by permission of Harcourt, Brace and World, Inc.

Cratylus

Plato

Many of the Greeks had much to say about language. In his dialogue, *Cratylus*, Plato pictures Socrates, Hermogenes, and Cratylus in a discussion on the nature of names. While here as elsewhere, it is impossible to tell where Socrates leaves off and Plato begins, we may assume that the thinking reflected general aspects of Greek thought.

Plato was born in 427 B.C. and died 347 B.C. Both sides of his family were distinguished Athenians in the Age of Pericles. Of the greatest importance in his life was his relationship to Socrates. The founding of the Academy marked a significant point in his development.

In the selections from *Cratylus* below, omissions are indicated by (. . .). The translation is that of the famous nineteenth century British scholar, Benjamin Jowett.

H*ermogenes.* Suppose that we make Socrates a party to the argument?

Cratylus. If you please.

Her. I should explain to you, Socrates, that our friend Cratylus has been arguing about names; he says that they are natural and not conventional; not a portion of the human voice which men agree to use; but that there is a truth or correctness in them, which is the same for Hellenes as for barbarians. Whereupon I ask him, whether his own name of Cratylus is a true name or not, and he answers 'Yes.' And Socrates? 'Yes.' Then every man's name, as I tell him, is that which he is called. To this he replies—'If all the world were to call you Hermogenes, that would not be your name.' And when I am anxious to have a further explanation he is ironical and mysterious, and seems to imply that he has a notion of his own about the matter, if he would only tell, and could entirely convince me, if he chose to be intelligible. Tell me, Socrates, what this oracle means; or rather tell me, if you will be so good, what is your own view of the truth or correctness of names, which I would far sooner hear.

Socrates. Son of Hipponicus, there is an ancient saying, that 'hard is the knowledge of the good.' And the knowledge of names is a great part of knowledge. If I had not been poor, I might have heard the fifty-drachma course of the great Prodicus, which is a complete education in grammar and language—these are his own words—and then I should have been at once able to answer your question about the correctness of names. But, indeed, I have only heard the single-drachma course, and therefore, I do not know the truth about such matters; I will, however, gladly assist you and Cratylus in the investigation of them. When he declares that your name is not really Hermogenes, I suspect that he is only making fun of you;—he means to say that you are no true son of Hermes, because you are always looking after a fortune and never in luck. But, as I was saying, there is a good deal of difficulty in this sort of knowledge, and therefore we had better leave the question open until we have heard both sides.

Her. I have often talked over this matter, both with Cratylus and others, and cannot convince myself that there is any principle of correctness in names other than convention and agreement; any name which you give, in my opinion, is the right one, and if you change that and give another, the new name is as correct as the old—we frequently change the names of our slaves, and the newly-imposed name is as good as the old: for there is no name given to anything but nature; all is convention and habit of the users; —such is my view. But if I am mistaken I shall be happy to hear and learn of Cratylus, or of any one else.

Soc. I dare say that you may be right, Hermogenes: let

us see;—Your meaning is, that the name of each thing is only that which anybody agrees to call it?

Her. That is my notion.

Soc. Whether the giver of the name be an individual or a city?

Her. Yes.

Soc. Well, now, let me take an instance;—suppose that I call a man a horse or a horse a man, you mean to say that a man will be rightly called a horse by me individually, and rightly called a man by the rest of the world; and a horse again would be rightly called a man by me and a horse by the world;—that is your meaning?

Her. He would, according to my view. . . .

Soc. And will there be so many names of each thing as everybody says that there are? and will they be true names at the time of uttering them?

Her. Yes, Socrates, I can conceive no correctness of names other than this; you give one name, and I another; and in different cities and countries there are different names for the same things; Hellenes differ from barbarians in their use of names, and the several Hellenic tribes from one another.

Soc. But would you say, Hermogenes, that the things differ as the names differ? and are they relative to individuals, as Protagoras tells us? For he says that man is the measure of all things, and that things are to me as they appear to me, and that they are to you as they appear to you. Do you agree with him, or would you say that things have a permanent essence of their own?

Her. There have been times, Socrates, when I have been driven in my perplexity to take refuge with Protagoras; not that I agree with him at all.

Soc. What! have you ever been driven to admit that there was no such thing as a bad man?

Her. No, indeed; but I have often had reason to think that there are very bad men, and a good many of them.

Soc. Well, and have you ever found any very good ones?

Her. Not many.

Soc. Still you have found them?

Her. Yes.

Soc. And would you hold that the very good were the very wise, and the very evil very foolish? Would that be your view?

Her. It would.

Soc. But if Protagoras is right, and the truth is that things are as they appear to any one, how can some of us be wise and some of us foolish?

Her. Impossible.

Soc. And if, on the other hand, wisdom and folly are really distinguishable, you will allow, I think, that the assertion of Protagoras can hardly be correct. For if what appears to each man is true to him, one man cannot in reality be wiser than another.

Her. He cannot.

Soc. Nor will you be disposed to say with Euthydemus, that all things equally belong to all men at the same moment and always; for neither of his view can there be some good and others bad, if virtue and vice are always equally to be attributed to all.

Her. There cannot.

Soc. But if neither is right, and things are not relative to individuals, and all things do not equally belong to all at the same moment and always, they must be supposed to have their own proper and permanent essence: they are not in relation to us, or influenced by us, fluctuating according to our fancy, but they are independent, and maintain to their own essence the relation prescribed by nature.

Her. I think, Socrates, that you have said the truth.

Soc. Does what I am saying apply only to the things themselves, or equally to the actions which proceed from them? Are not actions also a class of being?

Her. Yes, the actions are real as well as the things.

Soc. Then the actions also are done according to their proper nature, and not according to our opinion of them? In cutting, for example, we do not cut as we please, and with any chance instrument; but we cut with the proper instrument only, and according to the natural process of cutting; and the natural process is right and will succeed, but any other will fail and be of no use at all.

Her. I should say that the natural way is the right way.

Soc. Again, in burning, not every way is the right way; but the right way is the natural way, and the right instrument the natural instrument.

Her. True.

Soc. And this holds good of all actions?

Her. Yes.

Soc. And speech is a kind of action?

Her. True.

Soc. And will a man speak correctly who speaks as he pleases? Will not the successful speaker rather be he who speaks in the natural way of speaking, and as things ought to be spoken, and with the natural instrument? Any other mode of speaking will result in error and failure.

Her. I quite agree with you.

Soc. And is not naming a part of speaking? for in giving names men speak.

Her. That is true.

Soc. And if speaking is a sort of action and has a relation to acts, is not naming also a sort of action?

Her. True.

Soc. And we saw that actions were not relative to ourselves, but had a special nature of their own?

Her. Precisely.

Soc. Then the argument would lead us to infer that names ought to be given according to a natural process, and with a proper instrument, and not at our pleasure: in this and no other way shall we name with success.

Her. I agree. . . .

Soc. Then, Hermogenes, I should imagine this giving of names to be no such light matter as you fancy, or the work of light or chance persons; and Cratylus is right in saying that things have names by nature, and that not every man is an artificer of names, but he only who looks to the name which each thing by nature has, and is able to express the true forms of things in letters and syllables. . . .

Her. But I wish that you would tell me, Socrates, what sort of an imitation is a name?

Soc. In the first place, I should reply, not a musical imitation, although that is also vocal; nor, again, an imitation of what music imitates; these, in my judgment, would not be naming. Let me put the matter as follows: All objects have sound and figure, and many have colour?

Her. Certainly.

Soc. But the art of naming appears not to be concerned with imitations of this kind; the arts which have to do with them are music and drawing?

Her. True.

Soc. Again, is there not an essence of each thing, just as there is a colour, or sound? And is there not an essence of colour and sound as well as of anything else which may be said to have an essence?

Her. I should think so.

Soc. Well, and if any one could express the essence of each thing in letters and syllables, would he not express the nature of each thing?

Her. Quite so.

Soc. The musician and the painter were the two names which you gave to the two other imitators. What will this imitator be called?

Her. I imagine, Socrates, that he must be the namer, or name-giver, of whom we are in search.

Soc. If this is true, then I think that we are in a condition to consider the names ῥοη (stream), ἰέναι (to go), σχέσις (retention), about which you were asking; and we may see whether the namer has grasped the nature of them in letters and syllables in such a manner as to imitate the essence or not.

Her. Very good.

Soc. But are these the only primary names, or are there others?

Her. There must be others.

Soc. So I should expect. But how shall we further analyse them, and where does the imitator begin? Imitation of the essence is made by syllables and letters; ought we not, therefore, first to separate the letters, just as those who are beginning rhythm first distinguish the powers of elementary, and then of compound sounds, and when they have done so, but not before, they proceed to the consideration of rhythms?

Her. Yes.

Soc. Must we not begin in the same way with letters; first separating the vowels, and then the consonants and mutes,[1] into classes, according to the received distinctions of the learned; also the semi-vowels, which are neither vowels, nor yet mutes; and distinguishing into classes the vowels themselves? And when we have perfected the classification of things, we shall give them names, and see whether, as in the case of letters, there are any classes to which they may be all referred; and hence we shall see their natures, and see, too, whether they have in them classes as there are in the letters; and when we have well considered all this, we shall know how to apply them to what they resemble— whether one letter is used to denote one thing, or whether there is to be an admixture of several of them; just, as in painting, the painter who wants to depict anything sometimes uses purple only, or any other colour, and sometimes mixes up several colours, as his method is when he has to paint flesh colour or anything of that kind—he uses his colours as his figures appear to require them; and so, too, we shall apply letters to the expression of objects, either single letters when required, or several letters; and so we shall form syllables, as they are called, and from syllables make nouns and verbs; and thus, at last, from the combinations of nouns and verbs arrive at language, large and fair and whole; and as the painter made a figure, even so shall we

---

[1] Letters which are neither vowels nor semivowels.

make speech by the art of the namer or the rhetorician, or by some other art. Not that I am literally speaking of ourselves, but I was carried away—meaning to say that this was the way in which (not we but) the ancients formed language, and what they put together we must take to pieces in like manner, if we are to attain a scientific view of the whole subject; and we must see whether the primary and also whether the secondary elements are rightly given or not, for if they are not, the composition of them, my dear Hermogenes, will be a sorry piece of work, and in the wrong direction.

Her. That, Socrates, I can quite believe.

Soc. Well, but do you suppose that you will be able to analyse them in this way? for I am certain that I should not.

Her. Much less am I likely to be able.

Soc. Shall we leave them, then? or shall we seek to discover, if we can, something about them, according to the measure of our ability, saying by way of preface, as I said before of the Gods, that of the truth about them we know nothing, and do but entertain human notions of them. And in this present enquiry, let us say to ourselves, before we proceed, that the higher method is the one which we or others who would analyse language to any good purpose must follow; but under the circumstances, as men say, we must do as well as we can. What do you think?

Her. I very much approve.

Soc. That objects should be imitated in letters and syllables, and so find expression, may appear ridiculous, Hermogenes, but it cannot be avoided—there is no better principle to which we can look for the truth of first names. Deprived of this we must have recourse to divine help, like the tragic poets, who in any perplexity have their gods waiting in the air; and must get out of our difficulty in like fashion, by saying that 'the Gods gave the first names, and therefore they are right'. This will be the best contrivance, or perhaps that other notion may be even better still, of deriving them from some barbarous people, for the bar-

barians are older than we are; or we may say that antiquity
has cast a veil over them, which is the same sort of excuse
as the last; for all these are not reasons but only ingenious
excuses for having no reasons concerning the truth of words.
And yet any sort of ignorance of first or primitive names
involves an ignorance of secondary words; for they can
only be explained by the primary. Clearly then the professor of languages should be able to give a very lucid
explanation of first names, or let him be assured he will only
talk nonsense about the rest. Do you not suppose this to
be true?

Her. Certainly, Socrates.

Soc. My first notions of original names are truly wild and
ridiculous, though I have no objection to impart them to
you if you desire, and I hope that you will communicate to
me in return anything better which you may have.

Her. Fear not; I will do my best.

Soc. In the first place, the letter ῥ appears to me to be the
general instrument expressing all motion (κινησις). But I
have not yet explained the meaning of this latter word,
which is just ιεσις (going); for the letter η was not in use
among the ancients, who only employed ε; and the root is
κιειν which is a foreign form, the same as ιεναι. And the old
word κινησις will be correctly given as ιεσις in corresponding
modern letters. Assuming this foreign root κιειν, and allowing for the change of the η and the insertion of the ν, we
have κινησις, which should have been κιεινησις or εισις; and
στασις is the negative of ιεναι (or εισις), and has been improved into στασις. Now the letter ῥ as I was saying, appeared to
the imposer of names an excellent instrument for the expression of motion; and he frequently uses the letter for
this purpose: for example, in the actual words ῥειν and   ῥοη
he represents motion by ῥ; also in the words τρουσ (tremb-
ling), τραχυς (rugged); and again, in words such as κρουειν
(strike) σραυειν (crush), ἐρείκιν (bruise), θρύπτειν (break),
κερματίζειγ (crumble), ῥυμβειν (whirl): of all these sorts of
movements he generally finds an expression in the letter R,

because, as I imagine, he had observed that the tongue was most agitated and least at rest in the pronunciation of this letter, which he therefore used in order to express motion, just as by the letter ι he expresses the subtle elements which pass through all things. This is why he uses the letter ι as imitative of motion, ιεναί, ιεσθαί. And there is another class of letters, Φ, ψ, σ and ς, of which the pronunciation is accompanied by great expenditure of breath; these are used in the imitation of such notions as φνχρὸν (shivering), ζέον (seething), σείεσθαι (to be shaken), σεισμὸς (shock), and are always introduced by the giver of names when he wants to imitate what is Φνσῶδες (windy). He seems to have thought that the closing and pressure of the tongue in the utterance of δ and τ was expressive of binding and rest in a place: he further observed the liquid movement of λ, in the pronunciation of which the tongue slips, and in this he found the expression of smoothness, as in λειοs (level), and in the word ὀλισθάνειν (to slip) itself, λιπαρὸν (sleek), in the word κολλῶδες (gluey), and the like: the heavier sound of γ detained the slipping tongue, and the union of the two gave the notion of a glutinous clammy nature, as in γλίσχρος, γλνκνς, γλοιῶδες. The ν he observed to be sounded from within, and therefore to have a notion of inwardness; hence he introduced the sound in ενδον and ἐντος:α he assigned to the expression of size, and η of length, because they are great letters: *o* was the sign of roundness, and therefore there is plenty of *o* mixed up in the word γογγνλον (round). Thus did the legislator, reducing all things into letters and syllables, and impressing on them names and signs, and out of them by imitation compounding other signs. That is my view, Hermogenes, of the truth of names; but I should like to hear what Cratylus has more to say.

Her. But, Socrates, as I was telling you before, Cratylus mystifies me; he says that there is a fitness of names, but he never explains what is this fitness, so that I cannot tell whether his obscurity is intended or not. Tell me now, Cratylus, here in the presence of Socrates, do you agree in what Socrates has been saying about names, or have you something better of your own? and if you have, tell me what your view is, and then you will either learn of Socrates, or Socrates and I will learn of you.

Crat. Well, but surely, Hermogenes, you do not suppose that you can learn, or I explain, any subject of importance all in a moment; or any rate, not such a subject as language, which is, perhaps, the very greatest of all. . . .

Soc. Now then, as I am desirous that we being friends should have a good understanding about the argument, let me state my view to you: the first mode of assignment whether applied to figures or to names, I call right, and when applied to names only, true as well as right; and the other mode, of giving and assigning the name which is unlike, I call wrong, and in the case of names, false as well as wrong.

Crat. That may be true, Socrates, in the case of pictures; they may be wrongly assigned but not in the case of names —must they not always be right?

Soc. Why, what is the difference? May I not go to a man and say to him, 'This is your picture,' showing him his own likeness, or perhaps the likeness of a woman; and when I say 'show,' I mean bring before the sense of sight.

Crat. Certainly.

Soc. And may I not go to him again, and say, 'This is your name'?—for the name, like the picture, is an imitation. May I not say to him—'This is your name'? and may I not then bring to his sense of hearing the imitation of himself by saying, 'This is a man;' or of a female of the human species, by saying, 'This is a woman,' as the case may be? Is not all that quite possible?

Crat. I would fain agree with you, Socrates; and therefore I say, Granted.

Soc. That is very good of you, if I am right, which need hardly be disputed at present. But if I can assign names as well as pictures to objects, the right assignment of them we may call truth, and the wrong assignment of them falsehood. Now if there be such a wrong assignment of names, there may also be a wrong or inappropriate assignment of verbs; and if of names and verbs then of the sentences, which are made up of them. What do you say, Cratylus?

Crat. I agree; and think that what you say is very true.

Soc. And further, primitive nouns may be compared to pictures, and in pictures you may either give all the appropriate colours and figures, or you may not give them all—some may be wanting; or there may be too many or too much of them—may there not?

Crat. Very true. . . .

Soc. But let me ask you, what is the force of names, and what is the use of them?

Crat. The use of names, Socrates, as I should imagine, is to inform: the simple truth is, that he who knows names knows also the things which are expressed by them.

Soc. I suppose you mean to say, Cratylus, that as the name is, so also is the thing; and that he who knows the one will also know the other, because they are similars, and all similars fall under the same art or science; and therefore you would say that he who knows names will also know things.

Crat. That is precisely what I mean.

Soc. But let us consider what is the nature of this information about things which, according to you, is given us by names. Is it the best sort of information? or is there any other? What do you say?

Crat. I believe it to be both the only and the best sort of information about them; there can be no other.

Soc. But do you believe that in the discovery of them, he who discovers the names discovers also the things; or is this only the method of instruction, and is there some other method of enquiry and discovery?

Crat. I certainly believe that the methods of enquiry and discovery are of the same nature as instruction.

Soc. Well, but do you not see, Cratylus, that he who follows names in the search after things, and analyses their meaning, is in great danger of being deceived?

Crat. How so?

Soc. Why clearly he who first gave names gave them according to his conception of the things which they signified —did he not?

Crat. True.

Soc. And if his conception was erroneous, and he gave names according to his conception, in what position shall we who are his followers find ourselves? Shall we not be deceived by him?

Crat. But, Socrates, am I not right in thinking that he must surely have known; or else, as I was saying, his names would not be names at all? And you have a clear proof that he has not missed the truth, and the proof is—that he is perfectly consistent. Did you ever observe in speaking that all the words which you utter have a common character and purpose?

Soc. But that, friend Cratylus, is no answer. For if he did begin in error, he may have forced the remainder into agreement with the original error and with himself; there would be nothing strange in this, any more than in geometrical diagrams, which have often a slight and invisible flaw in the first part of the process, and are consistently mistaken in the long deductions which follow. And this is the reason why every man should expend his chief thought and attention on the consideration of first principles:—are they or are they not rightly laid down? and when he has duly sifted them, all the rest will follow.

Novum Organum

Francis Bacon

Born in 1561, Francis Bacon came from an illustrious family on both sides. His father, Sir Nicholas Bacon, was Keeper of the Great Seal; his mother was a sister of Lord Burghley. At age twelve, Bacon entered Cambridge University; at age sixteen he went to France with the Queen's ambassador. He returned to England, applied himself to the study of law and in 1584 was elected to Parliament. In years to follow, he became the friend to Lord Essex, but accepted albeit reluctantly a commission in 1601 to assist in the prosecution of his patron and friend. He was knighted by James I and in 1605 he published his *Advancement of Learning*. Later works were the *Novum Organum;* the *History of Henry VII; New Atlantis; Instauratio Magna;* and the *Essays*. He became Keeper of the Great Seal and subsequently Lord Chancellor. Accused of accepting bribes, he was removed from office and lived quietly until his death in 1626. The selection from Bacon used here is from *Novum Organum,* paragraphs 38 to 62 inclusive.

XXXVIII

T HE idols and false notions which are now in possession of the human understanding, and have taken deep root therein, not only beset men's minds that truth can hardly find entrance, but even after entrance obtained, they will again in the very instauration of the sciences meet and trouble us, unless men being forewarned of the danger fortify themselves as far as may be against their assaults.

XXXIX

There are four classes of idols which beset men's minds. To these for distinction's sake I have assigned names,—calling the first class *Idols of the Tribe;* the second, *Idols of the Cave;* the third, *Idols of the Market-place;* the fourth, *Idols of the Theater.*

XL

The formation of ideas and axioms by true induction is no doubt the proper remedy to be applied for the keeping off and clearing away of idols. To point them out, however, is of great use, for the doctrine of idols is to the interpretation of nature what the doctrine of the refutation of sophisms is to common logic.

XLI

The Idols of the Tribe have their foundation in human nature itself, and in the tribe or race of men. For it is a false assertion that the sense of man is the measure of things. On the contrary, all perceptions, as well of the sense as of the mind, are according to the measure of the individual and not according to the measure of the universe. And the human understanding is like a false mirror, which, receiving rays irregularly, distorts and discolors the nature of things by mingling its own nature with it.

XLII

The Idols of the Cave are the idols of the individual man. For everyone (besides the errors common to human nature in general) has a cave or den of his own, which refracts and discolors the light of nature; owing either to his own proper and peculiar nature or to his education and conversation with others; or to the reading of books, and the authority of those whom he esteems and admires; or to the differences of impressions, accordingly as they take place in a mind preoccupied and predisposed or in a mind indifferent and settled;

or the like. So that the spirit of man (according as it is meted out to different individuals) is in fact a thing variable and full of perturbation, and governed as it were by chance. Whence it was well observed by Heraclitus that men look for sciences in their own lesser worlds, and not in the greater or common world.

XLIII

There are also idols formed by the intercourse and association of men with each other, which I call Idols of the Marketplace, on account of the commerce and consort of men there. For it is by discourse that men associate; and words are imposed according to the apprehension of the vulgar. And therefore the ill and unfit choice of words wonderfully obstructs the understanding. Nor do the definitions or explanations wherewith in some things learned men are wont to guard and defend themselves, by any means set the matter right. But words plainly force and overrule the understanding, and throw all into confusion, and lead men away into numberless empty controversies and idle fancies.

XLIV

Lastly, there are idols which have immigrated into men's minds from the various dogmas of philosophies, and also from wrong laws of demonstration. These I call Idols of the Theater; because in my judgment all the received systems are but so many stage-plays, representing worlds of their own creation after an unreal and scenic fashion. Nor is it only of the systems now in vogue, or only of the ancient sects and philosophies, that I speak: for many more plays of the same kind may yet be composed and in like artificial manner set forth; seeing that errors the most widely different have nevertheless causes for the most part alike. Neither again do I mean this only of entire systems, but also of many principles and axioms in science, which by tradition, credulity, and negligence have come to be received.

But of these several kinds of idols I must speak more largely and exactly, that the understanding may be duly cautioned.

XLV

The human understanding is of its own nature prone to suppose the existence of more order and regularity in the world than it finds. And though there be many things in nature which are singular and unmatched, yet it devises for them parallels and conjugates and relatives which do not exist. Hence the fiction that all celestial bodies move in perfect circles; spirals and dragons being (except in name) utterly rejected. Hence too the element of fire with its orb is brought in, to make up the square with the other three which the sense perceives. Hence also the ratio of density of the so-called elements is arbitrarily fixed at ten to one. And so on of other dreams. And these fancies affect not dogmas only, but simple notions also.

XLVI

The human understanding when it has once adopted an opinion (either as being the received opinion or as being agreeable to itself) draws all things else to support and agree with it. And though there be a greater number and weight of instances to be found on the other side, yet these it either neglects and despises, or else by some distinction sets aside and rejects; in order that by this great and pernicious predetermination the authority of its former conclusions may remain inviolate. And therefore it was a good answer that was made by one who when they showed him hanging in a temple a picture of those who had paid their vows as having escaped shipwreck, and would have him say whether he did now acknowledge the power of the gods,—"Aye," asked he again, "but where are they painted that were drowned after their vows?" And such is the way of all superstition, whether in astrology, dreams, omens, divine judgments, or the like; wherein men, having a delight in such vanities, mark the events where they are fulfilled, but where they fail, though this happen much oftener, neglect and pass them by. But with far more subtlety does this mischief insinuate itself into philosophy and the sciences; in which the first conclusion colors and brings into conformity with itself all that come after, though far sounder and better. Besides, independently of that delight and vanity which I have described, it is the peculiar and perpetual error of the human intellect to be more moved and excited by affirmatives than by negatives; whereas it ought properly to hold itself indifferently disposed towards both alike. Indeed in the establishment of any true axiom, the negative instance is the more forcible of the two.

XLVII

The human understanding is moved by those things most which strike and enter the mind simultaneously and suddenly, and so fill the imagination; and then it feigns and supposes all other things to be somehow, though it cannot see how, similar to those few things by which it is surrounded. But for that going to and fro to remote and heterogeneous instances, by which axioms are tried as in the fire, the intellect is altogether slow and unfit, unless it be forced thereto by severe laws and overruling authority.

XLVIII

The human understanding is unquiet; it cannot stop or rest, and still presses onward, but in vain. Therefore it is that we cannot conceive of any end or limit to the world; but always as of necessity it occurs to us that there is something beyond. Neither again can it be conceived how eternity has flowed down to the present day: for that distinction which is commonly received of infinity in time past and in time to come can by no means hold; for it would thence follow that one infinity is greater than another, and that infinity is wasting away and tending to become finite. The like subtlety arises touching the infinite divisibility of lines, from the same inability of thought to stop. But this inability interferes more mischievously in the discovery of causes; for although the most general principles in nature ought to be held merely positive, as they are discovered, and cannot, with truth be referred to a cause; nevertheless the human understanding being unable to rest still seeks something prior in the order of nature. And then it is that in struggling towards that which is further off it falls back upon that which is more nigh at hand,— namely, on final causes; which have relation clearly to the nature of man rather than to the nature of the universe, and from this source have strangely defiled philosophy. But he is no less an unskilled and shallow philosopher who seeks causes of that which is most general, than he who in things subordinate and subaltern omits to do so.

XLIX

The human understanding is no dry light, but receives an infusion from the will and affections, whence proceed sciences which may be called "sciences as one would." For what a man had rather were true he more readily believes. Therefore he rejects difficult things from impatience of research; sober things, because they narrow hope; the deeper things of nature, from superstition; the light of experience, from arrogance and pride, lest his mind should seem to be occupied with things mean and transitory; things not commonly believed, out of deference to the opinion of the vulgar. Numberless in short are the ways, and sometimes imperceptible, in which the affections color and infect the understanding.

L

But by far the greatest hindrance and aberration of the human understanding proceeds from the dullness, incompetency, and deceptions of the senses; in that things which strike the sense outweigh things which do not immediately strike it, though they be more important. Hence it is that speculation commonly ceases where sight ceases, insomuch that of things invisible there is little or no observation. Hence all the working of the spirits inclosed in tangible bodies lies hid and unobserved of men. So also all the more subtle changes of form in the parts of coarser substances (which they commonly call alteration, though it is in truth local motion through exceedingly small spaces) is in like manner unobserved. And yet unless these two things just mentioned be searched out and brought to light, nothing great can be achieved in nature, as far as the production of works is concerned. So again the essential nature of our common air, and of all bodies less dense than air (which are very many), is almost unknown. For the sense by itself is a thing infirm and erring; neither can instruments for enlarging or sharpening the senses do much: but all the truer kind of interpretation of nature is effected by instances and experiments fit and opposite; wherein the sense decides touching the experiment only, and the experiment touching the point in nature and the thing itself.

LI

The human understanding is of its own nature prone to abstractions and gives a substance and reality to things which are fleeting. But to resolve nature into abstractions is less to our purpose than to dissect her into parts; as did the school of Democritus, which went further into nature than the rest. Matter rather than forms should be the object of our attention, its configurations and changes of configuration, and simple action, and law of action or motion; for forms are figments of the human mind, unless you will call those laws of action forms.

LII

Such then are the idols which I call Idols of the Tribe; and which take their rise either from the homogeneity of the substance of the human spirit, or from its preoccupation, or from its narrowness, or from its restless motion, or from an infusion of the affections, or from the incompetency of the senses, or from the mode of impression.

LIII

The Idols of the Cave take their rise in the peculiar constitution, mental or bodily, of each individual; and also in education, habit, and accident. Of this kind there is a great number and variety; but I will instance those the pointing out of which contains the most important caution, and which have most effect in disturbing the clearness of the under-standing.

LIV

Men become attached to certain particular sciences and speculations, either because they fancy themselves the authors and inventors thereof, or because they have bestowed the greatest pains upon them and become most habituated to them. But men of this kind, if they betake themselves to philosophy and contemplations of a general character, distort and color them in obedience to their former fancies; a thing especially to be noticed in Aristotle, who made his natural philosophy a mere bondservant to his logic, thereby rendering it contentious and well nigh useless. The race of chemists again out of a few experiments of the furnace have built up a fantastic philosophy, framed with reference to a few things; and Gilbert also, after he had employed himself most laboriously in the study and observation of the lodestone, proceeded at once to construct an entire system in accordance with his favorite subject.

LV

There is one principal and as it were radical distinction between different minds, in respect of philosophy and the sciences; which is this: that some minds are stronger and apter to mark the differences of things, others to mark their resemblances. The steady and acute mind can fix its contemplations and dwell and fasten on the subtlest distinctions; the lofty and discursive mind recognizes and puts together the finest and most general resemblances. Both kinds however easily err in excess, by catching the one at gradations, the other at shadows.

LVI

There are found some minds given to an extreme admiration of antiquity, others to an extreme love and appetite for novelty; but few so duly tempered that they can hold the mean, neither carping at what has been well laid down by the ancients, nor despising what is well introduced by the moderns. This however turns to the great injury of the sciences and philosophy: since these affectations of antiquity and novelty are the humors of partisans rather than judgments; and truth is to be sought for not in the felicity of any age, which is an unstable thing, but in the light of nature and experience, which is eternal. These factions therefore must be adjured, and care must be taken that the intellect be not hurried by them into assent.

LVII

Contemplations of nature and of bodies in their simple form break up and distract the understanding, while contemplations of nature and bodies in their composition and configuration overpower and dissolve the understanding: a distinction well seen in the school of Leucippus and Democritus as compared with the other philosophies. For that school is so busied with the particles that it hardly attends to the structure; while the others are so lost in admiration of the structure that they do not penetrate to the simplicity of nature. These kinds of contemplation should therefore be alternated and taken by turns; that so the understanding may be rendered at once penetrating and comprehensive, and the inconveniences above mentioned, with the idols which proceed from them, may be avoided.

LVIII

Let such then be our provision and contemplative prudence for keeping off and dislodging the Idols of the Cave, which grow for the most part either out of the predominance of a favorite subject, or out of an excessive tendency to compare or to distinguish, or out of partiality for particular ages, or out of the largeness or minuteness of the objects contemplated. And generally let every student of nature take this as a rule,—that whatever his mind seizes and dwells upon with peculiar satisfaction is to be held in suspicion, and that so much the more care is to be taken in dealing with such questions to keep the understanding even and clear.

LIX

But the Idols of the Market-place are the most troublesome of all: idols which have crept into the understanding through the alliances of words and names. For men believe that their reason governs words; but it is also true that words react on the understanding; and this it is that has rendered philosophy and the sciences sophistical and inactive. Now words, being commonly framed and applied according to the capacity of the vulgar, follow those lines of division which are most obvious to the vulgar understanding. And whenever an understanding of greater acuteness or a more diligent observation would alter those lines to suit the true divisions of nature, words stand in the way and resist the change. Whence it comes to pass that the high and formal discussions of learned men end oftentimes in disputes about words and names; with which (according to the use and wisdom of the mathematicians) it would be more prudent to begin, and so by means of definitions reduce them to order. Yet even definitions cannot cure this evil in dealing with natural and material things; since the definitions themselves consist of words, and those words beget others: so that it is necessary to recur to individual instances, and those in due series and order; as I shall say presently when I come to the method and scheme for the information of notions and axioms.

LX

The idols imposed by words on the understanding are of two kinds. They are either names of things which do not exist (for as there are things left unnamed through lack of observation, so likewise are there names which result from fantastic suppositions and to which nothing in reality corresponds), or they are names of things which exist, but yet confused and ill-defined, and hastily and irregularly derived from realities. Of the former kind are Fortune, the Prime Mover, Planetary Orbits, Elements of Fire, and like fictions which owe their origin to false and idle theories. And this class of idols is more easily expelled, because to get rid of them it is only necessary that all theories should be steadily rejected and dismissed as obsolete.

But the other class, which springs out of a faulty and unskillful abstraction, is intricate and deeply rooted. Let us take for example such a word as humid, and see how far the several things which the word is used to signify agree with each other; and we shall find the word humid to be nothing else than a mark loosely and confusedly applied to denote a variety of actions which will not bear to be reduced to any constant meaning. For it both signifies that which easily spreads itself round any other body; and that which in itself is indeterminate and cannot solidize; and that which readily yields in every direction; and that which easily divides and scatters itself; and that which easily unites and collects itself; and that which readily flows and is put in motion; and that which readily clings to another body and wets it; and that which is easily reduced to a liquid, or being solid easily melts. Accordingly when you come to apply the word,—if you take it in one sense, flame is humid; if in another, air is not humid; if in another, fine dust is humid; if in another, glass is humid. So that it is easy to see that the notion is taken by abstraction only from water and common and ordinary liquids, without any due verification.

There are however in words certain degrees of distortion and error. One of the least faulty kinds is that of names of substances, especially of lowest species and well-deduced (for the notion of chalk and of mud is good, of earth bad); a more faulty kind is that of actions, as to generate, to corrupt, to alter; the most faulty is of qualities (except such as are the immediate objects of the sense) as heavy, light, rare, dense, and the like. Yet in all these cases some notions are of necessity a little better than others, in proportion to the greater variety of subjects that fall within the range of the human sense.

LXI

But the Idols of the Theater are not innate, nor do they steal into the understanding secretly, but are plainly impressed and received into the mind from the play-books of philosophical systems and the perverted rules of demonstration. To attempt refutations in this case would be merely inconsistent with what I have already said: for since we agree neither upon principles nor upon demonstrations there is no place for argument. And this is so far well, inasmuch as it leaves the honor of the ancients untouched. For they are no wise disparaged—the question between them and me being only as to the way. For as the saying is, the lame man who keeps the right road outstrips the runner who takes a wrong one. Nay it is obvious that when a man runs the wrong way, the more active and swift he is the further he will go astray.

But the course I propose for the discovery of science is such as leaves but little to the acuteness and strength of wits, but places all wits and understandings nearly on a level. For as in the drawing of a straight line or a perfect circle, much depends on the steadiness and practice of the hand, if it be done by aim of hand only, but if with the aid of rule or compass, little or nothing; so is it exactly with my plan. But though particular confutations would be of no avail, yet touching the sects and general divisions of such systems I must say something; something also touching the external signs which show that they are unsound; and finally something touching the causes of such great infelicity and of such lasting and general agreement in error; that so the access to truth may be made less difficult, and the human understanding may the more willingly submit to its purgation and dismiss its idols.

LXII

Idols of the Theater, or of Systems, are many, and there can be and perhaps will be yet many more. For were it not that now for many ages men's minds have been busied with religion and theology; and were it not that civil governments, especially monarchies, have been averse to such novelties, even in matters speculative; so that men labor therein to the peril and harming of their fortunes,—not only unrewarded, but exposed also to contempt and envy: doubtless there would have arisen many other philosophical sects like to those which in great variety flourished once among the Greeks. For as on the phenomena of the heavens many hypotheses may be constructed, so likewise (and more also) many various dogmas may be set up and established on the phenomena of philosophy. And in the plays of this philosophical theater you may observe the same thing which is found in the theater of the poets, that stories invented for the stage are more compact and elegant, and more as one would wish them to be, than true stories out of history.

In general however there is taken for the material of philosophy either a great deal out of a few things, or a very little out of many things; so that on both sides philosophy is based on too narrow a foundation of experiment and natural history, and decides on the authority of too few cases. For the rational school of philosophers snatches from experience a variety of common instances, neither duly ascertained nor diligently examined and weighed, and leaves all the rest to meditation and agitation of wit.

There is also another class of philosophers, who having bestowed much diligent and careful labor on a few experiments, have thence made bold to educe and construct systems; wresting all other facts in a strange fashion to conformity therewith.

And there is yet a third class, consisting of those who out of faith and veneration mix their philosophy with theology and traditions; among whom the vanity of some has gone so far aside as to seek the origin of science among spirits and genii. So that this parent stock of errors—this false philosophy —is of three kinds; the sophistical, the empirical, and the superstitious.

"Of Speech"

Thomas Hobbes

Son of a poor English Vicar, Thomas Hobbes was born in 1588. He lived a long and active life of 91 years. He was educated at Oxford at a time when scholasticism still held sway—mathematics, for example, being considered a "black art." For many years he served the family of the Earl of Devonshire as tutor both in England and on the Continent. His works on politics and metaphysics were the center of considerable controversy, even in his lifetime. His best known work, *Leviathan, or, The Matter, Form and Power, of a Commonwealth,* came out in 1651. The selection here is Chapter IV from the book *Leviathan* by Thomas Hobbes. The text used is Everyman's Library edition. Reprinted by permission of E. P. Dutton & Co., Inc.

THE Invention of *Printing,* though ingenious, compared with the invention of *Letters,* is no great matter. But who was the first that found the use of Letters, is not known. He that first brought them into *Greece,* men say was *Cadmus,* the sonne of *Agenor,* King of Phaenicia. A profitable Invention for continuing the memory of time past, and the conjunction of mankind, dispersed into so many, and distant regions of the Earth; and with all difficult, as proceeding from a watchfull observation of the divers motions of the Tongue, Palat, Lips, and other organs of Speech; whereby to make as many differences of characters, to remember them. But the most noble and profitable invention of all other, was that of SPEECH, consisting of *Names* or *Appellations,* and their Connexion; whereby men register their Thoughts; recall them when they are past; and also declare them one to another for mutuall utility and conversation; without which, there had been amongst men, neither Common-wealth, nor Society, nor Contract, nor Peace, no more than amongst Lyons, Bears, and Wolves. The first author of Speech was *God* himself, that instructed *Adam* how to name such creatures as he presented to his sight; For the Scripture goeth no further in this matter. But this was sufficient to direct him to adde more names, as the experience and use of the creatures should give him occasion; and to joyn them in such manner by degrees, as to make himself understood; and so by succession of time, so much language might be gotten, as he had found use for; though not so copious as an Orator or Philosopher has need of. For I do not find any thing in the Scripture, out of which, directly or by consequence can be gathered, that *Adam* was taught the names of all Figures, Numbers, Measures, Colours, Sounds, Fancies, Relations; much less the names of Words and Speech, as *Generall, Speciall, Affirmative, Negative, Interrogative, Optative, Infinitive,* all which are usefull; and least of all, of *Entity, Intentionality, Quiddity,* and other insignificant words of the School.

But all this language gotten, and augmented by *Adam* and his posterity, was again lost at the tower of *Babel,* when by the hand of God, every man was stricken for his rebellion, with an oblivion of his former language. And being hereby forced to disperse themselves into severall parts of the world, it must needs be, that the diversity of Tongues that now is, proceeded by degrees from them, in such manner, as need (the mother of all inventions) taught them; and in tract of time grew every where more copious.

The generall use of Speech, is to transferre our Mentall Discourse, into Verbal; or the Trayne of our Thoughts, into a Trayne of Words; and that for two commodities; whereof one is, the Registring of the Consequences of our Thoughts; which being apt to slip out of our memory, and put us to a new labour, may again be recalled, by such words as they were marked by. So that the first use of names, is to serve for

Markes, or *Notes* of remembrance. Another is, when many use the same words, to signifie (by their connexion and order,) one to another, what they conceive, or think of each matter; and also what they desire, feare, or have any other passion for. And for this use they are called *Signes*. Speciall uses of Speech are these; First, to Register, what by cogitation, wee find to be the cause of any thing, present or past; and what we find things present or past may produce, or effect: which in summe, is acquiring of Arts. Secondly, to shew to others that knowledge which we have attained; which is, to Counsell, and Teach one another. Thirdly, to make known to others our wills, and purposes, that we may have the mutual help of one another. Fourthly, to please and delight our selves, and others, by playing with our words, for pleasure or ornament, innocently.

To these Uses, there are also foure correspondent Abuses. First, when men register their thoughts wrong, by the inconstancy of the signification of their words; by which they register for their conceptions, that which they never conceived; and so deceive themselves. Secondly, when they use words metaphorically; that is, in other sense than that they are ordained for; and thereby deceive others. Thirdly, when by words they declare that to be their will, which is not. Fourthly, when they use them to grieve one another: for seeing nature hath armed living creatures, some with teeth, some with horns, and some with hands, to grieve an enemy, it is but an abuse of Speech, to grieve him with the tongue, unlesse it be one whom wee are obliged to govern; and then it is not to grieve, but to correct and amend.

The manner how Speech serveth to the remembrance of the consequence of causes and effects, consisteth in the imposing of *Names,* and the *Connexion* of them.

Of Names, some are *Proper,* and singular to one onely thing; as *Peter, John, This Man, this Tree*: and some are *Common* to many things; as *Man, Horse, Tree;* every of which though but one Name, is nevertheless the name of divers particular things; in respect of all which together, it is called an *Universall;* there being nothing in the world Universall but Names; for the things named, are every one of them Individuall and Singular.

One Universall name is imposed on many things, for their similitude in some quality, or other accident: And whereas a Proper Name bringeth to mind one thing onely; Universals recall any one of those many.

And of Names Universall, some are of more, and some of lesse extent; the larger comprehending the lesse large: and some again of equall extent, comprehending each other reciprocally. As for example, the Name *Body* is of larger signification that the word *Man,* and comprehendeth it; and the names *Man* and *Rationall,* are of equall extent, comprehending mutually one another. But here wee must take notice, that by a Name is not alwayes understood, as in Grammar, one onely Word; but sometimes by circumlocution many words together. For all these words, *Hee that in his actions observeth the Lawes of his Country,* make but one Name, equivalent to this one word, *Just.*

By this imposition of Names, some of larger, some of stricter signification, we turn the reckoning of the consequences of things imagined in the mind, into a reckoning of the consequences of Appellations. For example, a man that hath no use of Speech at all, (such, as is born and remains perfectly deafe and dumb,) if he set before his eyes a triangle, and by it two right angles, (such as are the corners of a square figure,) he may by meditation compare and find, that the three angles of that triangle, are equall to those two right angles that stand by it. But if another triangle be shewn him different in shape from the former, he cannot know without a new labour, whether the three angles of that also be equall to the same. But he that hath the use of words, when he observes, that such equality was consequent, not to the length of the sides, nor to any other particular thing in his triangle; but onely to this, that the sides were straight, and the angles three; and that that was all, for which he named it a Triangle; will boldly conclude Universally, that such

equality of angles is in all triangles whatsoever; and register
his invention in these generall termes, *Every triangle hath its
three angles equall to two right angles.* And thus the consequence found in one particular, comes to be registered and
remembred, as an Universall rule; and discharges our mentall
reckoning, of time and place; and delivers us from all labour
of the mind, saving the first; and makes that which was
found true *here,* and *now,* to be true in *all times* and *places.*

But the use of the words in registering our thoughts, is in
nothing so evident as in Numbring. A naturall foole that
could never learn by heart the order of numerall words,
as *one, two,* and *three,* may observe every stroak of the
Clock, and nod to it, or say, one, one, one; but can never
know what houre it strikes. And it seems, there was a time
when those names of number were not in use; and men
were fayn to apply their fingers of one or both hand, to those
things they desired to keep account of; and that thence it
proceeded, that now our numerall words are but ten, in any
Nation, and in some but five, and then they begin again.
And he that can tell ten, if he recite them out of order, will
lose himself, and not know when he has done: Much lesse
will he be able to adde, and subtract, and performe all
other operations of Arithmetique. So that without words
there is no possibility of reckoning of Numbers; much lesse
of Magnitudes, of Swiftness, of Force, and other things, the
reckonings whereof are necessary to the being, or well-being of mankind.

When two Names are joyned together into a Consequence, or Affirmation; as thus, *A man is a living creature;*
or thus, *if he be a man, he is a living creature.* If the latter
name *Living creature,* signifie all that the former name *May*
signifieth, then the affirmation, or consequence is *true;* otherwise *false.* For *True* and *False* are attributes of Speech, not
of Things. And where Speech is not, there is neither *Truth*
nor *Falsehood.* Errour there may be, as when wee expect
that which shall not be; or suspect what has not been: but
in neither case can a man be charged with Untruth.

Seeing then that *truth* consisteth in the right ordering of names in our affirmations, a man that seeketh precise *truth*, had need to remember what every names he uses stands for; and to place it accordingly; or else he will find himselfe entangled in words, as a bird in lime-twiggs; the more he struggles, the more belimed. And therefore in Geometry, (which is the onely Science that it hath pleased God hitherto to bestow on mankind,) men begin at settling the significations of their words; which settling of significations, they call *Definitions;* and place them in the beginning of their reckoning.

By this it appears how necessary it is for any man that aspires to true Knowledge, to examine the Definitions of former Authors; and either to correct them, where they are negligently set down; or to make them himselfe. For the errours of Definitions multiply themselves, according as the reckoning proceeds; and lead men into absurdities, which at last they see, but cannot avoyd, without reckoning anew from the beginning; in which lyes the foundation of their errours. From whence it happens, that they which trust to books, do as they that cast up many little summs into a greater, without considering whether those little summes were rightly cast up or not; and at last finding the errour visible, and not mistrusting their first grounds, know not which way to cleere themselves; but spend time in fluttering over their bookes; as birds that entring by the chimney, and finding themselves inclosed in a chamber, flutter at the false light of a glasse window, for want of wit to consider which way they came in. So that in the right Definition of Names, lyes the first use of Speech; which is the Acquisition of Science: And in wrong, or no Definition, lyes the first abuse; from which proceed all false and senslesse Tenets; which make those men that take their instruction from the authority of books, and not from their own meditation, to be as much below the condition of ignorant men, and men endued with true Science are above it. For between true Science, and erroneous Doctrines, Ignorance is in the middle. Naturall sense and imagination are not subject to absurdity. Nature it selfe cannot erre: and as men abound in copiousness of language; so they become more wise, or more mad than ordinary. Nor is it possible without Letters for any man to become either excellently wise, or (unless his memory be hurt by disease, or ill constitution of organs) excellently foolish. For words are wise mens counters, they do but reckon by them: but they are the mony of fooles, that value them by the authority of an *Aristotle, a Cicero,* or a *Thomas,* or any other Doctor whatsoever, if but a man.

Subject to Names, is whatsoever can enter into, or be considered in an account; and be added one to another to make a summe; or substracted one from another, and leave a remainder. The Latines called Accounts of mony *Rationes,* and accounting, *Ratiocinatio*: and that which we in bills or books of account call *Items,* they called *Nomina;* that is, *Names*: and thence it seems to proceed, that they extended the word *Ratio,* to the faculty of Reckoning in all other things. The Greeks have but one word λόγος, for both *Speech* and *Reason;* not that they thought there was no Speech without Reason; but no Reasoning without Speech: And the act of reasoning they called *Syllogisme;* which signifieth summing up of the consequences of one saying to another. And because the same things may enter into account for divers accidents; their names are (to shew that diversity), diversly wrested, and diversified. This diversity of names may be reduced to foure generall heads.

First, a thing may enter into account for *Matter,* or *Body;* as *living, sensible, rationall, hot, cold, moved, quiet;* with all which names the word *Matter,* or *Body* is understood; all such, being names of Matter.

Secondly, it may enter into account, or be considered, for some accident or quality, which we conceive to be in it; as for *being moved,* for *being so long,* for *being hot,* etc; and then, of the name of the thing it selfe, by a little change or wresting, wee make a name for that accident, which we consider; and for *living* put into the account *life;* for *moved, motion;* for *hot, heat;* for *long, length,* and the like. And all such Names, are the names of the accidents and properties, by which one Matter, and Body is distinguished from another. These are called *names Abstract;* because severed (not from Matter, but) from the account of Matter.

Thirdly, we bring into account, the Properties of our own bodies, whereby we make such distinction: as when any thing is *Seen* for us, we reckon not the thing it selfe; but the *sight,* the *Colour,* the *Idea* of it in the fancy: and when any thing is *heard,* wee reckon it not; but the *hearing,* or *sound* onely, which is our fancy or conception of it by the Eare: and such are names of fancies.

Fourthly, we bring into account, consider, and give names to *Names* themselves, and to *Speeches*: For, *generall, universall, speciall, aequivocall,* are names of Names. And *Affirmation, Interrogation, Commandement, Narration, Syllogisme, Sermon, Oration,* and many other such, are names of Speeches. And this is all the variety of Names *Positive;* which are put to mark somewhat which is in Nature, or may be feigned by the mind of man, as Bodies that are, or may be conceived to be; or of bodies, the Properties that are, or may be feigned to be; or Words and Speech.

There be also other Names, called *Negative;* which are notes to signifie that a word is not the name of the thing in question: as these words *Nothing, no man, infinite, indocible, three want foure,* and the like; which are nevertheless of use in reckoning, or in correcting or reckoning; and call to mind our past cogitations, though they be not names of any thing; because they make us refuse to admit of Names not rightly used.

All other Names, are but insignificant sounds; and those of two sorts. One, when they are new, and yet their meaning not explained by Definition; whereof there have been abundance coyned by Schoole-men, and pusled Philosophers.

Another, when men make a name of two Names, whose significations are contradictory and inconsistent; as this name, an *incorporeall body,* or (which is all one) an *in-*

corporeall substance, and a great number more. For when-
soever any affirmation is false, the two names of which it is
composed, put together and made one, signifie nothing at
all. For example, if it be a false affirmation to say a *quadrangle is round,* the word *round quadrangle* signifies nothing;
but is a meere sound. So likewise if it be false, to say that
vertue can be powred, or blown up and down; the words
In-powred vertue, In-blown vertue, are as absurd and insignificant, as a *round quadrangle.* And therefore you shall
hardly meet with a senslesse and insignificant word, that is
not made up of some Latin or Greek names. A Frenchman
seldome hears our Saviour called by the name of *Parole,*
but by the name of *Verbe* often; yet *Verbe* and *Parole* differ
no more, but that one is Latin, the other French.

When a man upon the hearing of any Speech, hath those
thoughts which the words of that Speech, and their connexion, were ordained and constituted to signifie; Then he
is said to understand it: *Understanding* being nothing else,
but conception caused by Speech. And therefore if Speech
be peculiar to man (as for ought I know it is), then is
Understanding peculiar to him also. And therefore of absurd
and false affirmations, in case they be universall, there can
be no Understanding; though many think they understand,
then, when they do but repeat the words softly, or con them
in their mind.

What kinds of Speeches signifie the Appetites, Aversions
and Passions of mans mind; and of their use and abuse, I
shall speak when I have spoken of the Passions.

The names of such things as affect us, that is, which
please, and displease us, because all men be not alike affected with the same thing, nor the same man at all times,
are in the common discourses of men, of *inconstant* signification. For seeing all names are imposed to signifie our conceptions; and all our affections are but conceptions; when
we conceive the same things differently, we can hardly
avoyd different naming of them. For though the nature of
that we conceive, be the same; yet the diversity of our re-

ception of it, in respect of different constitutions of body, and prejudices of opinion, gives every thing a tincture of our different passions. And therefore in reasoning, a man must take heed of words; which besides the signification of what we imagine of their nature, have a signification also of the nature, disposition, and interest of the speaker; such as are the names of Vertues, and Vices; For one calleth *Wisdome*, what another calleth *feare;* and one *cruelty*, what another *justice;* one *prodigality*, what another *magnanimity;* and one *gravity* what another *stupidicy*, etc. And therefore such names can never be true grounds of any ratiocination. No more can Metaphors, and Tropes of speech: but these are less dangerous, because they profess their inconstancy; which the other do not.

"Of Words"

John Locke

John Locke was born in Somerset, England, in 1632, the son of an attorney who served as a captain in the Civil War. Locke was educated at Oxford University, taking his bachelor's degree in 1656 and his master's in 1658. He lectured for several years at Oxford, came under the influence of Descartes, was a friend of the scientist Boyle, and was elected to the Royal Society. Later he became physician, secretary, and friend to the First Earl of Shaftesbury, whom he followed into exile in 1682. They returned to England in 1689, where Locke lived until his death in 1704. His *Letters on Toleration,* on the necessity of separation of church and state, deeply influenced America; another great work was *Two Treatises on Government,* which contained the seeds of American independence. His *Essay Concerning Human Understanding* was the culmination of seventeen years of work. The selection used here is from Book III and Book IV of that work. A recent edition is in the Everyman's Library series, Introduction and editing copyright 1961 by J. M. Dent and Sons, Ltd. Reprinted here by permission of E. P. Dutton & Co., Inc.

OF WORDS AND LANGUAGE IN GENERAL

GOD, having designed man for a sociable creature, made him not only with an inclination and under a necessity to have fellowship with those of his own kind, but furnished him also with language, which was to be the great instrument and common tie of society. Man, therefore, had by nature his organs so fashioned, as to be fit to frame articulate sounds, which we call words. But this was not enough to produce language; for parrots, and several other birds, will be taught to make articulate sounds distinct enough, which yet by no means are capable of language.

Besides articulate sounds, therefore, it was further necessary that he should be able to use these sounds as signs of internal conceptions; and to make them stand as marks for the ideas within his own mind, whereby they might be made known to others, and the thoughts of men's minds be conveyed from one to another.

But neither was this sufficient to make words so useful as they ought to be. It is not enough for the perfection of language, that sounds can be made signs of ideas, unless those signs can be so made use of as to comprehend several particular things: for the multiplication of words would have perplexed their use, had every particular thing need of a distinct name to be signified by. To remedy this inconvenience, language had yet a further improvement in the use of *general terms*, whereby one word was made to mark a multitude of particular existences: which advantageous use of sounds was obtained only by the difference of the ideas they were made signs of: those names becoming general, which are made to stand for *general ideas*, and those remaining particular, where the *ideas* they are used for are *particular*.

Besides these names which stand for ideas, there be other words which men make use of, not to signify any idea, but the want or absence of some ideas, simple or complex, or all ideas together; such as are *nihil* in Latin, and in English, *ignorance* and *barrenness*. All which negative or private words cannot be said properly to belong to or signify no ideas: for then they would be perfectly insignificant sounds; but they relate to positive ideas, and signify their absence.

It may also lead us a little towards the original of all our notions and knowledge, if we remark how great a dependence our words have on common sensible ideas; and how those which are made use of to stand for actions and notions quite removed from sense, have their rise from thence, and from obvious sensible ideas are transferred to more abstruse significations, and made to stand for ideas that come not under the cognizance of our senses; v.g. to *imagine, apprehend, comprehend, adhere, conceive, instil, disgust, disturbance, tranquillity,* etc., are all words taken from the operations of sensible things, and applied to certain modes of thinking. *Spirit,* in its primary signification, is breath; *angel,* a messenger: and I doubt not but, if we could trace them to their sources, we should find, in all languages, the names which stand for things that fall not under our senses to have had their first rise from sensible ideas. By which we may give some kind of guess what kind of notions they were, and whence derived, which filled their minds who were the first beginners of languages, and how nature, even in the naming of things, unawares suggested to men the originals and principles of all their knowledge: whilst, to give names that might make known to others any operations they felt in themselves, or any other ideas that came not under their senses, they were fain to borrow words from ordinary known ideas of sensation, by that means to make others the more easily to conceive those operations they experimented in themselves, which made no outward sensible appearances; and then, when they had got known and agreed names to signify those internal operations of their own minds, they were sufficiently furnished to make known by words all their other ideas; since they could consist of nothing but either of outward sensible perceptions, or of the inward operations of their minds about them; we having, as has been proved, no ideas at all, but what originally come either from sensible objects without, or what we feel within ourselves, from the inward workings of our own spirits, of which we are conscious to ourselves within.

But to understand better the use and force of Language, as subservient to instruction and knowledge, it will be convenient to consider:

First, *To what it is that names, in the use of language, are immediately applied.*

Secondly, Since all (except proper) names are general, and so stand not particularly for this or that single thing, but for sorts and ranks of things, it will be necessary to consider, in the next place, what the sorts and kinds, or, if you rather like the Latin names, *what the Species and Genera of things are, wherein they consist, and how they come to be made*. These being (as they ought) well looked into, we shall the better come to find the right use of words; the natural advantages and defects of language; and the remedies that ought to be used, to avoid the inconveniences of obscurity or uncertainty in the signification of words: without which it is impossible to discourse with any clearness or order concerning knowledge: which, being conversant about propositions, and those most commonly universal ones, has greater connection with words than perhaps is suspected.

These considerations, therefore, shall be the matter of the following chapters.

OF THE SIGNIFICATION OF WORDS

Man, though he have great variety of thoughts, and such from which others as well as himself might receive profit and delight; yet they are all within his own breast, invisible and hidden from others, nor can of themselves be made to appear. The comfort and advantage of society not being to be had without communication of thoughts, it was necessary that man should find out some external sensible signs, whereof those invisible ideas, which his thoughts are made up of, might be made known to others. For this purpose nothing was so fit, either for plenty or quickness, as those articulate sounds, which with so much ease and variety he found himself able to make. Thus we may conceive how *words*, which were by nature so well adapted to that purpose, came to be made use of by men as the signs of their ideas; not by any natural connection that there is between particular articulate sounds and certain ideas, for then there would be but one language amongst all men; but by a voluntary imposition, whereby such a word is made arbitrarily the mark of such an idea. The use, then, of words, is to be sensible marks of ideas; and the ideas they stand for are their proper and immediate signification.

The use men have of these marks being either to record their own thoughts, for the assistance of their own memory; or, as it were, to bring out their ideas, and lay them before the view of others: words, in their primary or immediate signification, stand for nothing but *the ideas in the mind of him that uses them,* how imperfectly soever or carelessly those ideas are collected from the things which they are supposed to represent. When a man speaks to another, it is that he may be understood: and the end of speech is, that those sounds, as marks, may make known his ideas to the hearer. That then which words are the marks of are the ideas of the speaker: nor can any one apply them as marks, immediately, to anything else but the ideas that he himself hath: for this would be to make them signs of his own conceptions, and yet apply them to other ideas; which would be to make them signs and not signs of his ideas at the same time; and so in effect to have no signification at all. Words being voluntary signs, they cannot be voluntary signs imposed by him on things he knows not. That would be to make them signs of nothing, sounds without signification. A man cannot make his words the signs either of qualities in things, or of conceptions in the mind of another, whereof he has none in his own. Till he has some ideas of his own, he cannot suppose them to correspond with the conceptions of another mind. But when he represents to himself other mens' ideas by some of his own, if he consent to give them the same names that other men do, it is still to his own ideas; to ideas that he has, and not to ideas that he has not.

This is so necessary in the use of language, that in this respect the knowing and the ignorant, the learned and the unlearned, use the words they speak (with any meaning) all alike. They, in every man's mouth, stand for the ideas he has, and which he would express by them. A child having taken notice of nothing in the metal he hears called *gold,* but the bright shining yellow colour, he applies the word gold only to his own idea of that colour, and nothing else; and therefore calls the same colour in a peacock's tail gold. Another that hath better observed, adds to shining yellow great weight: and then the sound gold, when he uses it, stands for a complex idea of a shining yellow and a very weighty substance. Another adds to those qualities fusibility: and then the word gold signifies to him a body, bright, yellow, fusible, and very heavy. Another adds malleability. Each of these uses equally the word gold, when they have occasion to express the idea which they have applied it to: but it is evident that each can apply it only to his own idea; nor can he make it stand as a sign of such a complex idea as he has not.

But though words, as they are used by men, can properly and immediately signify nothing but the ideas that are in the mind of the speaker; yet they in their thoughts give them a secret reference to two other things.

First, *They suppose their words to be marks of the ideas in the minds also of other men, with whom they communicate*: for else they talk in vain, and could not be understood, if the sounds they applied to one idea were such as by the hearer were applied to another, which is to speak two languages.

Secondly, Because men would not be thought to talk barely of their own imagination, but of things as really they are; therefore they often suppose the *words to stand also for the reality of things*. We shall speak of different ways of applying words more at large, when we come to treat of the names of mixed modes and substances in particular: though give me leave here to say, that it is a perverting the use of words, and brings unavoidable obscurity and confusion into their signification, whenever we make them stand for anything but those ideas we have in our own minds.

Concerning words, also, it is further to be considered: First, that there comes, by constant use, to be such a connection between certain sounds and the ideas they stand for, that the names heard almost as readily excite certain ideas as if the objects themselves, which are apt to produce them, did actually affect the senses. Which is manifestly so in all obvious sensible qualities, and in all substances that frequently and familiarly occur to us.

Secondly, That through the proper and immediate signification of words are ideas in the mind of the speaker, yet, because by familiar use from our cradles, we come to learn certain articulate sounds very perfectly, and have them readily on our tongues, and always at hand in our memories, but yet are not always careful to examine or settle their significations perfectly; it often happens that men, even when they would apply themselves to an attentive consideration, do set their thoughts more on words than things.

Words, by long and familiar use, as has been said, come to excite in men certain ideas so constantly and readily, that they are apt to suppose a natural connection between them. But that they signify only men's peculiar ideas, and that *by a perfect arbitrary imposition,* is evident, in that they often fail to excite in others (even that use the same language) the same ideas we take them to be signs of: and every man has so inviolable a liberty to make words stand for what he pleases, that no one hath the power to make others have the same ideas in their minds that he has, when they use the same words that he does. And therefore the great Augustus himself, in the possession of that power which ruled the world, acknowledged he could not make a new Latin word: which was as much as to say, that he could not arbitrarily appoint what idea any sound should be a sign of, in the mouths and common language of his subjects. Whatever be the consequence of any man's using of words differently, either from their general meaning, or the particular sense of the person to whom he addressed them; this is certain, their signification, in his use of them, is limited to his ideas, and they can be signs of nothing else.

OF GENERAL TERMS

All things that exist being particulars, it may perhaps be

thought reasonable that words, which ought to be conformed to things, should be so too—I mean in their signification: but yet we find quite the contrary. The far greatest part of words that make all languages are general terms: which has not been the effect of neglect or chance, but of reason and necessity.

First, It is impossible that every particular thing should have a distinct peculiar name. For, the signification and use of words depending on that connection which the mind makes between its ideas and the sounds it uses as signs of them, it is necessary, in the application of names to things, that the mind should have distinct ideas of the things, and retain also the particular name that belongs to every one, with its peculiar appropriation to that idea. But it is beyond the power of human capacity to frame and retain distinct ideas of all the particular things we meet with: every bird and beast men saw, every tree and plant that affected the senses, could not find a place in the most capacious understanding.

Secondly, If it were possible, it would yet be useless; because it would not serve to the chief end of language. Men would in vain heap up names of particular things, that would not serve them to communicate their thoughts. The sound I make by the organs of speech excites, in another's man's mind who hears it, the idea I apply it to in mine when I speak it. This cannot be done by names applied to particular things; whereof I alone having the ideas in my mind, the names of them could not be significant or intelligible to another, who was not acquainted with all those very particular things which had fallen under my notice.

Thirdly, A distinct name for every particular thing would not be of any great use for the improvement of knowledge: which, though founded in particular things, enlarges itself by general views; to which things reduced into sorts, under general names, are properly subservient. These, with the names belonging to them, come within some compass, and do not multiply every moment, beyond what either the mind can contain, or use requires. And therefore, in these, men have for the most part stopped: but yet not so as to hinder themselves from distinguishing particular things by appropriated names, where convenience demands it. And therefore in his own species, which they have most to do with, and wherein they have often occasion to mention particular persons, they make use of proper names; and there distinct individuals have distinct denominations.

Since all things that exist are only particulars, how come we by general terms, or where find we those general natures they are supposed to stand for? Words become general by being made the signs of general ideas: and ideas become general by separating from them the circumstances of time and place, and any other ideas that may determine them to this or that particular existence. By this way of abstraction they are made capable of representing more individuals than one; each of which having in it a conformity to that abstract idea, is (as we call it) of that sort.

There is nothing more evident, than that the ideas of the persons children converse with (to instance in them alone) are, like the persons themselves, only particular. The ideas of the nurse and the mother are well framed in their minds; and, like pictures of them there, represent only those individuals. The names they first gave to them are confined to these individuals; and the names of *nurse* and *mamma* the child uses, determine themselves to those persons. Afterwards, when time and a larger acquaintance have made them observe that there are a great many other things in the world, that in some common agreements of shape, and several other qualities, resemble their father and mother, and those persons they have been used to, they frame an idea, which they find those many particulars do partake in; and to that they give, with others, the name *man,* for example. And thus they come to have a general name, and a general idea. Wherein they make nothing new; but only leave out of the complex idea that they had of Peter and James, Mary and Jane, that which is peculiar to each, and retain only what is common to them all.

By the same way that they come by the general name and idea of *man*, they easily advance to more general names and notions. For, observing that several things that differ from their idea of man, and cannot therefore be comprehended under that name, have yet certain qualities wherein they agree with man, by retaining only those qualities, and uniting them into one idea, they have again another and more general idea; to which having given a name they make a term of a more comprehensive extension: which new idea is made, not by any new addition, but only as before, by leaving out the shape, and some other properties signified by the name man, and retaining only a body, with life, sense, and spontaneous motion, comprehended under the name animal.

That this is the way whereby men first formed general ideas, and general names to them, I think is so evident, that there needs no other proof of it but the considering of a man's self, or others, and the ordinary proceedings of their minds in knowledge. And he that thinks *general natures* or *notions* are anything else but such abstract and partial ideas of more complex ones, taken at first from particular existences, will, I fear, be at a loss where to find them. For let any one reflect, and then tell me wherein does his idea of *man* differ from that of *Peter* and *Paul*, or his idea of *horse* from that of *Bucephalus*, but in the leaving out something that is peculiar to each individual, and retaining so much of those particular complex ideas of several particular existences as they are found to agree in. Of the complex ideas signified by the names *man* and *horse*, leaving out but those particulars wherein they differ, and retaining only those wherein they agree, and of those making a new distinct complex idea, and giving the name *animal* to it, one has a more general term, that comprehends with man several other creatures. Leave out of the idea of *animal*, sense and spontaneous motion, and the remaining complex idea, made up of the remaining simple ones of body, life, and nourishment, becomes a more general one, under the more comprehensive term, *vivens*. And not to dwell longer upon this particular, so evident in itself; by the same way the mind proceeds to *body, substance*, and at last to *being, thing*, and such universal terms, which stand for any of our ideas whatsoever. To conclude: this whole mystery of genera and species, which make such a noise in the schools, are with justice so little regarded out of them, is nothing else but *abstract ideas*, more or less comprehensive, with names annexed to them. In all which this is constant and unvariable, that every more general term stands for such an idea, and is but a part of any of those contained under it.

This may show us the reason why, in the defining of words, which is nothing but declaring their signification, we make use of the *genus*, or next general word that comprehends it. Which is not out of necessity, but only to save the labour of enumerating the several simple ideas which the next general word or *genus* stands for. Definition being nothing but making another understand by words what idea the term defined stands for, a definition is best made by enumerating those simple ideas that are combined in the signification of the term defined: and if, instead of such an enumeration, men have accustomed themselves to use the next general term, it has not been out of necessity, or for greater clearness, but for quickness and dispatch sake. For I think that, to one who desired to know what idea the word *man* stood for; if it should be said, that man was a solid extended substance, having life, sense, spontaneous motion, and the faculty of reasoning, I doubt not but the meaning of the term man would be as well understood, and the idea it stands for be at least as clearly made known, as when it is defined to be a rational animal: which, by the several definitions of *animal, vivens*, and *corpus*, resolves itself into those enumerated ideas. I have, in explaining the term *man*, followed here the ordinary definition of the schools; which,

though perhaps not the most exact, yet serves well enough
to my present purpose. And one may, in this instance, see
what gave occasion to the rule, that a definition must consist
of *genus* and *differentia;* and it suffices to show us the little
necessity there is of such a rule, or advantage in the strict
observing of it.

To return to general words: it is plain, by what has been
said, that *general* and *universal* belong not to the real existence of things; but are the inventions and creatures of
the understanding, made by it for its own use, and concern
only signs, whether words or ideas. Words are general, as
has been said, when used for signs of general ideas, and so
are applicable indifferently to many particular things; and
ideas are general when they are set up as the representatives
of many particular things: but universality belongs not to
things themselves, which are all of them particular in their
existence, even those words and ideas which in their signification are general. When therefore we quit particulars,
the generals that rest are only creatures of our own making;
their general nature being nothing but the capacity they
are put into, by the understanding, of signifying or representing many particulars. For the signification they have is
nothing but a relation that, by the mind of man, is added
to them.

That then which general words signify is a *sort* of things;
and each of them does that, by being a sign of an abstract
idea in the mind; to which idea, as things existing are found
to agree, so they come to be ranked under that name, or,
which is all one, be of that sort. Whereby it is evident that
the *essences* of the sorts, or, if the Latin word pleases better,
species of things, are nothing else but these abstract ideas.
Since nothing can be a man, or have a right to the name
man, but what has a conformity to the abstract idea the
name man stands for, nor anything be a man, or have a right
to the species man, but what has the essence of that species;
it follows, that the abstract idea for which the name stands,
and the essence of the species, is one and the same. From

whence it is easy to observe, that the essences of the sorts of things, and, consequently, the sorting of things, is the workmanship of the understanding that abstracts and makes those general ideas.

I would not here be thought to forget, much less to deny, that nature, in the production of things, makes several of them alike: there is nothing more obvious, especially in the races of animals, and all things propagated by seed. But yet I think we may say, *the sorting of them under names is the workmanship of the understanding, taking occasion, from the similitude it observes amongst them, to make abstract general ideas,* and set them up in the mind, with names annexed to them, as patterns or forms, to which as particular things existing are found to agree, so they come to be of that species. Therefore the supposed real essences of substances, if different from our abstract ideas, cannot be the essences of the species *we* rank things into. For two species may be one, as rationally as two different essences be the essence of one species: and I demand, What are the alterations which may or may not be made in a *horse* or *lead*, without making either of them to be of another species? In determining the species of things by *our* abstract ideas, this is easy to resolve: but if any one will regulate himself herein by supposed *real* essences, he will, I suppose, be at a loss: and he will never be able to know when anything precisely ceases to be of the species of a *horse* or *lead*.

In truth, every distinct abstract idea is a distinct essence; and the names that stand for such distinct ideas are the names of things essentially different. Thus a circle is as essentially different from an oval as a sheep from a goat; and rain is as essentially different from snow as water from earth: that abstract idea which is the essence of one being impossible to be communicated to the other.

But since the essences of things are thought by some (and not without reason) to be wholly unknown, it may not be amiss to consider the several significations of the word *essence.*

First, Essence may be taken for the very being of any-thing, whereby it is what it is. And thus the real internal, but generally (in substances) unknown constitution of things, whereon their discoverable qualities depend, may be called their essence. This is the proper original signifi-cation of the word, as is evident from the formation of it; *essentia*, in its primary notation, signifying properly, being. And in this sense it is still used, when we speak of the es-sence of *particular* things, without giving them any name.

Secondly, The learning and disputes of the schools having been much busied about *genus* and *species*, the word *essence* has almost lost its primary signification: and, instead of a real constitution of things, has been almost wholly applied to the artificial constitution of *genus* and *species*. It is true, there is ordinarily supposed a real constitution of the sorts of things; and it is past doubt there must be some real con-stitution, on which any collection of simple ideas co-exist-ing must depend. But, it being evident that things are ranked under names into sorts or species, only as they agree to certain abstract ideas, to which we have annexed those names, the essence of each *genus*, or sort, comes to be nothing but that abstract idea which the general, or sortal (if I may have leave so to call it from sort, as I do general from genus), name stands for. And this we shall find to be that which the word essence imports in its most familiar use.

These two sorts of essences, I suppose, may not unfitly be termed, the one the *real*, the other *nominal essence*.

Between the *nominal essence* and the *name* there is so near a connection, that the name of any sort of things can-not be attributed to any particular being but what has this essence, whereby it answers that abstract idea whereof that name is the sign.

Concerning the *real essences* of corporeal substances there are, if I mistake not, two opinions. The one is of those who, using the word essence for they know not what, suppose a certain number of those essences, according to which all na-

tural things are made, and wherein they do exactly every one
of them partake, and so become of this or that species. The
other and more rational opinion is of those who look on all
natural things to have a real, but unknown, constitution of
their insensible parts; from which flow those sensible qualities which serve us to distinguish them one from another,
according as we have occasion to rank them into sorts, under
common denominations. The former of these opinions, which
supposes these essences as a certain number of forms or
moulds, wherein all natural things that exist are cast, and do
equally partake, has, I imagine, very much perplexed the
knowledge of natural things. The frequent productions of
monsters, in all the species of animals, and of changelings,
and other strange issues of human birth, carry with them
difficulties, not possible to consist with this hypothesis; since
it is as impossible that two things partaking exactly of the
same real essence should have different properties, as that
two figures partaking of the same real essence of a circle
should have different properties. But were there no other
reason against it, yet the supposition of essences that cannot
be known, and the making of them, nevertheless, to be that
which distinguishes the species of things, is so wholly useless and unserviceable to any part of our knowledge, that that
alone, were sufficient to make us lay it by, and content ourselves with such essences of the sorts or species of things as
come within the reach of our knowledge: which, when seriously considered, will be found, as I have said, to be
nothing else but those *abstract* complex ideas to which we
have annexed distinct general names.

Essences being thus distinguished into nominal and real,
we may further observe, that, in the species of simple ideas
and modes, they are always the same; but in substances always quite different. Thus, a figure including a space between three lines, is the real as well as nominal essence of
a triangle; it being not only the abstract idea to which the
general name is annexed, but the very *essentia* or being of
the thing itself; that foundation from which all its prop-

erties flow, and to which they are all inseparably annexed. But it is far otherwise concerning that parcel of matter which makes the ring on my finger; wherein these two essences are apparently different. For it is the real constitution of its insensible parts, on which depend all those properties of colour, weight, fusibility, fixedness, etc., which are to be found in it: which constitution we know not, and so, having no particular idea of, having no name that is the sign of it. But yet it is its colour, weight, fusibility, fixedness, etc., which makes it to be gold, or gives it a right to that name, which is therefore its nominal essence.

That such abstract ideas, with names to them, as we have been speaking of are essences, may further appear by what we are told concerning essences, viz. that they are all ingenerable and incorruptible. Which cannot be true of the real constitutions of things, which begin and perish with them. All things that exist, besides their Author, are all liable to change; especially those things we are acquainted with, and have ranked into bands under distinct names or ensigns. Thus, that which was grass to-day is to-morrow the flesh of a sheep: and, within a few days after, becomes part of a man: in all which and the like changes, it is evident their real essence—i.e. that constitution whereon the properties of these several things depended—is destroyed, and perishes with them. But essences being taken for ideas established in the mind, with names annexed to them, they are supposed to remain steadily the same, whatever mutations the particular substances are liable to. For, were there now no circle existing anywhere in the world (as perhaps that figure exists not anywhere exactly marked out), yet the idea annexed to that name would not cease to be what it is.

To conclude. This is that which in short I would say, viz. that all the great business of *genera* and *species*, and their *essences*, amounts to no more but this: that men making abstract ideas, and settling them in their minds with names annexed to them, do thereby enable themselves to consider things, and discourse of them, as it were in bundles, for the

easier and readier improvement and communication of their
knowledge, which would advance but slowly were their
words and thoughts confined only to particulars. . . .

OF TRUTH IN GENERAL

Truth seems to me, in the proper import of the word, to
signify but *the joining or separating of signs, as the things
signified by them do agree or disagree one with another.*
The joining or separating of signs here meant, is what by another name we call *proposition.* So that truth properly belongs only to propositions: whereof there are two sorts, viz.
mental and verbal; as there are two sorts of signs commonly
made use of, viz. ideas and words.

To form a clear notion of truth, it is very necessary to consider truth of thought, and truth of words, distinctly one
from another: but yet it is very difficult to treat of them
asunder. Because it is unavoidable, in treating of mental
propositions, to make use of words: and then the instances
given of mental propositions cease immediately to be barely
mental, and become verbal. For a *mental proposition* being
nothing but a bare consideration of the ideas, as they are in
our minds, stripped of names, they lose the nature of purely
mental propositions as soon as they are put into words.

And that which makes it yet harder to treat of mental and
verbal propositions separately is, that most men, if not all, in
their thinking and reasonings within themselves, make use of
words instead of ideas; at least when the subject of their
meditation contains in it complex ideas. When we make any
propositions within our own thoughts about *white* or *black,
sweet* or *bitter,* a *triangle* or a *circle,* we can and often do
frame in our minds the ideas themselves, without reflecting
on the names. But when we would consider or make propositions about the more complex ideas, as of a *man, vitriol, for-
titude, glory,* we usually put the name for the idea: because
the ideas these names stand for being for the most part imperfect, confused, and undetermined, we reflect on the
names themselves, because they are more clear, certain, and

distinct, and readier occur to our thoughts than the pure ideas: and so we make use of these words instead of the ideas themselves, even when we would meditate and reason within ourselves, and make tacit mental propositions.

But to return to the consideration of truth: we must, I say, observe two sorts of propositions that we are capable of making:

First, *Mental,* wherein the ideas in our understandings are without the use of words, put together or separated by the mind perceiving or judging of their agreement or disagreement.

Secondly, *Verbal* propositions, which are words, the signs of our ideas, put together or separated in affirmative or negative sentences. By which way of affirming or denying, these signs, made by sounds, are, as it were, put together or separated one from another. So that proposition consists in joining or separating signs; and truth consists in the putting together or separating those signs, according as the things which they stand for agree or disagree.

Every one's experience will satisfy him, that the mind, either by perceiving, or supposing, the agreement or disagreement of any of its ideas, does tacitly within itself put them into a kind of proposition affirmative or negative; which I have endeavoured to express by the terms putting together and separating. When ideas are so put together or separated in the mind, as they or the things they stand for do agree or not, that is, as I may call it, *mental truth.* But *truth of words* is something more; and that is the affirming or denying of words one of another, as the ideas they stand for agree or disagree: and this again is twofold: either purely verbal and trifling, or real and instructive.

But here again will be apt to occur the same doubt about truth, that did about knowledge: and it will be objected, that if truth be nothing but the joining and separating of words in propositions, as the ideas they stand for agree or disagree in men's minds, the knowledge of truth is not so valuable a thing as it is taken to be, nor worth the pains and time men employ in the search of it: since by this account it amounts to no more than the conformity of words to the chimeras of men's brains. But of what use is all such truth to us?

Though our words signify nothing but our ideas, yet being designed by them to signify things, the truth they contain when put into propositions will be only verbal, when they stand for ideas in the mind that have not an agreement with the reality of things. And therefore truth as well as knowledge may well come under the distinction of verbal and real; that being only verbal truth, wherein terms are joined according to the agreement or disagreement of the ideas they stand for; without regarding whether our ideas are such as really have, or are capable of having, an existence in nature. But then it is they contain *real truth*, when these signs are joined, as our ideas agree; and when our ideas are such as we know are capable of having an existence in nature: which in substances we cannot know, but by knowing that such have existed.

Truth is the marking down in words the agreement or disagreement of ideas as it is. Falsehood is the marking down in words the agreement or disagreement of ideas otherwise than it is. And so far as these ideas, thus marked by sounds, agree to their archetypes, so far only is the truth real. The knowledge of this truth consists in knowing what ideas the words stand for, and the perception of the agreement or disagreement of those ideas, according as it is marked by those words.

"Introduction"

George Berkeley

George Berkeley was born in Ireland in 1685, and was educated at Trinity College, Dublin, where he graduated with honors in 1704. His first important work, *A New Theory of Vision*, appeared in 1709. His most famous work was published in 1710—*A Treatise concerning the Principles of Human Knowledge*. From 1728 to 1731 he was in Rhode Island planning a missionary college in Bermuda. When an expected government grant from England failed, he returned home and in 1734 was made Bishop of Cloyne. He died at Oxford in 1753. The selection below is the Introduction to *A Treatise*.

I. PHILOSOPHY being nothing else but *the study of wisdom and truth*, it may with reason be expected, that those who have spent most time and pains in it should enjoy a greater calm and serenity of mind, a greater clearness and evidence of knowledge, and be less disturbed with doubts and difficulties than other men. Yet so it is, we see the illiterate bulk of mankind, that walk the high road of plain, common sense, and are governed by the dictates of nature, for the most part easy and undisturbed. To them nothing *that is familiar* appears unaccountable or difficult to comprehend. They complain not of any want of evidence in their senses, and are out of all danger of becoming *sceptics*. But no sooner do we depart from sense and instinct to follow the light of a superior principle, to reason, meditate, and reflect on the nature of things, but a thousand scruples spring up in our minds, concerning those things which before we seemed fully to comprehend. Prejudices and errors of sense do from all parts discover themselves to our view; and endeavouring to correct these by reason, we are insensibly drawn into uncouth paradoxes, difficulties, and inconsistences, which multiply and grow upon us as we advance in speculation; till at length, having wandered through many intricate mazes, we find ourselves just where we were, or, which is worse, sit down in a forlorn scepticism.

II. The cause of this is thought to be (1) the obscurity of things, or the natural weakness and imperfection of our understandings. It is said the faculties we have are few, and those designed by nature for the *support* and comfort (pleasure) of life, and not to penetrate into the *inward essence* and constitution of things. Besides, (2) the mind of man being finite, when it treats of things which partake of infinity, it is not to be wondered at if it run into absurdities and contradictions; out of which it is impossible it should ever extricate itself, it being of the nature of infinite not to be comprehended by that which is finite.

III. But perhaps we may be too partial to ourselves in placing the fault originally in our faculties, and not rather in the wrong use we make of them. *It is a hard thing to suppose, that right deductions from true principles should ever end in consequences which cannot be maintained* or made consistent. We should believe that God has dealt more bountifully with the sons of men, than to give them a strong desire for that knowledge which he had placed quite out of their reach. This were not agreeable to the wonted indulgent methods of Providence, which, whatever appetites it may have implanted in the creatures, doth usually furnish them with such means as, if rightly made use of, will not fail to satisfy them. Upon the whole I am inclined to think that the far greater part, if not all, of those difficulties which have hitherto amused philosophers, and blocked up the way to knowledge, are entirely owing to ourselves. That we have first raised a dust, and then complain we cannot see.

IV. My purpose therefore, is, to try if I can discover what those principles are, which have introduced all that doubtfulness and uncertainty, those absurdities and contradictions into the several sects of philosophy; insomuch that the wisest men have thought our ignorance incurable, conceiving it to arise from the natural dullness and limitation of our faculties. And surely it is a work well deserving our pains, to make a strict inquiry concerning the first principles of human knowledge, to sift and examine them on all sides: especially since there may be some grounds to suspect that those lets and difficulties, which stay and embarrass the mind in its search after truth, do not spring from any darkness and intricacy in the objects, or natural defect in the understanding, so much as from false principles which have been insisted on, and might have been avoided.

V. How difficult and discouraging soever this attempt may seem, when I consider how many great and extraordinary men have gone before me in the same designs: yet I am not without some hopes, upon the consideration that the largest views are not always the clearest, and that he who is short-sighted will be obliged to draw the object nearer, and may, perhaps, by a close and narrow survey, discern that which had escaped far better eyes.

VI. *A chief source of error in all parts of knowledge.*— In order to prepare the mind of the reader for the easier conceiving what follows, it is proper to premise somewhat, by way of introduction, concerning the nature and abuse of language. But the unravelling this matter leads me in some measure to anticipate my design, by taking notice of what seems to have had a chief part in rendering speculation intricate and perplexed, and to have occasioned innumerable errors and difficulties in almost all parts of knowledge. And that is the opinion that the mind hath a power of framing *abstract ideas* or notions of things. He who is not a perfect stranger to the writings and disputes of philosophers, must needs acknowledge that no small part of them are spent about abstract ideas. These are, in a more especial manner, thought to be the object of those sciences which go by the name of *logic* and *metaphysics,* and of all that which passes under the notion of the most abstracted and sublime learning, in all which one shall scarce find any question handled in such a manner, as does not suppose their existence in the mind, and that it is well acquainted with them.

VII. *Proper acceptation of abstraction.*—It is agreed, on all hands, that the qualities or modes of things do never *really exist each of them apart by itself*, and separated from all others, but are mixed, as it were, and blended together, several in the same object. But we are told, the mind being able to consider each quality singly, or abstracted from those other qualities with which it is united, does by that means frame to itself abstract ideas. For example, there is perceived by sight an object extended, coloured, and moved: this mixed or compound idea the mind resolving into its simple, constituent parts, and viewing each by itself, exclusive of the rest, does frame the abstract ideas of extension, colour, and motion. Not that it is possible for colour or motion to exist without extension: but only that the mind can frame to itself by *abstraction* the idea of colour exclusive of extension, and of motion exclusive of both colour and extension.

VIII.—*Of generalizing*—Again, the mind having observed that in the particular extensions perceived by sense, there is something *common* and alike *in all*, and some other things peculiar, as this or that figure or magnitude, which distinguish them one from another; it considers apart or singles out by itself that which is common, making thereof a most abstract idea of extension, which is neither line, surface, nor solid, nor has any figure or magnitude, but is an idea entirely prescinded from all these. So likewise the mind, by leaving out of the particular colours perceived by sense, that which distinguishes them one from another, and retaining that only which is *common to all*, makes an idea of colour in abstract, which is neither red, nor blue, nor white, nor any other determinate colour. And in like manner, by considering motion abstractedly not only from the body moved, but likewise from the figure it describes, and all particular directions and velocities, the abstract idea of motion is framed; which equally corresponds to all particular motions whatsoever that may be perceived by sense.

IX. *Of compounding.*—And as the mind frames to itself abstract ideas of qualities or *modes,* so does it, by the same precision or mental separation, attain abstract ideas of the more compounded *beings,* which include several coexistent qualities. For example, the mind having observed that Peter, James, and John resemble each other, in certain common agreements of shape and other qualities, leaves out of the complex or compounded idea it has of Peter, James, and any other particular man, that which is peculiar to each, retaining only what is common to all; and so makes an abstract idea wherein all the particulars equally partake, abstracting entirely from the cutting off all those circumstances and differences, which might determine it to any particular existence. And after this manner it is said we come by the abstract idea of *man,* or, if you please, humanity or human nature; wherein it is true there is included colour, because there is no man but has some colour, but then it can be neither white, nor black, nor any particular colour; because there is no one particular colour wherein all men partake. So likewise there is included stature, but then it is neither tall stature nor low stature, nor yet middle stature, but something abstracted from all these. And so of the rest. Moreover, there being a great variety of other creatures that partake in some parts, but not all, of the complex idea of *man,* the mind leaving out those parts which are peculiar to men, and retaining those only which are common to all the living creatures, frameth the idea of *animal,* which abstracts not only from all particular men, but also all birds, beasts, fishes, and insects. The constituent parts of the abstract idea of animal are body, life, sense, and spontaneous motion. By *body* is meant, body without any particular shape or figure, there being no one shape or figure common to all animals, without covering, either of hair or feathers, or scales, &c., nor yet naked: hair, feathers, scales, and nakedness being the distinguishing properties of particular animals, and for that reason left out of the *abstract idea.* Upon the same account the spontaneous motion must be neither walking, nor flying, nor creeping; it is nevertheless a motion, but what that motion is, it is not easy to conceive.

X. *Two objections to the existence of abstract ideas.*— Whether others have this wonderful faculty of *abstracting their ideas,* they best can tell: for myself I find indeed I have a faculty of imagining, or representing to myself the ideas of those particular things I have perceived, and of variously compounding and dividing them. I can imagine a man with two heads, or the upper parts of a man joined to the body of a horse. I can consider the hand, the eye, the nose, each by itself abstracted or separated from the rest of the body. But then whatever hand or eye I imagine, it must have some particular shape and colour. Likewise the idea of man that I frame to myself, must be either of a white, or a black, or a tawny, a straight, or a crooked, a tall, or a low, or a middle-sized man. I cannot by any effort of thought conceive the abstract idea above described. And it is equally impossible for me to form the abstract idea of motion distinct from the body moving, and which is neither swift nor slow, curvilinear nor rectilinear; and the like may be said of all other abstract general ideas whatsoever. To be plain, I own myself able to abstract *in one sense,* as when I consider some particular parts or qualities separated from others, with which though they are united in some object, yet it is possible they may really exist without them. But I deny that I can abstract one from another, or conceive separately, those qualities which it is impossible should exist so separated; or that I can frame a general notion by abstracting from particulars in the manner aforesaid. Which two last are the proper acceptations of *abstraction.* And there are grounds to think most men will acknowledge themselves to be in my case. The generality of men which are simple and illiterate never pretend to *abstract notions.* (1) It is said they are difficult, and not to be attained without pains and study. We may therefore reasonably conclude that, if such there be, they are confined only to the learned.

XI. I proceed to examine what can be alleged in *defence*

of the doctrine of abstraction, and try if I can discover what it is that inclines the men of speculation to embrace an opinion so remote from common sense as that seems to be. There has been a late deservedly esteemed philosopher, who, no doubt, has given it very much countenance by seeming to think the having abstract general ideas is what puts the widest difference in point of understanding betwixt man and beast. "The having of general ideas," saith he, "is that which puts a perfect distinction betwixt man and brutes, and is an excellency which the faculties of brutes do by no means attain unto. For it is evident we observe no footsteps in them of making use of general signs for universal ideas; from which we have reason to imagine that they have not the faculty of *abstracting,* or making general ideas, since they have no use of words or any other general signs." And a little after: "Therefore, I think, we may suppose that it is in this that the species of brutes are discriminated from men and it is that proper difference wherein they are wholly separated, and which at last widens to so wide a distance. For if they have any ideas at all, and are not bare machines (as some would have them), we cannot deny them to have some reason. It seems as evident to me that they do some of them in certain instances reason as that they have sense, but it is only in particular ideas, just as they receive them from their senses. They are the best of them tied up within those narrow bounds, and have not (as I think) the faculty to enlarge them by any kind of *abstraction.*" Essay on Hum. Underst., b. ii. ch. xi. sect. 10, 11. I readily agree with this learned author, that the faculties of brutes can by no means attain to *abstraction.* But then if this be made the distinguishing property of that sort of animals, I fear a great many of those that pass for men must be reckoned into their number. The reason that is here assigned why we have no grounds to think brutes have abstract general ideas, is that we observe in them no use of words or any other general signs; which is built on this supposition, to wit, that the making use of words implies the having general ideas. From which it follows, that men who use language are able to *abstract* or *generalize* their ideas. That this is the sense and arguing of the author will further appear by his answering the question he in another place puts. "Since all things that exist are only particulars, how come we by general terms?" His answer is, "Words become general by being made the signs of general ideas." Essay on Hum. Underst., b. iii. ch. iii. sect. 6. But it seems that (2) a word becomes general by being made the sign, not of an *abstract* general idea, but of several particular ideas, any one of which it indifferently suggests to the mind. For example, when it is said *the change of motion is proportional to the impressed force*, or that *whatever has extension is divisible;* these propositions are to be understood of motion and extension in general, and nevertheless it will not follow that they suggest to my thoughts an idea of motion without a body moved, or any determinate direction and velocity, or that I must conceive an abstract general idea of extension, which is neither line, surface, nor solid, neither great nor small, black, white, nor red, nor of any other determinate colour. It is only implied that whatever motion I consider, whether it be swift or slow, perpendicular, horizontal, or oblique, or in whatever object, the axiom concerning it holds equally true. As does the other of every particular extension, it matters not whether line, surface, or solid, whether of this or that magnitude or figure.

XII. *Existence of general ideas admitted.*—By observing how ideas become general, we may the better judge how words are made so. And here it is to be noted that I do not deny absolutely there are general ideas, but only that there are any *abstract general ideas*: for in the passages above quoted, wherein there is mention of general ideas, it is always supposed that they are formed by *abstraction*, after the manner set forth in Sects. viii and ix. Now if we will annex a meaning to our words, and speak only of what we can conceive, I believe we shall acknowledge, that an idea, which considered in itself is particular, becomes general, by being made to represent or stand for all other particular ideas of the *same sort*. To make this plain by an example, suppose a geometrician is demonstrating the method of cutting a line in two equal parts. He draws, for instance, a black line of an inch in length; this, which in itself is a particular line, is nevertheless with regard to its signification general, since, as it is there used, it represents all particular lines whatsoever; so that what is demonstrated of it, is demonstrated of all lines, or, in other words, of a line in general. And as that particular line becomes general, by being made a sign, so the name *line*, which taken absolutely is *particular*, by being a sign is made *general*. And as the former owes its generality, not to its being the sign of an abstract or general line, but of *all particular* right lines that may possibly exist; so the latter must be thought to derive its generality from the same cause, namely, the *various particular* lines which it indifferently denotes.

XIII. *Abstract general ideas necessary, according to Locke.* —To give the reader a yet clearer view of the nature of abstract ideas, and the uses they are thought necessary to, I shall add one more passage out of the Essay on Human Understanding, which is as follows. "*Abstract ideas* are not so obvious or easy to children or the yet unexercised mind as particular ones. If they seem so to grown men, it is only because by constant and familiar use they are made so. For when we nicely reflect upon them, we shall find that general ideas are fictions and contrivances of the mind, that carry difficulty with them, and do not so easily offer themselves as we are apt to imagine. For example, does it not require some pains and skill to form the general idea of a triangle? (which is yet none of the most abstract, comprehensive, and difficult;) for it must be neither oblique nor rectangle, neither equilateral, equicrural, nor scalenon, but *all and none* of these at once. In effect, it is something imperfect that cannot exist, an idea wherein some parts of several different and *inconsistent* ideas are put together. It is true the mind in this imperfect state has need of such ideas, and makes all the haste to them it can, for the (1) *conveniency of communication and* (2) *enlargement of knowledge,* to both which it is naturally very much inclined. But yet one has reason to suspect such ideas are marks of our imperfection. At least this is enough to show that the most abstract and general ideas are not those that the mind is first and most easily acquainted with, nor such as its earliest knowledge is conversant about." Book iv. ch. vii. sect. 9. If any man has the faculty of framing in his mind such an idea of a triangle as is here described, it is in vain to pretend to dispute him out of it, nor would I go about it. All I desire is, that the reader would fully and certainly inform himself whether he has such an idea or no. And this, methinks, can be no hard task for any one to perform. What more easy than for any one to look a little into his own thoughts, and there try whether he has, or can attain to have, an idea that shall correspond with the description that is here given of the general idea of a triangle, which is, *neither oblique, nor rectangle, equilateral, equicrural, nor scalenon, but all and none of these at once?*

XIV. *But they are not necessary for communication.—* Much is here said of the difficulty that abstract ideas carry with them, and the pains and skill requisite to the forming them. And it is on all hands agreed that there is need of great toil and labour of the mind, to emancipate our thoughts from particular objects, and raise them to those sublime speculations that are conversant about abstract ideas. From all which the natural consequence should seem to be, that so *difficult* a thing as the forming abstract ideas was not necessary for *communication*, which is so *easy* and familiar to *all sorts of men.* But we are told, if they seem obvious and easy to grown men, *it is only because by constant and familiar use they are made so.* Now I would fain know at what time it is men are employed in surmounting that difficulty, and furnishing themselves with those necessary helps for discourse. It cannot be when they are grown-up, for then it seems they are not conscious of any such painstaking; it remains therefore to be the business of their childhood. And surely, the great and multiplied labour of framing abstract notions will be found a hard task for that tender age. Is it not a hard thing to imagine, that a couple of children cannot prate together of their sugarplums, and rattles, and the rest of their little trinkets, till they have first tacked together numberless inconsistencies, and so framed in their minds *abstract general ideas,* and annexed them to every common name they make use of?

XV. *Nor for the enlargement of knowledge.*—Nor do I think them a whit more needful for the *enlargement of knowledge* than for *communication.* It is, I know, a point much insisted on, that all knowledge and demonstration are about universal notions, to which I fully agree: but then it doth not appear to me that these notions are formed by *abstraction* in the manner premised; *universality,* so far as I can comprehend, not consisting in the absolute, *positive* nature or conception of any thing, but in the *relation* it bears to the particulars signified or represented by it: by virtue whereof it is that things, names, or notions, being in their own nature *particular* are rendered *universal.* Thus when I demonstrate any propositions concerning triangles, it is to be supposed that I have in view the universal idea of a triangle; which ought not to be understood as if I could frame an idea of a triangle which was neither equilateral, nor scalenon, nor equicrural. But only that the particular triangle I consider, whether of this or that sort it matters not, doth equally stand for and represent all rectilinear triangles whatsoever, and is, in that sense, *universal.* All which seems very plain, and not to include any difficulty in it.

XVI. *Objection.—Answer.*—But here it will be demanded, *how we can know any proposition to be true of all particular triangles, except* we have first seen it *demonstrated of the abstract idea of a triangle* which equally agrees to all? For, because a property may be demonstrated to agree to some one particular triangle, it will not thence follow that it equally belongs to any other triangle, which in all respects is not the same with it. For example, having demonstrated that the three angles of an isosceles rectangular triangle are equal to two right ones, I cannot therefore conclude this affection agrees to all other triangles, which have neither a right angle, nor two equal sides. It seems therefore that, to be certain this proposition is universally true, we must either make a particular demonstration for every particular triangle, which is impossible, or once for all demonstrate it of the *abstract idea of a triangle*, in which all the particulars do indifferently partake, and by which they are all equally represented. To which I answer, that though the idea I have in view whilst I make the demonstration, be, for instance, that of an isosceles rectangular triangle, whose sides are of a determinate length, I may nevertheless be certain it extends to all other rectilinear triangles, of what sort of bigness soever. And that, because neither the right angle, nor the equality, nor determinate length of the sides, are at all concerned in the demonstration. It is true, the diagram I have in view includes all these particulars, but then there is not the least mention made of them in the proof of the proposition. It is not said, the three angles are equal to two right ones, because one of them is a right angle, or because the sides comprehending it are of the same length. Which sufficiently shows that the right angle might have been oblique, and the sides unequal, and for all that the demonstration have held good. And for this reason it is, that I conclude that to be true of any obliquangular or scalenon, which I had demonstrated of a particular right-angled, equicrural triangle; and not because I demonstrated the proposition of the abstract idea of a triangle. And here it must be acknowledged, that a man may consider a figure merely as triangular, without attending to the particular qualities of the angles, or relations of the sides. So far he may abstract: but this will never prove that he can frame an abstract general inconsistent idea of a triangle. In like manner we may consider Peter so far forth as man, or so far forth as animal, without framing the forementioned abstract idea, either of man or of animal, inasmuch as all that is perceived is not considered.

XVII. *Advantage of investigating the doctrine of abstract general ideas.*—It were an endless, as well as a useless thing, to trace the *schoolmen,* those great masters of abstraction, through all the manifold, inextricable labyrinths of error and dispute, which their doctrine of abstract natures and notions seems to have led them into. What bickerings and controversies, and what a learned dust have been raised about those matters, and what mighty advantage hath been from thence derived to mankind, are things at this day too clearly known to need being insisted on. And it had been well if the ill effects of that doctrine were confined to those only who make the most avowed profession of it. When men consider the great pains, industry, and parts, that have, for so many ages, been laid out on the cultivation and advancement of the sciences, and that nothwithstanding all this, the far greater part of them remain full of darkness and uncertainty, and disputes that are like never to have an end, and even those that are thought to be supported by the most clear and cogent demonstrations, contain in them paradoxes which are perfectly irreconcilable to the understandings of men, and that, taking all together, a small portion of them doth supply any real benefit to mankind, otherwise than by being an innocent diversion and amusement: I say, the consideration of all this is apt to throw them into a despondency, and perfect contempt of all study. But this may perhaps cease, upon a view of the false principles that have obtained in the world, amongst all which there is none, methinks, hath a more wide influence over the thoughts of speculative men, than this of abstract general ideas.

XVIII. I come now to consider the *source of this prevailing notion,* and that seems to me to be *language.* And surely nothing of less extent than reason itself could have been the source of an opinion so universally received. The truth of this appears as from other reasons, so also from the plain confession of the ablest patrons of abstract ideas, who acknowledge that they are made in order to naming; from which it is a clear consequence, that if there had been no such thing as speech or universal signs, there never had been any thought of abstraction. See book iii. ch. vi. sect. 39, and elsewhere, of the Essay on Human Understanding. Let us therefore examine the manner wherein words have contributed to the origin of that mistake. First, then, it is thought that every name hath, or ought to have, *one only* precise and settled signification, which inclines men to think there are certain *abstract, determinate ideas,* which constitute the true and only immediate signification of each general name. And that it is by the mediation of these abstract ideas, that a general name comes to signify any particular thing. Whereas, in truth, there is no such thing as one precise and definite signification annexed to any general name, they all signifiying indifferently a great number of particular ideas. All which doth evidently follow from what has been already said, and will clearly appear to any one by a little reflection. To this it will be *objected*, that every name that has a definition, is thereby restrained to one certain signification. For example, a *triangle* is defined to be a *plain surface comprehended by three right lines;* by which that name is limited to denote one certain idea and no other. To which I answer, that in the definition it is not said whether the surface be great or small, black or white, nor whether the sides are long or short, equal or unequal, nor with what angles they are inclined to each other; in all which there may be great variety, and consequently there is *no one settled idea* which limits the signification of the word *triangle*. It is one thing for to keep a name constantly to the same definition, and another to make it stand every where for the same idea: the one is necessary, the other useless and impracticable.

XIX. *Secondly,* But to give a further account how *words* came to *produce the doctrine of abstract ideas,* it must be observed that it is a received opinion, that language has *no other end* but the communicating our ideas, and that every significant name stands for an idea. This being so, and it being withal certain, that names, which yet are not thought altogether insignificant, do not always mark out *particular* conceivable ideas, it is straightway concluded that *they stand for abstract notions.* That there are many names in use amongst speculative men, which do not always suggest to others determinate particular ideas, is what nobody will deny. And a little attention will discover, that it is not necessary (even in the strictest reasonings) significant names which stand for ideas should, every time they are used, excite in the understanding the ideas they are made to stand for: in reading and discoursing, names being, for the most

part, used as letters are in *algebra*, in which, though a particular quantity be marked by each letter, yet to proceed right
it is not requisite that in every step each letter suggest to
your thoughts that particular quantity it was appointed to
stand for.

XX. *Some of the ends of language.*—Besides, the (1) communicating of ideas marked by words is not the chief and
only end of language, as is commonly supposed. There are
other ends, as the (2) raising of some passion, the exciting
to, or (3) deterring from an action, the (4) putting the mind
in some particular disposition; to which the former is, in
many cases, barely subservient, and sometimes entirely omitted, when these can be obtained without it, as I think doth
not infrequently happen in the familiar use of language. I
entreat the reader to reflect with himself, and see if it doth
not often happen, either in hearing or reading a discourse,
that the passions of fear, love, hatred, admiration, disdain,
and the like, arise immediately in his mind upon the perception of certain words, without any ideas coming between. At
first, indeed, the words might have occasioned ideas that
were fit to produce those emotions; but, if I mistake not, it
will be found that when language is once grown familiar, the
hearing of the sounds or sight of the characters is oft immediately attended with those passions, which at first were wont
to be produced by the intervention of ideas, that are now
quite omitted. May we not, for example, be affected with the
promise of a *good thing,* though we have not an idea of what
it is? Or is not the being threatened with danger sufficient
to excite a dread, though we think not of any particular evil
likely to befall us, nor yet frame to ourselves an idea of danger in abstract? If any one shall join ever so little reflection
of his own to what has been said, I believe it will evidently
appear to him, that general names are often used in the
propriety of language without the speaker's designing them
for marks of ideas in his own, which he would have them
raise in the mind of the hearer. Even proper names themselves do not seem always spoken with a design to bring into
our view the ideas of those individuals that are supposed to

be marked by them. For example, when a schoolman tells me "Aristotle hath said it," all I conceive he means by it, is to dispose me to embrace his opinion with the deference and submission which custom has annexed to that name. And this effect may be so instantly produced in the minds of those who are accustomed to resign their judgment to the authority of that philosopher, as it is impossible any idea either of his person, writings, or reputation, should go before. Innumerable examples of this kind may be given, but why should I insist on those things which every one's experience will, I doubt not, plentifully suggest unto him?

XXI. *Caution in the use of language necessary.*—We have, I think shown (1) the impossibility of *abstract ideas.* We have considered (2) what has been said for them by their ablest patrons; and endeavoured to show they are of no use for those ends to which they are thought necessary. And lastly, we have (3) traced them to the source from whence they flow, which appears to be language. It cannot be denied that words are of excellent use; in that, by their means, all that stock of knowledge, which has been purchased by the joint labours of inquisitive men in all ages and nations, may be drawn into the view and made the possession of one single person. But at the same time it must be owned that most parts of knowledge have been strangely perplexed and darkened by the abuse of words, and general ways of speech wherein they are delivered. Since, therefore, words are so apt to impose on the understanding, whatever ideas I consider, I shall endeavour to take them bare and naked into my view, keeping out of my thoughts, so far as I am able, those names which long and constant use hath so strictly united with them; from which I may expect to derive the following advantages:—

XXII. *First,* I shall be sure to get clear of all controversies *purely verbal;* the springing up of which weeds in almost all the sciences has been a main hindrance to the growth of true and sound knowledge. *Secondly.* this seems to be a sure way to extricate myself out of that fine and subtile net of *abstract ideas,* which has so miserably perplexed and entangled the

minds of men, and that with this peculiar circumstance, that
by how much the finer and more curious was the wit of any
man, by so much the deeper was he like to be ensnared, and
faster held therein. *Thirdly,* so long as I confine my thoughts
to my own ideas divested of words, I do not see how I can
be easily mistaken. The objects, I consider, I clearly and
adequately know. I cannot be deceived in thinking I have an
idea which I have not. It is not possible for me to imagine,
that any of my own ideas are like or unlike, that are not truly
so. To discern the agreements or disagreements that are between my ideas, to see what ideas are included in any compound idea, and what not, there is nothing more requisite,
than an attentive perception of what passes in my own understanding.

XXIII. But the attainment of all *these advantages* doth
presuppose an entire deliverance from the deception of words,
which I dare hardly promise myself; so difficult a thing it is
to dissolve a union so early begun, and confirmed by so long
a habit as that betwixt words and ideas. Which difficulty
seems to have been very much increased by the doctrine of
abstraction. For so long as men thought abstract ideas were
annexed to their words, it doth not seem strange that they
should use words for ideas: it being found an impracticable
thing to lay aside the word, and *retain the abstract idea in
the mind, which in itself was perfectly inconceivable.* This
seems to me the principal cause, why those men who have so
emphatically recommended to others the laying aside all use
of words in their meditations, and contemplating their bare
ideas, have yet failed to perform it themselves. Of late many
have been very sensible of the absurd opinions and insignificant disputes, which grow out of the abuse of words. And in
order to remedy these evils they advise well, that we attend
to the ideas signified, and draw off our attention from the
words which signify them. But how good soever this advice
may be they have given others, it is plain they could not
have a due regard to it themselves, so long as they thought
(1) the only immediate use of words was to signify ideas,

and that (2) the immediate signification of every general name was a *determinate, abstract idea.*

XXIV. But *these being known to be mistakes, a man may* with greater ease *prevent his being imposed on by words.* He that knows he has no other than particular ideas, will not puzzle himself in vain to find out and conceive the abstract idea, annexed to any name. And he that knows names do not always stand for ideas, will spare himself the labour of looking for ideas, where there are none to be had. It were therefore to be wished that every one would use his utmost endeavours, to obtain a clear view of the ideas he would consider, separating from them all that dress and encumbrance of words which so much contribute to blind the judgment and divide the attention. In vain do we extend our view into the heavens, and pry into the entrails of the earth; in vain do we consult the writings of learned men, and trace the dark footsteps of antiquity; we need only draw the curtain of words, to behold the fairest tree of knowledge, whose fruit is excellent, and within the reach of our hand.

XXV. Unless we take care *to clear the first principles of knowledge, from the* embarrass and *delusion of words,* we may make infinite reasonings upon them to no purpose: we may draw consequences from consequences, and be never the wiser. The further we go, we shall only lose ourselves the more irrecoverably, and be the deeper entangled in difficulties and mistakes. Whoever therefore designs to read the following sheets, I entreat him to make my words the occasion of his own thinking, and endeavour to attain the same train of thoughts in reading, that I had in writing them. By this means it will be easy for him to discover the truth or falsity of what I say. He will be out of all danger of being deceived by my words, and I do not see how he can be led into an error by considering his own naked, undisguised ideas.

"Of the Origin of Our Ideas"

David Hume

David Hume was born in Edinburgh in 1711—as he says in *My Own Life*, "of a good Family both by Father and Mother. . . . My Family, however, was not rich." He entered Edinburgh University in 1723, and apparently left without taking a degree. For several years he studied law. Increasingly, however, he grew interested in philosophy-literature. His *Treatise of Human Nature* may have been projected before he left college—but certainly by the time he was twenty-one. It was published in 1739-40. Later works were *Political Discourses, History of England,* and *Dialogues on Natural Religion.* He died in 1776. The selection here is Section 1 of Part I of *A Treatise of Human Nature.*

ALL the perceptions of the human mind resolve themselves into two distinct kinds, which I shall call *impressions* and *ideas.* The difference betwixt these consists in the degrees of force and liveliness, with which they strike upon the mind, and make their way into our thought or consciousness. Those perceptions which enter with most force and violence, we may name *impressions;* and, under this name, I comprehend all our sensations, passions, and emotions, as they make their first appearance in the soul. By *ideas,* I mean the faint images of these in thinking and reasoning; such as, for instance, are all the perceptions excited by the present discourse, excepting only those which arise from the sight and touch, and excepting the immediate pleasure or uneasiness it may occasion. I believe it will not be very necessary to employ many words in explaining this distinction. Every one of himself will readily perceive the difference betwixt feeling and thinking. The common degrees of these are easily distinguished; though it is not impossible but, in particular instances, they may very nearly approach to each other. Thus, in sleep, in a fever, in madness, or in any very violent emotions of soul, our ideas may approach to our impressions: as, on the other hand, it sometimes happens, that our impressions are so faint and low, that we cannot distinguish them from our ideas. But, notwithstanding this near resemblance in a few instances, they are in general so very different, that no one can make a scruple to rank them under distinct heads, and assign to each a peculiar name to mark the difference.

There is another division of our perceptions, which it will be convenient to observe, and which extends itself both to our impressions and ideas. This division is into *simple* and *complex*. Simple perceptions, or impressions and ideas, are such as admit of no distinction nor separation. The complex are the contrary to these, and may be distinguished into parts. Though a particular colour, taste, and smell, are qualities all united together in this apple, it is easy to perceive they are not the same, but are at least distinguishable from each other.

Having, by these divisions, given an order and arrangement to our objects, we may now apply ourselves to consider, with the more accuracy, their qualities and relations. The first circumstance that strikes my eye, is the great resemblance betwixt our impressions and ideas in every other particular, except their degree of force and vivacity. The one seems to be, in a manner, the reflection of the other; so that all the perceptions of the mind are double, and appear both as impressions and ideas. When I shut my eyes, and think of my chamber, the ideas I form are exact representations of the impressions I felt; nor is there any circumstance of the one, which is not to be found in the other. In running over my other perceptions, I find still the same resemblance and representation. Ideas and impressions appear always to correspond to each other. This circumstance seems to me remarkable, and engages my attention for a moment.

Upon a more accurate survey I find I have been carried away too far by the first appearance, and that I must make use of the distinction of perceptions into *simple* and *complex,* to limit this general decision, *that all our ideas and impressions are resembling.* I observe that many of our complex ideas never had impressions that corresponded to them, and that many of our complex impressions never are exactly copied in ideas. I can imagine to myself such a city as the New Jerusalem, whose pavement is gold, and walls are rubies, though I never saw any such. I have seen Paris; but shall I affirm I can form such an idea of that city, as will perfectly represent all its streets and houses in their real and just proportions?

I perceive, therefore, that though there is, in general, a great resemblance betwixt our *complex* impressions and ideas, yet the rule is not universally true, that they are exact copies of each other. We may next consider, how the case stands with our *simple* perceptions. After the most accurate examination of which I am capable, I venture to affirm, that the rule here holds without any exception, and that every simple idea has a simple impression, which resembles it, and every simple impression a correspondent idea. That idea of red, which we form in the dark, and that impression which strikes our eyes in sunshine, differ only in degree, not in nature. That the case is the same with all our simple impressions and ideas, it is impossible to prove by a particular enumeration of them. Every one may satisfy himself in this point by running over as many as he pleases. But if any one should deny this universal resemblance, I know no way of convincing him, but by desiring him to show a simple impression that has not a correspondent idea, or a simple idea that has not a correspondent impression. If he does not answer this challenge, as it is certain he cannot, we may, from his silence and our own observation, establish our conclusion.

Thus we find, that all simple ideas and impressions resemble each other; and, as the complex are formed from them, we affirm in general, that these two species of perception are exactly correspondent. Having discovered this relation, which requires no further examination, I am curious to find some other of their qualities. Let us consider, how they stand with regard to their existence, and which of the impressions and ideas are causes, and which effects.

The full examination of this question is the subject of the present treatise; and, therefore, we shall here content ourselves with establishing one general proposition, *That all our simple ideas in their first appearance, are derived from simple impressions, which are correspondent to them, and which they exactly represent.*

In seeking for phenomena to prove this proposition, I find only those of two kinds; but, in each kind the phenomena are obvious, numerous, and conclusive. I first make myself certain, by a new review, of what I have already asserted, that every simple impression is attended with a correspondent idea, and every simple idea with a correspondent impression. From this constant conjunction of resembling perceptions I immediately conclude, that there is a great connection betwixt our correspondent impressions and ideas, and that the existence of the one has a considerable influence upon that of the other. Such a constant conjunction, in such an infinite number of instances, can never arise from chance; but clearly proves a dependence of the impressions on the ideas, or of the ideas on the impressions. That I may know on which side this dependence lies, I consider the order of their *first appearance;* and find, by constant experience, that the simple impressions always take the precedence of their correspondent ideas, but never appear in the contrary order. To give a child an idea of scarlet or orange, of sweet or bitter, I present the objects, or, in other words, convey to him these impressions; but proceed not so absurdly, as to endeavour to produce the impressions by exciting the ideas. Our ideas, upon their appearance, produce not their correspondent impressions, nor do we perceive any colour, or feel any sensation merely upon thinking of them. On the other hand we find, that any impression, either of the mind or body, is constantly followed by an idea, which resembles it, and is only different in the degrees of force and liveliness. The constant conjunction of our resembling perceptions, is a convincing proof, that the one are the causes of the other; and this priority of the impressions is an equal proof, that our impressions are the cause of our ideas, not our ideas of our impressions.

To confirm this, I consider another plain and convincing phenomenon; which is, that wherever, by any accident, the faculties which give rise to any impressions are obstructed in their operations, as when one is born blind or deaf, not only the impressions are lost, but also their correspondent ideas; so that there never appear in the mind the least trace of either of them. Nor is this only true, where the organs of sensations are entirely destroyed, but likewise where they have never been put in action to produce a particular impression. We cannot form to ourselves a just idea of the taste of a pineapple, without having actually tasted it.

There is, however, one contradictory phenomenon, which may prove, that it is not absolutely impossible for ideas to go before their correspondent impressions. I believe it will readily be allowed, that the several distinct ideas of colours, which enter by the eyes, or those of sounds, which are conveyed by the hearing, are really different from each other, though, at the same time, resembling. Now, if this be true of different colours, it must be no less so of the different shades of the same colour, that each of them produces a distinct idea, independent of the rest. For if this should be denied, it is possible, by the continual gradation of shades, to run a colour insensibly into what is most remote from it; and, if you will not allow any of the means to be different, you cannot, without absurdity, deny the extremes to be the same. Suppose, therefore, a person to have enjoyed his sight for thirty years, and to have become perfectly well acquainted with colours of all kinds, excepting one particular shade of blue, for instance, which it never has been his fortune to meet with. Let all the different shades of that colour, except that single one, be placed before him, descending gradually from the deepest to the lightest; it is plain, that he will perceive a blank, where that shade is wanting, and will be sensible that there is a greater distance in that place, betwixt the contiguous colours, than in any other. Now I ask, whether it is possible for him, from his own imagination, to supply this deficiency, and raise up to himself the idea of that particular shade, though it had never been conveyed to him by his senses? I believe there are few but will be of opinion that he can; and this may serve as a proof, that the simple ideas are not always derived from the correspondent impressions; though the instance is so particular and singular, that it is scarce worth our observing, and does not merit that, for it alone, we should alter our general maxim.

But, besides this exception, it may not be amiss to remark, on this head, that the principle of the priority of impressions to ideas, must be understood with another limitation, viz. that as our ideas are images of our impressions, so we can form secondary ideas, which are images of the primary, as appears from this very reasoning concerning them. This is not, properly speaking, an exception to the rule so much as an explanation of it. Ideas produce the images of themselves in new ideas; but as the first ideas are supposed to be derived from impressions, it still remains true, that all our simple ideas proceed, either mediately or immediately, from their correspondent impressions.

This, then, is the first principle I establish in the science of human nature; nor ought we to despise it because of the simplicity of its appearance. For it is remarkable, that the present question concerning the precedency of our impressions or ideas, is the same with what has made so much noise in other terms, when it has been disputed whether there be any *innate ideas,* or whether all ideas be derived from sensation and reflection. We may observe, that in order to prove the ideas of extension and colour not to be innate, philosophers do nothing but show that they are conveyed by our senses. To prove the ideas of passion and desire not to be innate, they observe, that we have a preceding experience of these emotions in ourselves. Now, if we carefully examine these arguments, we shall find that they prove nothing but that ideas are preceded by other more lively perceptions, from which they are derived, and which they represent. I hope this clear stating of the question will remove all disputes concerning it, and will render this principle of more use in our reasonings, than it seems hitherto to have been.

A Treatise on Language

Alexander Bryan Johnson

A. B. Johnson is often referred to as America's first semanticist. Born in England in 1786, he came to Utica, New
York, to join his father in 1801. From that time onward he
was almost entirely self-educated. For many years he was
successful in business, especially in banking. He died in
1867. During his leisure hours he was reticent and studious,
writing copiously in many fields, from finance to language.
The Philosophy of Human Knowledge appeared in 1828; it
was revised and enlarged, and published by Harper and
Brothers in 1836 under the title, *A Treatise on Language: or
the Relation Which Words Bear to Things*. The selections
from the work used here are Lecture I and Lecture II.

Lecture I

INTRODUCTION

§ 1.—*To know the extent of our powers will save us from
impracticable pursuits.*

Man exists in a world of his own creation. He cannot step,
but on ground transformed by culture; nor look, but on objects produced by art. The animals which constitute his food
are unknown to nature, while trees, fruits, and herbs, are the
trophies of his labour. In himself nearly every natural impulse is suppressed as vicious, and every mortification solicit-
ed as a virtue. His language, actions, sentiments, and desires,
are nearly all factitious. Stupendous in achievement, he is
boundless in attempt. Having subdued the earth's surface,
he would explore its centre; having vanquished diseases, he

would subdue death. Unsatisfied with recording the past, he would anticipate the future. Uncontented with subjugating the ocean, he would traverse the air. Success but sharpens his avidity, and facility but augments his impatience. To know the extent of our powers is therefore important, that in our restlessness for further acquisitions we may neither dissipate strength in designs for which our faculties are unsuited, nor attempt practicabilities by incompetent methods.

§ 2.—*We are in little danger from the pursuit of physical impracticabilities.*

What we can accomplish in physicks, may be safely left to the development of experiment; for though alchymy and perpetual motion have occasioned some waste of time, tangible bodies oppose so sturdily our errours when we attempt physical incongruities, that we lose little by such attempts. Even royalty, which seldom hears unsophisticated truths, is treated by physical bodies as unceremoniously as the commonalty.

§ 3.—*We are in danger of wasting time in verbal investigations.*

Speculative researches are accommodating to human weakness. From geology, which teaches us what exists in the centre of the earth, to astronomy, which reveals what is transpiring in the empyrean;—and from physicks, which discourse about the body, to metaphysicks, which treat of the mind; the mass of verbal doctrine assumes any shape which ingenuity strives to create:—like the pebbles of Rockaway, that change their position as every wave, rising on the ruins of its predecessor, rushes, (lord of the moment,) proudly over the beach.

§ 4.—*To ascertain the capacity that language possesses for discoursing of external existences which our senses cannot discover, will enable us, more understandingly than at present, as estimated theories.*

To fix the fluctuating mass of theories, no man has suggested any other expedient than the construction of some new theory, to whose authority, (like to Johnson's orthography,) all persons shall submit. The remedy is constantly augmenting the disease. I shall not imitate so unsuccessful a procedure; but as theories are the means by which we attempt to discourse of external existences that our senses cannot discover; and as the desire for such discourse originates a large portion of our theories; I will teach you the capacity of language for such an employment, and thereby enable you to judge more understandingly than you can at present, the utility of most theories, and the signification of all.

§ 5.—*No knowledge is more important than a correct appreciation of language.*

But not in theories only is a correct understanding desirable of the capacity of language. Words constitute a great part of all our thoughts. An infusion of words is the means of nearly all instruction, and an ability to repeat words is the substance of much of our learning. When a man is distressed, we administer to him words for his consolation; and when he rejoices, we proffer words to heighten his felicity. Even when medicine admits itself vanquished,—when wealth can no longer purchase a gratification, nor power excite ambition, —words not only maintain their influence, but their potency is augmented by the surrounding desolation.

§ 6.—*Verbal discourse contains defects which have escaped detection.*

Language possessing this important relation to man, the duty is imperative of becoming acquainted with its defects; especially if it contain any which have hitherto escaped detection:—and such it actually contains.

§ 7.—*Significant verbal inquisition is not unlimited.*

Language possesses also an illimitable power of interrogation. Nothing is too sacred to escape its inquires,—nothing too remote,—nothing too minute. We employ it, if not without suspicion that it contains any latent incapacity for unlimited inquisition, with certainly a very indefinite apprehension of its limitations:—hence the importance of defining the limits, (if it possess any,) within which interrogatories are significant. I am prepared to show both that it possesses limited powers in these particulars, and to define the limits.

§ 8.—*Language may be formed into propositions whose results, though incontrovertible by logick, are irreconcileable with our senses.*

Language is also mouldable into propositions that can neither be controverted by any known rules of logick, nor credited without violence to the evidence of our senses:—hence the importance of ascertaining whether language, when thus employed, possesses not a covert signification that will save us from the alternative of either disbelieving our senses, or disbelieving the best demonstrated conclusions. I will satisfy you that it possesses such a signification, and I will teach you the signification of language that is thus sophistically employed. The propositions to which I allude may be known from the following examples:—

1. Mathematicks assures us that the water which placidly flows in our canal, is no where level;—that the walls which constitute the sides of this chamber, are not parallel;—that a line no longer than an inch, is diminishable interminably.

2. Astronomy declares that we are whirled momentarily a thousand miles in one direction, and fifteen miles in another; and in this giddy rotation, our heads travel faster and further than our bodies:—that a portion of mankind walk with their feet diametrically opposite to ours;—that the world is a ball, and assumes at a given distance the appearance of a star;— that comets are hotter than red hot iron, and the sun a body of fire thirteen hundred thousand times larger than the earth; —that tides are caused by the attraction of the moon, and weight produced by the attraction of the earth.

3. Opticks assert that while I look around, and perceive distant hills, spacious streets, lofty buildings, and prosperous activity, I truly see neither spaciousness nor distance, but a miniature, not an inch in diameter, that is painted on the retina of my eyes.

4. Physiology affirms that a ray of light, though it seems colourless, is iridescent; while roses are a mere blank apparatus, display the tints which exist latently in light. Botany has, however, compensated the queen of flowers for this dispar-

agement. Botany insists that plants eat, drink, sleep, and breathe;—that they are male and female;—that their fragrance is amorous sighs, and their motions nervous irritability.

5. Chymistry is peculiarly the science of enchantment. It asserts that water is principally composed of the most inflammable substance in nature;—that our flesh is but a combination of disgustful gases, and diamonds but a preparation of charcoal.

§ 9.—*The verbal defects which these discourses will discuss, are inseparable from language, and differ from any defects that you may anticipate.*

You must not expect that I can, at present, make you understand the defects of the foregoing propositions. All that I shall say hereafter, I deem necessary to convey that information. Indeed, I can afford no better guide to lead you ultimately to a correct understanding of the defects of language, than to say, at a hazard, that I allude to no defects that you ever heard of or conceived. I also allude to none that can be obviated. The most that I hope to perform is to make them known; as we erect a beacon, to denote the presence of a shoal which we cannot remove.

§ 10.—But though you know not the defects to which I refer, still, when you read the conclusions of astronomy that I have above adduced, the conclusions of opticks, of physiology, and chymistry, may you not infer, that if such doctrines are incontestible by logick the doctrines are more repugnant to reason, than the belief that some latent sophistry exists in the language by which the doctrines are expressed, or in the processes by which the doctrines are sustained?

§ 11.—When you hear further, not as an item of revelation to which the judgment is bound to submit, but as a reality, elaborated proudly by the judgment itself, that all things were created out of nothing;—that every existence had a beginning, except the first, which had no beginning;—that every existence sprang from some cause, except the first, which is uncaused;—may we not catch some glimmering of a suspicion, that our words have lost their intelligence in these heights of speculation?—as we read in a book of ingenious absurdities, that a man in a balloon ascended so high, that his hat, which he accidentally removed from his head, flew upwards, having lost its original gravity, and become attracted by the moon's.

§ 12.—*These discourses concern not the relative meaning which words bear to each other, but the relation which words bear to created existences.*

I have gained my present object, if I have excited your attention to the succeeding discourses, and removed some prepossessions that would have prevented you from discovering in language the defects to which I refer; for when I speak of defects in language, most persons suppose that I allude to the admitted ambiguity of speech. My remarks will not concern the relative meaning which words bear to each other, but the relation that words bear to the phenomena of the universe.

§ 13.—*We translate sensible existences into words, instead of interpreting words by the information of our senses.*

When an Englishman is learning to read French, he learns to translate French words into English words. A French word he estimates as a mere representative of some English word. We translate creation much in the same way. Every natural existence we deem a mere representative of some word. Language usurps thus, to an astonishing extent, the dignity which truly belongs to creation. I know we usually say that words are signs of things. Practically, we make things the signs of words.

§ 14.—*We must make our senses the expositors of words, instead of making words the expositors of what our senses reveal.*

Our misuse of language may be illustrated by another simile:—we estimate creation by means of words, much in the same way as we estimate the gravity of bodies by means of weights. My lectures will endeavour to subordinate language to nature,—to make nature the expositor of words, instead of making words the expositors of nature. If I succeed, the success will ultimately accomplish a great revolution in every branch of learning.

§ 15.—*To understand these discourses, a slight perusal of detached parts, or of the whole, will be insufficient.*

That language will eventually receive the construction for which I shall contend, I feel no doubt, though I may not possess the talent to introduce the reformation. Before we commence our discussions, I must warn you, that the perverted estimation of language is so habitual, that you will be constantly liable to misapprehend my remarks. Should a person, unacquainted with geometry, read Euclid's Elements, he may meet with no word for which he possesses not a definite signification; yet when he shall have read to the end of the volume, he will know but little of geometry. To understand geometry, it must be studied slowly and painfully. No effort of mine can indoctrinate you with the knowledge of language on any easier conditions.

§ 16.—I will labour intently to state my views as intelligibly as possible, and as concisely; and as I am aware that in oral instruction to voluntary auditors, the speaker must conciliate his hearers, or be taught by the solitude which will soon environ him, that his labours are vain, I will endeavour to believe that Philosophy is not necessarily so frowning and sluggish a divinity as her ministers usually represent. Her limbs are masculine I admit, and her discourse is grave; but her language may be tasteful, and her decorations gay. I pause at these promises. All the stimulation which you can yield will probably be necessary to my perseverance. If I stagnate in the midst of your kindest efforts, the result should disappoint my hopes, rather than your expectations.

§ 17.—When fame has produced for an individual an elevation to which all eyes are continually directed;—when his opinions are impatiently expected, and rapidly disseminated; —when they are applauded in anticipation, and their adoption secured by prepossessions;—the labour of composition assimilates to the progress through Spain of the Duke of Angoulême,—a progress in which every city was approached but to be entered with a bloodless triumph; and every enemy pursued, but to be received by a resistless surrender—a progress whose labour is only the fatigue of pleasure, and whose dangers are merely the inebriation of success.

§ 18.—Startled at the difference between such a writer and me, I have more than once cast aside my pen as an insidious enemy, that lures me from the substantial pursuits of life. Even the consolation of yielding an amusement to you cannot well be expected; and while I have been distracted in seeking a worthy motive for exertion, I have not been exempt from apprehensions that I may, unconsciously, be influenced by the demon who delights to revel in our infirmities: the demon who makes the taciturn exult at his own dulness, and the loquacious enamoured of his own frivolity; who makes ill-timed gravity increase its frown, and incessant levity augment its laughter.

§ 19.—The demon at whose pernicious suggestions even moral deformities are heightened. Surgeons, thus induced, will boast of an insensibility that they cannot feel; and libertines, of profligacy that they never practised. The avaricious will falsely magnify his selfishness, and the prodigal his expenses. The liar will laugh at an exaggerated recital of his infamy, and the extortioner at an aggravated list of his oppressions. Nor escape personal deformities, the malice of this evil counsellor. Dwarfs, at his suggestion, endeavour to appear smaller than nature intended, and giants larger. The stammerer he urges to incessant conversation, and the freckled to an unnecessary nudity.

§ 20.—While I was reflecting on the eccentricities which proceed from his persuasion, imagination presented him unexpectedly before me. His language was harmonious,—his actions were profoundly respectful. Delight hung upon his lips, and conviction attended his communication. An unusual complacency expanded my breast. I extended my arms in the attitude of oratory, and prepared to welcome him with all the figures of rhetorick; when suddenly, approaching the fiend, his eyes were averted, and his face was distorted in ridicule. He dissolved into air, and, as he vanished, I discovered his name Vanity, stamped upon his back.

Lecture II

EXTERNAL SENSIBLE EXISTENCES ARE SUSCEPTIBLE OF A CLASSIFICATION WHICH SHALL REFER EACH EXISTENCE TO THE SENSE THROUGH WHOSE AGENCY WE ACQUIRE OUR KNOWLEDGE OF THE EXISTENCE

§ 1.—CREATION is boundless, whether we estimate its objects numerically, or its extent superficially. We cannot, by penetrating the earth, discover a vacuity;—we cannot exalt our vision beyond created objects;—we cannot fathom the fullness of the ocean.

§ 2.—To bring this immensity of existences within our definite comprehension, naturalists divide the whole into a vegetable kingdom, a mineral kingdom, and an animal kingdom: with various subdivisions of classes, orders, species, &c.

§ 3.—Chymists subject creation to a still more concise classification. All subjects are convertible, chymically, into about forty different substances; and chymists classify objects with reference to the substances into which they are thus convertible;—hence, with chymists, the universe is reduced into about forty different substances.

§ 4.—*To understand the relation which words bear to created existences, we must contemplate creation apart from words.*

Creation is susceptible of a classification more definite, and even less multifarious, than that of chymistry. This classification will constitute the present discourse. You must understand it, because I cannot teach you the relation that words bear to created existences, till you can contemplate the existences apart from words.

§ 5.—*The external universe may be divided into sights, sounds, tastes, feels, and smells.*

The classification which I propose, refers to our senses.

We derive from them our knowledge of the external universe; hence, by marshalling under each of our five senses, all the information that the sense reveals to us, our knowledge of the external universe becomes divided into five classes. Each class can be confounded with no other. A triangle is not more distinguishable from a circle, than the information of one sense is distinguishable from the information of every other. To make each class as distinct in name, as in nature, every information that is revealed to me by hearing, I shall call a sound;—every information that is revealed to me by seeing, a sight;—every information that is revealed to me by feeling, a feel;—every information that is revealed to me by smelling, a smell;—and every information that is revealed to me by tasting, a taste.

§ 6.—*Sights, feels, &c., are presented to us by nature in certain groups.*

When considered with reference to our senses, and divested of names, the external universe is a mass of sights, sounds, tastes, feels, and smells. Nature presents these to us in certain groups. A sight and a feel that are invariably associated, we call fire. Another group, consisting of a certain sight, feel, taste, and smell, (associated in a manner peculiar to nature,) we call an orange. Another group, consisting of a certain sight, feel, and taste, we call bread. Another group, consisting wholly of sights, we call a rainbow.

§ 7.—*Sights and feels are the most frequently associated.*

The associations which are most frequent in nature, are sights associated with feels. Of these associations, one sight and feel we call silver; another, gold; another, mahogany; another, marble; and another, wool.

§ 8.—*Sights, feels, tastes, and smells, are frequently associated.*

The associations which are next in frequency, are composed of a sight, feel, taste, and smell. The word lemon names an association of this description, and the words brandy, apple, grass, sulphur, oil, tar, tobacco, cheese, beef, cinnamon, &c.

§ 9.—Sights, feels, and tastes, are found in frequent association. To some of the associations we apply the words salt, sugar, water, honey, milk, wheat, chalk, &c.

§ 10.—*Sights, sounds, tastes, feels, and smells, nature sometimes presents singly to us.*

In some cases, sights, sounds, tastes, feels, and smells, are presented to us disjunctively. One sight, which is thus presented to us, we call moon. Another sight we call light; and another, aurora borealis, meteor, ignis fatuus, &c. A certain unassociated feel, we call air. Another feel, we call wind; and another, cold. A certain unassociated sound, we call echo. Thunder can hardly be designated as an unassociated sound, for it is usually associated with a sight which we call lightning. Tastes and smells are never presented to us, unless in association with some other existence. I recollect only one exception, and we designate it, when it occurs, by saying, we have an unpleasant taste in our mouths.

§ 11.—*We must discriminate between the extent and variety of creation, and the paucity of language.*

The number of unassociated sights is very small, if we estimate them by the number of words which name such sights. They are, however, far more numerous than this mode of estimating them will imply. The word star, for instance, names an unassociated sight, (a sight not associated with any feel, &c.;) but the word which thus seems to name but one sight, names a great number of sights, that differ in magnitude, brilliancy, colour, shape, &c. I state this, to enable you to perceive, that verbal designations are an inadequate means of estimating the variety and number of natural existences.

§ 12.—The sights which are presented to us in association with feels, &c., are also far more numerous and various than language implies. Colours alone are almost infinite in variety, while our names for them are comparatively a few words. But a large portion of sights, we never attempt to designate by specifick appellations. When I look at a chair, I discern a different sight from what I see when I look at fire; still, for the sight alone of neither the chair nor the fire, language possesses no name. The words chair and fire apply severally to an associated sight and feel. When we speak of the sight alone, we employ a periphrasis, and say the appearance of the fire, the appearance of the chair, &c.

§ 13.—*Tastes, smells, sounds, and feels, are seldom designated specifically by names.*

Men have been more sparing of names to tastes, smells, sounds, and feels, than even to sights. Fragrant, fetid, and a few other words, are all that we have deigned to appropriate to the information of the sense of smelling. Hot, cold, pain, &c., are all which we have appropriated to specifick feels, though nature presents them to us in boundless variety. When I touch iron, I realize a different feel from what I experience when I touch wood, silk, wool, linen, &c.; but to none of these feels is a name appropriated. The word iron names an associated sight and feel. The same may be said of the words wood, silk, wool, linen, &c.

§ 14.—*We create names when we deem them useful.*

But not only numerous sights, sounds, tastes, feels, and smells, possess separately no name; many associations of them possess no name. We name such associations only as utility requires us to designate. A certain associated sight and feel we designate by the word square, and others we name round, flat, &c.; but a hundred shapes which may be assumed by a piece of glass, on its accidental fractures, we have not designated by any name.

§15. —*The associations of nature are sometimes separable.*

If a piece of gold is held in front of a mirror, the mirror will exhibit the sight, gold, separated from the feel. In many other instances, art can separate the sights and feels which nature associates. If you thrust a stick into water, and leave a part unimmersed, the stick will exhibit the sight, crooked, without the feel, crooked. If you look at a candle, and press with your finger against the external angle of one of your eyes, you will experience the sight, two candles, unaccompanied by the feel, two. If you look at the sun, and then close your eyes; or, without looking at the sun, if you press for a moment rather painfully against either of your eyes; you will see various colours, unaccompanied by any of the feels with which colours are generally associated. If you whirl your body, and produce dizziness, every object on which you look will exhibit the sight, rotation, unaccompanied by the feel.

§ 16.—*Feels can also be separated from the sights with which they are naturally associated.*

If you cross the third and fourth fingers of your right hand, and rest the tips of the crossed fingers on a bullet, you will experience the feel, two bullets, unaccompanied by the sight, two. I have seen a wheel whirl so rapidly and evenly, as to present the feel, motion, without the sight. Blindness and darkness effectually separate all feels from their associated sights. To the blind, iron is a feel only, fire a feel only, sunshine a feel only.

§ 17.—*Painting, sleight of hand, natural magick, & c., consist in the separation, either artificially or spontaneously, of the sensible existences which nature usually associates.*

The art of painting consists principally in producing sights separated from their usually attendant feels:—the sight, prominence, without the feel,—the sight, distance, without the feel,—the sight, shape, without the feel. Perfumery consists in separating the smell, rose, jessamine, &c., from the sights and feels with which the smells are naturally associated. Ventriloquism and mimickry consist in separating sounds from the sights and feels with which the sounds are naturally associated. Sleight of hand and natural magick are either the apparent or actual separation of phenomena which nature generally associates:—usually some sight separated from its associated feel. If a wine glass be half filled with cotton wool, and immersed, (in an inverted position,) in a bowl of water, the cotton will exhibit the sight, wet, as you slowly emerge the wine glass. To the feel, the cotton will be dry. Sights are far more frequently and easily separated from their associated feels, than feels are from their associated sights.

§ 18.—*When we see a sight, experience alone induces us to expect that it is associated with a feel.*

An ignis fatuus is the sight, fire, without the feel. Our surprise at the phenomenon, and the alarm of the ignorant, is not occasioned by the sight, but at the absence of any associated feel. We forget that experience is all the warrant which we possess, in any case, for expecting a feel, where we discover a sight. We erroneously deem the sight a proof that a feel exists, and hence we suspect no possibility of mistake when we predicate tangibility of the sun, moon, and stars. We suppose that we can see their tangibility; a supposition which involves the absurdity that we can feel with our sight. When we look at space, and know that our hand will encounter no resistance in passing through it; and when we look at glass, and know that our hand will encounter resistance in passing through it; the knowledge in both cases is experimental, and no part of the sight of either the glass or space. That a fog is not tangible, and that a stone wall is; that the moon cannot be reached by our hand, and that the table can be; are all revelations of feeling, and not revelations of vision.

§ 19.—*When we perceive a feel, experience alone induces us to expect that it is associated with a sight.*

Should we feel a violent external pressure, and discover no accompanying sight, we should be alarmed at the invisible annoyance;—still, experience alone induces us to expect a visible accompaniment, when we experience a feel; and hence, an external pressure produced by a gust of wind, disconcerts no person by its invisibility. External feels, unassociated with a sight, are very few. The wind is such an existence; and temperature, both hot and cold, is another. A person unaccustomed to the experiment, to whom you should exhibit a bladder inflated with air, would expect its contents to be visible, as strongly as he would were the bladder filled with stone;—he would in both cases believe that the feel of the bladder testified to a visible contents:— a belief that involves the absurdity, that we can feel visibility. In the dark, when we place our hand on a window, and know that what we feel is visible; and when, at the same time, we feel a current of wind rushing through a broken window, and know that what we feel is invisible; the knowledge in both cases is experimental, and no part of the feel of either the window or the wind:—the knowledge is a revelation of vision, and not of feeling.

§ 20.—*Language refers to the groups which nature presents to us, and not to the individual phenomena of any group.*

I shall not pursue these remarks, as they belong more properly to the future physical investigations referred to in my preface. I introduced them here with no object but to enable you, amid the group of sensible existences which compose the external universe, to discriminate the separate existences of each group. The discrimination is peculiarly important, language referring to the groups, and seldom regarding the individual phenomena which compose any group. All the incidents which I have stated are mere illustrations of the proposed discrimination, and probably I need not burden you with further examples.

§ 21.—*Words are confounded with things.*

The benefits which you are to derive from the discrimination will be gradually disclosed in our progress; but the first benefit is to enable you to contemplate created existences apart from their names. The names are at present so identified and confounded with the external existences, that we cannot discover the subordinates which language bears to the realities of nature, but are continually, (as I shall show hereafter,) imputing to nature limitations, classifications, ambiguities, imperfections, and properties, of various kinds, which truly belong to language alone. A child comprehends with difficulty, that in France, the people eat apples, and still know not the meaning of the word apple. We smile at the child, but we all conform more nearly to the child than we imagine, in our identification of language with the existences to which we apply it.

§ 22.—*We should endeavour to regard words as merely the names of things.*

Should a person point to an object, and ask me what it is, I might answer, it is a sight and a feel. My children are so accustomed to such answers from me, that they never address me as above. They ask me to tell them the name of the object. This question keeps the name distinct from the object, and gives language its proper subordination to created existences.

§ 23.—Besides, by answering that the object is a sight and a feel, I direct your attention, not to the name, but to the group of existences, to which the name refers. Examine it, and discover the sight. Handle the object, and discover the feel. Elicit all the sights and feel which it presents. Try if it possesses a taste and smell. This category conduces to physical knowledge, and at least separates distinctly physical existences from language.

§ 24.—For the same purposes, when a child reverses the inquiry, and asks me what is a rose; I reply, it is a word with which we name an associated sight, feel, and smell. For the sensible existence itself, I refer him to his senses, as alone able to communicate the information:—words being unable to perform the functions of our senses. Words can refer us to sensible information which we have experienced; but they cannot reveal to us what we have not experienced.

§ 25.—If you have succeeded in catching my analysis, you no longer see in the heavens, light, clouds, sun, galaxy, moon, stars, meteors, space, vacuity, distance, shape, &c.; but you see various sights, to which the above words are names. You no longer feel, in a knife, iron, hardness, weight, matter, substance, impenetrability, external, cold, edge, sharpness, &c.; but you experience various feels, to which Englishmen apply the above words, and Frenchmen apply other words, and uneducated mutes no words.

§ 26.—To investigate the sights, sounds, feels, tastes, and smells, which separately, and in various associations, constitute the external universe, is not my present object; nor shall I discuss whether sights, sounds, tastes, feels, and smells, are words which appropriately designate external existences. I adopt the phraseology, as a means of investigating the nature of language; and if I shall establish the utility of the adoption, I trust you will tolerate the expressions, how much so ever they may offend against euphony and custom.

"Of Definition"

John Stuart Mill

John Stuart Mill was born on May 20, 1806, in London.
An infant prodigy, thanks partly to an innate capacity for
learning and partly to the rigorous training given to him by
his father, Mill had no formal education in his life. However, through systematic reading and rigorous study he
became one of England's greatest philosophers. By vocation he was a clerk in the examiner's office in the India
House of London. He began writing for the *Westminster
Review,* a periodical of the philosophical radicals. An early
devotee to the philosophy of Jeremy Bentham, Mill later
described himself as a liberal utilitarian. He became unof-
ficial editor of the *London Review* and many of his early
essays appeared in this publication. After retirement from
the India Company in 1865, Mill was elected to parliament
and was instrumental in the passage of the Reform Bill of
1867. He died in London on May 8, 1873. Among his chief
works are *On Liberty,* 1859; *A System of Logic,* 1843; *An
Autobiography,* 1873. "Of Definition" is Chapter 8 in his
System of Logic, Vol. I, published by Longmans, Green,
Reader and Dyer in 1868.

ONE necessary part of the theory of Names and of Propositions remains to be treated of in this place: the theory
of Definitions. As being the most important of the class by
propositions which we have characterized as purely verbal,
they have already received some notice in the chapter preceding the last. But their fuller treatment was at that time
postponed, because definition is so closely connected with
classification, that, until the nature of the latter process is
in some measure understood, the former cannot be discussed to much purpose.

The simplest and most correct notion of a Definition is, a proposition declaratory of the meaning of a word; namely, either the meaning which it bears in common acceptation, or that which the speaker or writer, for the particular purposes of his discourse, intends to annex to it.

The definition of a word being the proposition which enunciates its meaning, words which have no meaning are unsusceptible of definition. Proper names, therefore, cannot be defined. A proper name being a mere mark put upon an individual, and of which it is the characteristic property to be destitute of meaning, its meaning cannot of course be declared; though we may indicate by language, as we might indicate still more conveniently by pointing with the finger, upon what individual that particular mark has been, or is intended to be, put. It is no definition of "John Thomson" to say he is "the son of General Thomson;" for the name John Thomson does not express this. Neither is it any definition of "John Thomson" to say he is "the man now crossing the street." These propositions may serve to make known who is the particular man to whom the name belongs, but that may be done still more unambiguously by pointing to him, which, however, has not been esteemed one of the modes of definition.

In the case of connotative names, the meaning, as has been so often observed, is the connotation; and the definition of a connotative name, is the proposition which declares its connotation. This might be done either directly or indirectly. The direct mode would be by a proposition in this form: "Man" (or whatsoever the word may be) "is a name connoting such and such attributes," or "is a name which, when predicated of anything, signifies the possession of such and such attributes by that thing." Or thus: Man is everything which possesses such and such attributes: Man is everything which possesses corporeity, organization, life, rationality, and certain peculiarities of external form.

This form of definition is the most precise and least equivocal of any; but it is not brief enough, and is besides too technical for common discourse. The more usual mode of declaring the connotation of a name, is to predicate of it another name or names of known signification, which connote the same aggregation of attributes. This may be done either by predicating of the name intended to be defined, another connotative name exactly synonymous, as, "Man is a human being," which is not commonly accounted a definition at all; or by predicating two or more connotative names, which make up among them the whole connotation of the name to be defined. In this last case, again, we may either compose our definition of as many connotative names as there are attributes, each attribute being connotated by one, as, Man is a corporeal, organized, animated, rational being, shaped so and so; or we may employ names which connote several of the attributes at once, as, Man is a rational *animal*, shaped so and so.

The definition of a name, according to this view of it, is the sum total of all the *essential* propositions which can be framed with that name for their subject. All propositions the truth of which is implied in the name, all those which we are made aware of by merely hearing the name, are included in the definition, if complete, and may be evolved from it without the aid of any other premises; where the definition expresses them in two or three words, or in a larger number. It is, therefore, not without reason that Condillac and other writers have affirmed a definition to be an *analysis*. To resolve any complex whole into the elements of which it is compounded, is the meaning of analysis: and this we do when we replace one word which connotes a set of attributes collectively, by two or more which connote the same attributes singly, or in smaller groups.

From this, however, the question naturally arises, in what manner are we to define a name which connotes only a single attribute: for instance, "white," which connotes nothing but whiteness; "rational," which connotes nothing but the possession of reason. It might seem that the meaning of such names could only be declared in two ways; by a synonymous term, if any such can be found; or in the direct way already alluded to: "White is a name connoting the attribute whiteness." Let us see, however, whether the analysis of the meaning of the name, that is, the breaking down of that meaning into several parts, admits of being carried farther. Without at present deciding this question as to the word *white*, it is obvious that in the case of *rational* some further explanation may be given of its meaning than is contained in the proposition, "Rational is that which possesses the attribute of reason;" since the attribute reason itself admits of being defined. And here we must turn our attention to the definitions of attributes, or rather of the names of attributes, that is, of abstract names.

In regard to such names of attributes as are connotative, and express attributes of those attributes, there is no difficulty; like other connotative names they are defined by declaring their connotation. Thus, the word *fault* may be defined, "a quality productive of evil or inconvenience." Sometimes, again, the attribute to be defined is not one attribute, but an union of several: we have only, therefore, to put together the names of all the attributes taken separately, and we obtain the definition of the name which belongs to them all taken together; a definition which will correspond exactly to that of the corresponding concrete name. For, as we define a concrete name by enumerating the attributes which it connotes, and as the attributes connoted by a concrete name form the entire signification of the corresponding abstract name, the same enumeration will serve for the definition of both. Thus, if the definition of a *human being* be this, "a being, corporeal, animated, rational, shaped so and so," the definition of *humanity* will be corporeity and animal life, combined with rationality, and with such and such a shape.

When, on the other hand, the abstract name does not express a complication of attributes, but a single attribute, we must remember that every attribute is grounded on some fact or phenomenon, from which, and which alone, it derives its meaning. To that fact or phenomenon, called in a former chapter the foundation of the attitude, we must, therefore, have recourse for its definition. Now, the foundation of the attribute may be a phenomenon of any degree of complexity, consisting of many different parts, either coexistent or in succession. To obtain a definition of the attribute, we must analyse the phenomenon into these parts. Eloquence, for example, is the name of one attribute only; but this attribute is grounded on external effects of a complicated nature, flowing from acts of the person to whom we ascribed the attitude; and by resolving this phenomenon of causation into its two parts, the cause and the effect, we obtain a definition of eloquence, viz. the power of influencing the feelings by speech or writing.

A name, therefore, whether concrete or abstract, admits of definition, provided we are able to analyse, that is, to distinguish into parts, the attribute or set of attributes which constitute the meaning both of the concrete name and of the corresponding abstract: if a set of attributes, by enumerating them; if a single attribute, by dissecting the fact or phenomenon (whether of perception or of internal consciousness) which is the foundation of the attribute. But, further, even when the fact is one of our simple feelings or states of consciousness, and therefore unsusceptible of analysis, the names both of the object and of the attribute still admit of definition: or rather, would do so if all our simple feelings had names. Whiteness may be defined, the property or power of exciting the sensation of white. A white object may be defined, an object which excites the sensation of white. The only names which are unsusceptible of definition, because their meaning is unsusceptible of analysis, are the names of the simple feelings themselves. These are in the same condition as proper names. They are not indeed, like proper names, unmeaning; for the words *sensation of white* signify, that the sensation which I so denominate resembles other sensations which I remember to have had before, and to have called by that name. But as we have no words by which to recall those former sensations, except the very word which we seek to define, or some other which, being exactly synonymous with it, requires definition as much, words cannot unfold the signification of this class of names;

and we are obliged to make a direct appeal to the personal experience of the individual whom we address.

Having stated what seems to be the true idea of a Definition, we proceed to examine some opinions of philosophers, and some popular conceptions on the subject, which conflict more or less with that idea.

The only adequate definition of a name is, as already remarked, one which declares the facts, and the whole of the facts, which the name involves in its signification. But with most persons the object of a definition does not embrace so much; they look for nothing more, in a definition, than a guide to the correct use of the term—a protection against applying it in a manner inconsistent with custom and convention. Anything, therefore, is to them a sufficient definition of a term, which will serve as a correct index to what the term *de*notes; though not embracing the whole, and sometimes, perhaps, not even any part, of what it connotes. This gives rise to two sorts of imperfect, or unscientific definition; Essential but incomplete Definitions, and Accidental Definitions, or Descriptions. In the former, a connotative name is defined by a part only of its connotation; in the latter, by something which forms no part of the connotation at all.

An example of the first kind of imperfect definitions is the following:—Man is a rational animal. It is impossible to consider this as a complete definition of the word Man, since (as before remarked) if we adhered to it we should be obliged to call the Houyhnhnms men; but as there happen to be no Houyhnhnms, this imperfect definition is sufficient to mark out and distinguish from all other things, the objects at present denoted by "man;" all the beings actually known to exist, of whom the name is predicable. Though the word is defined by some only among the attributes which it connotes, not by all, it happens that all known objects which possess the enumerated attributes, possess also those which are omitted; so that the field of predication which the word covers, and the employment of it which is conformable to usage, are as well indicated by the inadequate definition as by an adequate one. Such definitions, however, are always liable to be overthrown by the discovery of new objects in nature.

Definitions of this kind are what logicians have had in view, when they laid down the rule, that the definition of a species should be *per genus et differentiam*. Differentia being seldom taken to mean the whole of the peculiarities constitutive of the species, but some of those peculiarities only, a complete definition would be *per genus et differentias*, rather that *differentiam*. It would include, with the name of the superior genus, not merely *some* attribute which distinguishes that species intended to be defined from all other species of the same genus, but *all* the attributes implied in the name of the species, which the name of the superior genus has not already implied. The assertion, however, that a definition must of necessity consist of a genus and differentiae, is not tenable. It was early remarked by logicians, that the *summum genus* in any classification, having no genus superior to itself, could not be defined in this manner. Yet we have seen that all names, except those of our elementary feelings, are susceptible of definition in the strictest sense; by setting forth in words the constituent parts of the fact or phenomenon, of which the connotation of every word is ultimately composed.

Although the first kind of imperfect definition, (which defines a connotative term by a part only of what it connotes, but a part sufficient to mark out correctly the boundaries of its denotation,) has been considered by the ancients, and by logicians in general, as a complete definition; it has always been deemed necessary that the attributes employed should really form part of the connotation; for the rule was that the definition must be drawn from the *essence* of the class; and this would not have been the case if it had been in any degree made up of attributes not connoted by the name. The second kind of imperfect definition, therefore, in which the name of a class is defined by any of its accidents,—that is, by attributes which are not included in its connotation,—has been rejected from the rank of genuine Definition by all logicians and has been termed Description.

This kind of imperfect definition, however, takes its rise from the same cause as the other, namely, the willingness to accept as a definition anything which, whether it expounds the meaning of the name or not, enables us to discriminate the things denoted by the name from all other things, and consequently to employ the term in predication without deviating from established usages. This purpose is duly answered by stating any (no matter what) of the attributes which are common to the whole of the class, and peculiar to it; or any combination of attributes which happens to be peculiar to it, though separately each of those attributes may be common to it with some other things. It is only necessary that the definition (or description) thus formed, should be *convertible* with the name which it professes to define; that is, should be exactly co-extensive with it, being predicable of everything of which it is predicable, and of nothing of which it is not predicable; though the attributes specified may have no connexion with those which mankind had in view when they formed or recognised the class, and gave it a name. The following are correct definitions of Man, according to this test: Man is a mammiferous animal, having (by nature) two hands (for the human species answers to this description, and no other animal does): Man is an animal who cooks his food: Man is a featherless biped.

What would otherwise be a mere description, may be raised to the rank of a real definition by the peculiar purpose which the speaker or writer has in view. As was seen in the preceding chapter, it may, for the ends of a particular art or science, or for the more convenient statement of an author's particular doctrines, be advisable to give to some general name, without altering its denotation, a special connotation, different from its ordinary one. When this is done, a definition of the name by means of the attributes which make up the special connotation, though in general a mere accidental definition or description, becomes on the particular occasion and for the particular purpose a complete and genuine definition. This actually occurs with respect to one of the preceding examples, "Man is a mammiferous animal having two hands," which is the scientific definition of man, considered as one of the species in Cuvier's distribution of the animal kingdom.

In cases of this sort, though the definition is still a declaration of the meaning which in the particular instance the name is appointed to convey, it cannot be said that to state the meaning of the word is the purpose of the definition. The purpose is not to expound a name, but a classification. The special meaning which Cuvier assigned to the word Man, (quite foreign to its ordinary meaning, though involving no change in the denotation of the word,) was incidental to a plan of arranging animals into classes on a certain principle, that is, according to a certain set of distinctions. And since the definition of Man according to the ordinary connotation of the word, though it would have answered every other purpose of a definition, would not have pointed out the place which the species ought to occupy in that particular classification; he gave the word a special connotation, that he might be able to define it by the kind of attributes on which, for reasons of scientific convenience, he had resolved to found his division of animated nature.

Scientific definitions, whether they are definitions of scientific terms, or of common terms used in a scientific sense, are almost always of the kind last spoken of: their main purpose is to serve as the landmarks of scientific classification. And since the classifications in any science are continually modified as scientific knowledge advances, the definitions in the sciences are also constantly varying. A striking instance is afforded by the words Acid and Alkali, especially the former. As experimental discovery advanced, the substances classed with acids have been constantly multiplying, and by a natural consequence the attributes connoted by the word have receded and become fewer. At first it connoted the attributes, of combining with an alkali to form a neutral substance (called a salt); being compounded of a base and oxygen;

causticity to the taste and touch; fluidity, &c. The true analysis of muriatic acid, into chlorine and hydrogen, caused the second property, composition from a base and oxygen, to be excluded from the connotation. The same discovery fixed the attention of chemists upon hydrogen as an important element in acids; and more recent discoveries having led to the recognition of its presence in sulphuric, nitric, and many other acids, where its existence was not previously suspected, there is now a tendency to include the presence of this element in the connotation of the word. But carbonic acid, silica, sulphurous acid, have no hydrogen in their composition; that property cannot therefore be connoted by the term, unless those substances are no longer to be considered acids. Causticity and fluidity have long since been excluded from the characteristics of the class, by the inclusion of silica and many other substances in it; and the formation of neutral bodies by combination with alkalis, together with such electro-chemical peculiarities as this is supposed to imply, are now the only *differentiae* which form the fixed connotation of the word Acid, as a term of chemical science.

What is true of the definition of any term of science, is of course true of the definition of a science itself: and accordingly, (as observed in the Introductory Chapter of this work,) the definition of a science must necessarily be progressive and provisional. Any extension of knowledge or alteration in the current opinions respecting the subject matter, may lead to a change more or less extensive in the particulars included in the science; and its composition being thus altered, it may easily happen that a different set of characteristics will be found better adapted as differentiæ for defining its name.

In the same manner in which a special or technical definition has for its object to expound the artificial classification out of which it grows; the Aristotelian logicians seem to have imagined that it was also the business of ordinary definition to expound the ordinary, and what they deemed the natural, classification of things, namely, the division of them into Kinds; and to show the place which each Kind occupies, as superior, collateral, or subordinate, among other Kinds. This notion would account for the rule that all definition must necessarily be *per genus et differentiam,* and would also explain why a single differentia was deemed sufficient. But to expound, or express in words, a distinction of Kind, has already been shown to be an impossibility: the very meaning of a Kind is, that the properties which distinguish it do not grow out of one another, and cannot therefore be set forth in words, even by implication, otherwise than by enumerating them all: and all are not known, nor are ever likely to be so. It is idle, therefore, to look to this as one of the purposes of a definition: while, if it be only required that the definition of a Kind should indicate what Kinds include it or are included by it, any definitions which expound the connotation of the names will do this: for the name of each class must necessarily connote enough of its properties to fix the boundaries of the class. If the definition, therefore, be a full statement of the connotation, it is all that a definition can be required to be.

Of the two incomplete and popular modes of definition, and in what they differ from the complete or philosophical mode, enough has now been said. We shall next examine an ancient doctrine, once generally prevalent and still by no means exploded, which I regard as the source of a great part of the obscurity hanging over some of the most important processes of the understanding in the pursuit of truth. According to this, the definitions of which we have now treated are only one of two sorts into which definitions may be divided, viz. definitions of names, and definitions of things. The former are intended to explain the meaning of a term; the latter, the nature of thing; the last being incomparably the most important.

This opinion was held by the ancient philosophers, and by their followers, with the exception of the Nominalists; but as the spirit of modern metaphysics, until a recent period, has been on the whole a Nominalist spirit, the notion of definitions of things has been to a certain extent in abeyance, still continuing, however, to breed confusion in logic, by its consequences indeed rather than by itself. Yet the doctrine in its own proper form now and then breaks out, and has appeared (among other places) where it was scarcely to be expected, in a justly admired work, Archbishop Whately's *Logic*.* In a review of that work published by me in the *Westminster Review* for January 1828, and containing some opinions which I no longer entertain, I find the following observations on the question now before us; observations with which my present view of that question is still sufficiently in accordance.

"The distinction between nominal and real definitions, between definitions of words and what are called definitions of things, though conformable to the ideas of most of the Aristotelian logicians, cannot, as it appears to us, be maintained. We apprehend that no definition is ever intended to 'explain and unfold the nature of a thing.' It is some confirmation of our opinion, that none of those writers who have thought that there were definitions of things, have ever succeeded in dis-

---

* In the fuller discussion which Archbishop Whately has given to this subject in his later editions, he almost ceases to regard the definitions of names and those of things as, in any important sense, distinct. He seems (9th ed. p. 145) to limit the notion of a Real Definition to one which "explains anything *more* of the nature of the thing than is implied in the name;" (including under the word "implied," not only what the name connotes, but everything which can be deduced by reasoning from the attributes connoted). Even this, as he adds, is usually called, not a Definition, but a Description; and (as it seems to me) rightly so called. A Description, I conceive, can only be ranked among Definitions, when taken (as in the case of the zoological definition of man) to fulfil the true office of a Definition, by declaring the connotation given to a word in some special use, as a term of science or art: which special connotation of course would not be expressed by the proper definition of the word in its ordinary employment.

Mr. De Morgan, exactly reversing the doctrine of Archbishop Whately, understands by a Real Definition one which contains *less* than the Nominal Definition, provided only that what it contains is sufficient for distinction. "By *real* definition I mean such an explanation of the word, be it the whole of the meaning or only part, as will be sufficient to separate the things contained under that word from all others. Thus the following, I believe, is a complete definition of an elephant: An animal which naturally drinks by drawing the water into its nose, and then spurting it into its mouth."—*Formal Logic*, p. 36. Mr. De Morgan's general proposition and his example are at variance; for the peculiar mode of drinking of the elephant certainly forms no part of the meaning of the word elephant. It could not be said, because a person happened to be ignorant of this property, that he did not know what an elephant means.

covering any criterion by which the definition of a thing can be distinguished from any other proposition relating to the thing. The definition, they say, unfolds the nature of the thing: but no definition can unfold its whole nature; and every proposition in which any quality whatever is predicated of the thing, unfolds some part of its nature. The true state of the case we take to be this. All definitions are of names, and of names only; but, in some definitions, it is clearly apparent, that nothing is intended except to explain the meaning of the word; while in others, besides explaining the meaning of the word, it is intended to be implied that there exists a thing, corresponding to the word. Whether this be or be not implied in any given case, cannot be collected from the mere form of the expression. 'A centaur is an animal with the upper parts of a man and the lower parts of a horse,' and 'A triangle is a rectilineal figure with three sides,' are, in form, expressions precisely similar; although in the former it is not implied that any *thing*, conformable to the term, really exists, while in the latter it is; as may be seen by substituting, in both definitions, the word *means* for *is*. In the first expression, 'A centaur means an animal,' &c., the sense would remain unchanged: in the second, 'A triangle means,' &c., the meaning would be altered, since it would be obviously impossible to deduce any of the truths of geometry from a proposition expressive only of the manner in which we intend to employ a particular sign.

"There are, therefore, expressions, commonly passing for definitions, which include in themselves more than the mere explanation of the meaning of a term. But it is not correct to call an expression of this sort a peculiar kind of definition. Its difference from the other kind consists in this, that it is not a definition, but a definition and something more. The definition above given of a triangle, obviously comprises not one, but two propositions, perfectly distinguishable. The one is, 'There may exist a figure, bounded by three straight lines;' the other, 'And this figure may be termed a triangle.' The former of these propositions is not a definition at all: the latter is a mere nominal definition, or explanation of the use and application of a term. The first is susceptible of truth or falsehood, and may therefore be made the foundation of a train of reasoning. The latter can neither be true nor false; the only character it is susceptible of is that of conformity or disconformity to the ordinary usage of language."

There is a real distinction, then, between definitions of names, and what are erroneously called definitions of things; but it is, that the latter, along with the meaning of a name, covertly asserts a matter of fact. This covert assertion is not a definition, but a postulate. The definition is a mere identical proposition, which gives information only about the use of language, and from which no conclusions affecting matters of fact can possibly be drawn. The accompanying postulate, on the other hand, affirms a fact, which may lead to consequences of every degree of importance. It affirms the actual or possible existence of Things possessing the combination of attributes set forth in the definition; and this, if true, may be foundation sufficient on which to build a whole fabric of scientific truth.

We have already made, and shall often have to repeat, the remark, that the philosophers who overthrew Realism by no means got rid of the consequences of Realism, but retained long afterwards, in their own philosophy, numerous propositions which could only have a rational meaning as part of a Realistic system. It had been handed down from Aristotle, and probably from earlier times, as an obvious truth, that the science of Geometry is deduced from definitions. This, so long as a definition was considered to be a proposition "unfolding the nature of the thing," did well enough. But Hobbes followed, and rejected utterly the notion that a definition declares the nature of the thing, or does anything but state the meaning of a name; yet he continued to affirm as broadly as any of his predecessors, that the $\alpha\rho\chi\alpha\iota$, *principia*, or original premises of mathematics, and even of all science, are definitions; producing the singular paradox, that systems of scientific truth, nay, all truths whatever at which we arrive by reasoning, are deduced from the arbitrary conventions of mankind concerning the signification of words.

To save the credit of the doctrine that definitions are the premises of scientific knowledge, the proviso is sometimes added, that they are so only under a certain condition, namely, that they be framed conformably to the phenomena of nature; that is, that they ascribe such meanings to terms as shall suit objects actually existing. But this is only an instance of the attempt so often made, to escape from the necessity of abandoning old language after the ideas which it expresses have been exchanged for contrary ones. From the meaning of a name (we are told) it is possible to infer physical facts, provided the name has corresponding to it an existing thing. But if this proviso be necessary, from which of the two is the inference really drawn? From the existence of a thing having the properties, or from the existence of a name meaning them?

Take, for instance, any of the definitions laid down as premises in Euclid's Elements; the definition, let us say, of a circle. This, being analysed, consists of two propositions; the one an assumption with respect to a matter of fact, the other a genuine definition. "A figure may exist, having all the points in the line which bounds it equally distant from a single point within it:" "Any figure possessing this property is called a circle." Let us look at one of the demonstrations which are said to depend on this definition, and observe to which of the two propositions contained in it the demonstration really appeals. "About the centre A, describe the circle B C D." Here is an assumption that a figure, such as the definition expresses, *may* be described; which is no other than the postulate, or covert assumption, involved in the so-called definition. But whether that figure be called a circle or not is quite immaterial. The purpose would be as well answered, in all respects except brevity, were we to say, "Through the point B, draw a line returning into itself, of which every point shall be at an equal distance from the point A." By this the definition of a circle would be got rid of, and rendered needless; but not the postulate implied in it; without that the demonstration could not stand. The circle being now described, let us proceed to the consequence.

"Since B C D is a circle, the radius B A is equal to the radius C A." B A is equal to C A, not because B C D is a circle, but because B C D is a figure with the radii equal. Our warrant for assuming that such a figure about the centre A, with the radius B A, may be made to exist, is the postulate. Whether the admissibility of these postulates rests on intuition, or on proof, may be a matter of dispute; but in either case they are the premises on which the theorems depend; and while these are retained it would make no difference in the certainty of geometrical truths, though every definition in Euclid, and every technical term therein defined, were laid aside.

It is, perhaps, superfluous to dwell at so much length on what is so nearly self-evident; but when a distinction, obvious as it may appear, has been confounded, and by powerful intellects, it is better to say too much than too little for the purpose of rendering such mistakes impossible in future. I will, therefore, detain the reader while I point out one of the absurd consequences flowing from the supposition the definitions, as such, are the premises in any of our reasonings, except such as relate to words only. If this supposition were true, we might argue correctly from true premises, and arrive at a false conclusion. We should only have to assume as a premise the definition of a nonentity; or rather of a name which has no entity corresponding to it. Let this, for instance, be our definition:

A dragon is a serpent breathing flame.

This proposition, considered only as a definition, is indisputably correct. A dragon *is* a serpent breathing flame: the word *means* that. The tacit assumption, indeed, (if there were any such understood assertion), of the existence of an object with properties corresponding to the definition, would, in the present instance, be false. Out of this definition we may carve the premises of the following syllogism:

A dragon is a thing which breathes flame:

A dragon is a serpent:

From which the conclusion is,

Therefore some serpent or serpents breathe flame:—
an unexceptionable syllogism in the first mode of the third

figure, in which both premises are true and yet the conclusion false; which every logician knows to be an absurdity. The conclusion being false and the syllogism correct, the premises cannot be true. But the premises, considered as parts of a definition, are true. Therefore, the premises considered as parts of a definition cannot be the real ones. The real premises must be—

A dragon is a *really existing* thing which breathes flame:
A dragon is a *really existing* serpent:
which implied premises being false, the falsity of the conclusion presents no absurdity.

If we would determine what conclusion follows from the same ostensible premises when the tacit assumption of real existence is left out, let us, according to the recommendation in a previous page, substitute *means* for *is*. We then have—

Dragon is a *word meaning* a thing which breathes flame:
Dragon is *a word meaning* a serpent:

From which the conclusion is,

Some *word or words which mean* a serpent, also mean a thing which breathes flame:
where the conclusion (as well as the premises) is true, and is the only kind of conclusion which can ever follow from a definition, namely, a proposition relating to the meaning of words.

There is still another shape into which we may transform this syllogism. We may suppose the middle term to be the designation neither of a thing nor of a name, but of an idea. We then have—

The *idea of* a dragon is *an idea of* a thing which breathes flame:
The *idea of* a dragon is *an idea of* a serpent:
Therefore, there is *an idea of* a serpent, which is *an idea of* a thing breathing flame.

There the conclusion is true, and also the premises; but the premises are not definitions. They are propositions affirming that an idea existing in the mind, includes certain ideal elements. The truth of the conclusion follows from the existence of the psychological phenomenon called the idea of a dragon; and therefore still from the tacit assumption of a matter of fact. *

When, as in this last syllogism, the conclusion is a proposition respecting an idea, the assumption on which it depends may be merely that of the existence of an idea. But when the conclusion is a proposition concerning a Thing, the postulate involved in the definition which stands as the apparent premise, is the existence of a thing conformable to the definition, and not merely of an idea conformable to it. This assumption of real existence will always convey the impression that we intend to make, when we profess to define any name which is already known to be a name of really existing objects. On this account it is, that the assumption was not necessarily implied in the definition of a dragon, while

----

* In the only attempt which, so far as I know, has been made to refute the preceding argumentation, it is maintained that in the first form of the syllogism,

A dragon is a thing which breathes flame,

A dragon is a serpent,

Therefore some serpent or serpents breathe flame,

"there is just as much truth in the conclusion as there is in the premises, or rather, no more in the latter than in the former. If the general name serpent includes both real and imaginary serpents, there is no falsity in the conclusion; if not, there is falsity in the minor premise."

Let us, then, try to set out the syllogism on the hypothesis that the name serpent includes imaginary serpents. We shall find that it is now necessary to alter the predicates; for it cannot be asserted that an imaginary creature breathes flame: in predicating of it such a fact, we assert by the most positive implication that it is real and not imaginary. The conclusion must run thus, "Some serpent or serpents either do or are *imagined* to breathe flame." And to prove this conclusion by the instance of dragons, the premises must be, A dragon is *imagined* as breathing flame, A dragon is a (real or imaginary) serpent: from which it undoubtedly follows, that there are serpents which are imagined to breathe flame; but the major premise is not a definition, nor part of a definition; which is all that I am concerned to prove.

Let us now examine the other assertion—that if the word serpent stands for none but real serpents, the minor premise (a dragon is a serpent) is false. This is exactly what I have myself said of the premise, considered as a statement of fact: but it is not false as part of the definition of a dragon; and since the premises, or one of them, must be false, (the conclusion being so,) the real premise cannot be the definition, which is true, but the statement of fact, which is false.

there was no doubt of its being included in the definition of a circle.

One of the circumstances which have contributed to keep up the notion, that demonstrative truths follow from definitions rather than from the postulates implied in those definitions, is, that the postulates, even in those sciences which are considered to surpass all others in demonstrative certainty, are not always exactly true. It is not true that a circle exists, or can be described, which has all its radii *exactly* equal. Such accuracy is ideal only; it is not found in nature, still less can it be realized by art. People had a difficulty, therefore, in conceiving that the most certain of all conclusions could rest on premises which, instead of being certainly true, are certainly not true to the full extent asserted. This apparent paradox will be examined when we come to treat of Demonstration; where we shall be able to show that as much of the postulate is true, as is required to support as much is true of the conclusion. Philosophers, however, to whom this view had not occurred, or whom it did not satisfy, have thought it indispensable that there should be found in definitions something *more* certain, or at least more accurately true, than the implied postulate of the real existence of a corresponding object. And this something they flattered themselves they had found, when they laid it down that a definition is a statement and analysis not of the mere meaning of a word, nor yet of the nature of a thing, but of an idea. Thus, the proposition, "A circle is a plane figure bounded by a line all the points of which are at an equal distance from a given point within it," was considered by them, not as an assertion that any real circle has that property, (which would not be exactly true,) but that we *conceive* a circle as having it; that our abstract idea of a circle is an idea of a figure with its radii exactly equal.

Conformably to this it is said, that the subject-matter of mathematics, and of every other demonstrative science, is not things as they really exist, but abstractions of the mind. A geometrical line is a line without breadth; but no such line exists in nature; it is a notion merely suggested to the mind by its experience of nature. The definition (it is said) is a definition of this mental line, not of any actual line: and it is only of the mental line, not of any line existing in nature, that the theorems of geometry are accurately true.

Allowing this doctrine respecting the nature of demonstrative truth to be correct (which, in a subsequent place, I shall endeavour to prove that it is not;) even on that supposition, the conclusions which seem to follow from a definition, do not follow from the definition as such, but from an implied postulate. Even if it be true that there is no object in nature answering to the definition of a line, and that the geometrical properties of lines are not true of any lines in nature, but only of the idea of a line; the definition, at all events, postulates the real existence of such an idea: it assumes that the mind can frame, or rather has framed, the notion of length without breadth, and without any other sensible property whatever. To me, indeed, it appears that the mind cannot form any such notion; it cannot conceive length without breadth; it can only, in contemplating objects, attend to their length, exclusively of their other sensible qualities, and so determine what properties may be predicated of them in virtue of their length alone. If this be true, the postulate involved in the geometrical definition of a line, is the real existence, not of length without breadth, but merely of length, that is, of long objects. This is quite enough to support all the truths of geometry, since every property of a geometrical line is really a property of all physical objects in so far as possessing length. But even what I hold to be the false doctrine on the subject, leaves the conclusion that our reasonings are grounded on the matters of fact postulated in definitions, and not on the definitions themselves, entirely unaffected; and accordingly this conclusion is one which I have in common with Dr. Whewell, in his *Philosophy of the Inductive Sciences*: though, on the nature of demonstrative truth, Dr. Whewell's opinions are greatly at variance with mine. And here, as in many other instances, I gladly acknowledge that his writings are eminently serviceable in clearing from confusion the initial steps in the analysis of the mental processes, even where his views respecting the ultimate analysis are such as (though with unfeigned respect) I cannot but regard as fundamentally erroneous.

Although, according to the opinion here presented, Definitions are properly of names only, and not of things, it does not follow from this that definitions are arbitrary. How to define a name, may not only be an inquiry of considerable difficulty and intricacy, but may involve considerations going deep into the nature of the things which are denoted by the name. Such, for instance, are the inquiries which form the subjects of the most important of Plato's Dialogues; as "What is rhetoric?" the topic of the Gorgias, or "What is justice?" that of the Republic. Such, also, is the question scornfully asked by Pilate, "What is truth?" and the fundamental question with speculative moralists in all ages, "What is virtue?"

It would be a mistake to represent these difficult and noble inquiries as having nothing in view beyond ascertaining the conventional meaning of a name. They are inquiries not so much to determine what is, as what should be, the meaning of a name; which, like other practical questions of terminology, requires for its solution that we should enter, and sometimes enter very deeply, into the properties not merely of names but of the things named.

Although the meaning of every concrete general name resides in the attributes which it connotes, the objects were named before the attributes; as appears from the fact that in all languages, abstract names are mostly compounds or other derivatives of the concrete names which correspond to them. Connotative names, therefore, were, after proper names, the first which were used: and in the simpler cases, no doubt, a distinct connotation was present to the minds of those who first used the name, and was distinctly intended by them to be conveyed by it. The first person who used the word white, as applied to snow or to any other object, knew, no doubt, very well what quality he intended to predicate, and had a perfectly distinct conception in his mind of the attribute signified by the name.

But where the resemblances and differences on which our

classifications are founded are not of this palpable and easily determinable kind; especially where they consist not in any one quality but in a number of qualities, the effects of which being blended together are not very easily discriminated, and referred each to its true source; it often happens that names are applied to nameable objects, with no distinct connotation present to the minds of those who apply them. They are only influenced by a general resemblance between the new object and all or some of the old familiar objects which they have been accustomed to call by that name. This, as we have seen, is the law which even the mind of the philosopher must follow, in giving names to the simple elementary feelings of our nature: but, where the things to be named are complex wholes, a philosopher is not content with noticing a general resemblance; he examines what the resemblance consists in: and he only gives the same name to things which resemble one another in the same definite particulars. The philosopher, therefore, habitually employs his general names with a definite connotation. But language was not made, and can only in some small degree be mended, by philosophers. In the minds of the real arbiters of language, general names, especially when the classes they denote cannot be brought before the tribunal of the outward senses to be identified and discriminated, connote little more than a vague gross resemblance to the things which they were earliest, or have been most, accustomed to call by those names. When, for instance, ordinary persons predicate the words *just* or *unjust* of any action, *noble* or *mean* of any sentiment, expression, or demeanour, *statesman* or *charlatan* of any personage figuring in politics, do they mean to affirm of those various subjects any determinate attributes, of whatever kind? No: they merely recognise, as they think, some likeness, more or less vague and loose, between these and some other things which they have been accustomed to denominate or to hear denominated by those appellations.

Language, as Sir James Mackintosh used to say of governments, "is not made, but grows." A name is not imposed at once and by previous purpose upon a *class* of objects, but is

first applied to one thing, and then extended by a series of
transitions to another and another. By this process (as has
been remarked by several writers, and illustrated with great
force and clearness by Dugald Stewart in his Philosophical
Essays) a name not unfrequently passes by successive links
of resemblance from one object to another, until it becomes
applied to things having nothing in common with the first
things to which the name was given; which, however, do not,
for that reason, drop the name; so that it at last denotes a
confused huddle of objects, having nothing whatever in common; and connotes nothing, not even a vague and general
resemblance. When a name has fallen into this state, in which
by predicating it of any object we assert literally nothing
about the object, it has become unfit for the purposes either
of thought or of the communication of thought; and can only
be made serviceable by stripping it of some part of its multifarious denotation, and confining it to objects possessed of
some attributes in common, which it may be made to connote. Such are the inconveniences of a language which "is
not made, but grows." Like the governments which are in a
similar case, it may be compared to a road which is not made
but has made itself: it requires continual mending in order
to be passable.

From this it is already evident, why the question respecting the definition of an abstract name is often one of so much
difficulty. The question, What is justice? is, in other words,
What is the attribute which mankind mean to predicate
when they call an action just? To which the first answer is,
that having come to no precise agreement on the point, they
do not mean to predicate distinctly any attribute at all. Nevertheless, all believe that there is some common attribute
belonging to all the actions which they are in the habit of
calling just. The question then must be, whether there is any
such common attribute? and, in the first place, whether mankind agree sufficiently with one another as to the particular
actions which they do or do not call just, to render the inquiry, what quality those actions have in common, a possible
one: if so, whether the actions really have any quality in

common; and if they have, what it is. Of these three, the first alone is an inquiry into usage and convention; the other two are inquiries into matters of fact. And if the second question (whether the actions form a class at all) has been answered negatively, there remains a fourth, often more arduous than all the rest, namely, how best to form a class artificially, which the name may denote.

And here it is fitting to remark, that the study of the spontaneous growth of languages is of the utmost importance to those who would logically remodel them. The classifications rudely made by established language, when retouched, as they almost all require to be, by the hands of the logician, are often in themselves excellently suited to his purposes. As compared with the classifications of a philosopher, they are like the customary law of a country, which has grown up as it were spontaneously, compared with laws methodized and digested into a code: the former are a far less perfect instrument than the latter; but being the result of a long, though unscientific, course of experience, they contain a mass of materials which may be made very usefully available in the formation of the systematic body of written law. In like manner, the established grouping of objects under a common name, even when founded only on a gross and general resemblance, is evidence, in the first place, that the resemblance is obvious, and therefore considerable; and, in the next place, that it is a resemblance which has struck great numbers of persons during a series of years and ages. Even when a name, by successive extensions, has come to be applied to things among which there does not exist this gross resemblance common to them all, still at every step in its progress we shall find such a resemblance. And these transitions of the meaning of words are often an index to real connexions between the things denoted by them, which might otherwise escape the notice of thinkers; of those at least who, from using a different language, or from any difference in their habitual associations, have fixed their attention in preference on some other aspect of the things. The history of philosophy abounds in examples of such oversights, committed for want of per-

ceiving the hidden link that connected together the seemingly disparate meanings of some ambiguous word.*

Whenever the inquiry into the definition of the name of
any real object consists of anything else than a mere comparison of authorities, we tacitly assume that a meaning must
be found for the name, compatible with its continuing to
denote, if possible all, but at any rate the greater or the more
important part, of the things of which it is commonly predicated. The inquiry, therefore, into the definition, is an
inquiry into the resemblances and differences among those
things: whether there be any resemblance running through
them all; if not, through what portion of them such a general
resemblance can be traced: and finally, what are the common
attributes, the possession of which gives to them all, or to
that portion of them, the character of resemblance which has
led to their being classed together. When these common attributes have been ascertained and specified, the name which
belongs in common to the resembling objects acquires a distinct instead of a vague connotation; and by possessing this
distinct connotation, becomes susceptible of definition.

In giving a distinct connotation to the general name, the
philosopher will endeavour to fix upon such attributes as,
while they are common to all the things usually denoted by
the name, are also of greatest importance in themselves;
either directly, or from the number, the conspicuousness, or
the interesting character, of the consequences to which they

---

* "Few people" (I have said in another place) "have reflected how
great a knowledge of Things is required to enable a man to affirm that any
given argument turns wholly upon words. There is, perhaps, not one of
the leading terms of philosophy which is not used in almost innumerable
shades of meaning, to express ideas more or less widely different from
one another. Between two of these ideas a sagacious and penetrating mind
will discern, as it were intuitively, an unobvious link of connexion, upon
which, though perhaps unable to give a logical account of it, he will
found a perfectly valid argument, which his critic, not having so keen an
insight into the Things, will mistake for a fallacy turning on the double
meaning of a term. And the greater the genius of him who thus safely
leaps over the chasm, the greater will probably be the crowing and vain-
glory of the mere logician, who, hobbling after him, evinces his own
superior wisdom by pausing on its brink, and giving up as desperate his
proper business of bridging it over."

lead. He will select, as far as possible, such *differentiæ* as lead to the greatest number of interesting *propria*. For these, rather than the more obscure and recondite qualities on which they often depend, give that general character and aspect to a set of objects, which determine the groups into which they naturally fall. But to penetrate to the more hidden agreement on which these obvious and superficial agreements depend, is often one of the most difficult of scientific problems. As it is among the most difficult, so it seldom fails to be among the most important. And since upon the result of this inquiry respecting the causes of the properties of a class of things, there incidentally depends the question what shall be the meaning of a word; some of the most profound and most valuable investigations which philosophy presents to us, have been introduced by, and have offered themselves under the guise of, inquiries into the definition of a name.

Life of Language

"How Each Individual Acquires His Language"

WILLIAM DWIGHT WHITNEY

William Dwight Whitney was born February 1827 in
Northampton, Massachusetts. He graduated from Williams
College in 1845. Although he was first interested in a medical career, he became fascinated with the then new Sanskrit studies of Sir William Jones. He did graduate work at
Yale University where he studied philology with Professor
Edward Salisbury, and later studied in Germany, then the
fountainhead of the new linguistic science. Returning to the
United States he became professor of Sanskrit and philosophy at Yale University. He was instrumental in the founding of the American Philological Society and served as first
president of the organization. Among his important publications are *Sanskrit Grammar*, in 1879; *The Life and
Growth of Language* in 1867; and *Max Müller and the
Science of Language*, 1892. He died June 7, 1894.

The selection used here is Chapter II of *The Life and
Growth of Language*, published by D. Appleton and Com-
pany in 1875. The sub-title of this work is "an Outline of
Linguistic Science."

T HERE can be asked respecting language no other question of a more elementary and at the same time of a more
fundamentally important character than this: how is language obtained by us? how does each speaking individual
become possessed of his speech? Its true answer involves
and determines well-nigh the whole of linguistic philosophy.

There are probably few who would not at once reply that

we learn our language; it is taught us by those among whom our lot is cast in childhood. And this obvious and common-sense answer is also, as we shall find on a more careful and considerate inquiry, the correct one. We have to look to see what is implied in it.

In the first place, it sets aside and denies two other conceivable answers: that language is a race-characteristic, and, as such, inherited from one's ancestry, along with color, physical constitution, traits of character, and the like; and that it is independently produced by each individual, in the natural course of his bodily and mental growth.

Against both these excluded views of the acquisition of language may be brought such an array of facts so familiar and undeniable that they cannot be seriously upheld. Against the theory of language as a race-characteristic may be simply set, as sufficient rebutting evidence, the existence of a community like the American, where there are in abundance descendants of African, of Irish, of German, of southern European, of Asiatic, as well as of English ancestors, all using the same dialect, without other variety than comes of differences of locality and education, none showing a trace of any other "mother-tongue" or "native speech." But the world is full of such cases, on the small scale and on the large. Any child of parents living in a foreign country grows up to speak the foreign speech, unless carefully guarded from doing so; or, it speaks both this and the tongue of its parents, with equal readiness. The children of missionary families furnish the most striking examples of this class: no matter where they may be in the world, among what remotely kindred or wholly unrelated dialects, they acquire the local speech as "naturally" as do the children of the natives. And it is only necessary that the child of English or German or Russian parents, born in their native country, should (as is often done) be put with a French nurse, and hear French alone spoken about it, and it will grow up to speak French first and French only, just as if it were a French child. And what is French, and who are its speakers? The mass of the people of France are Celts by descent, with characteristic Celtic traits which no mixture or education has been able to obliterate; but there is hardly an appreciable element of Celtic in the French language; this is almost purely a Romanic dialect, a modern representative of the ancient Latin. There are few unmixed languages in the world, as there are few unmixed races; but the one mixture does not at all determine the other, or measure it. The English is a very striking proof of this; the preponderating French-Latin element in our vocabulary gets its most familiar and indispensable part from the Normans, a Germanic race, who got it from the French, a Celtic race, who got it from the Italians, among whom the Latin-speaking community were at first a very insignificant element, numerically. It is useless to bring up further examples; the force of those here given will be sufficiently supported by our later inquiry into the actual processes of acquisition of language.

So far as the other theory, that of independent production by each person of his own speech, implies that each inherits from his ancestors a physical constitution which makes him develop unconsciously the same speech as theirs, it is virtually coincident with the first theory, and the same facts tell with crushing weight against it; so far as it is meant to imply that there is a general likeness in intellectual constitution between members of the same community which leads them to frame accordant systems of expression, it is equally without support from facts; for the distribution of human dialects is as irreconcilable with that of natural capacity and bent as with that of physical form among human beings. Every variety of gift is found among those who employ, each with his own degree of skill and capacity, the same speech; and souls of commensurate calibre in different communities are unable to have intercourse together.

We come, then, to consider directly the process by which the child becomes able—to speak a certain language—a process sufficiently under every one's observation to allow of general and competent criticism of any attempted description of it. We cannot, it is true, follow with entire comprehension all the steps of evolution of the infantile and childish powers; but we can understand them well enough for our purpose.

The first thing which the child has to learn, before speech is possible, is to observe and distinguish; to recognize the persons and things about him, in their concrete individuality, and to notice as belonging to them some of their characteristic qualities and acts. This is a very brief description of a very intricate psychological process—which, however, it does not belong to the student of language to draw out in greater detail. There is involved in it, we may further remark in passing, nothing which some of the lower animals may not achieve. At the same time, the child is exercising his organs of utterance, and gaining conscious command of them, partly by a mere native impulse to the exertion of all his native powers, partly by imitation of the sound-making persons about him: the child brought up in solitude would be comparatively silent. This physical process is quite analogous with the training of the hands: for some six months the child tosses them about, he knows not how or why; then he begins to notice them and work them under command, till at length he can do by conscious volition whatever is within their power. Control and management of the organs of utterance comes much more slowly; but the time arrives when the child can imitate at least some of the audible as well as the visible acts of others; can reproduce a given sound, as a given gesture. But before this, he has learned to associate with some of the objects familiar to him the names by which they are called; a result of much putting of the two together on the part of his instructors. Here is seen more markedly, at least in degree, the superiority of human endowment. The association in question is doubtless at the outset no easy thing, even for the child; he does not readily catch the idea that a set of sounds belongs to and represents a thing—any more than, when older, the idea that a series of written characters represents a word; but their connection is set so often and so distinctly before him as to be learned at last, just as the connection is learned between sugar and pleasure to the taste, between a rod and retribution for misbehavior. And every child begins to know things by their names long before he begins to call them. The next step is to imitate and reproduce the familiar name, usually at first in the most imperfect way, by a mere hint of the true sound, intelligible only to the child's constant attendants; and when that step is taken, then for the first time is made a real beginning of the acquisition of language.

Though not all children start with the acquisition of precisely the same words, yet their limit of variety is but a narrow one. We may take as fair examples of at least the very early ones the childish names for 'father' and 'mother,' namely *papa* and *mamma*, and the words *water, milk, good*. And we have to notice especially both how wholly external is the process which makes the child connect these particular names with their respective ideas, and how empirical and imperfect are the ideas themselves. What is really implied in *papa* and *mamma*, the child does not in the least know; to him they are only signs for certain loving and caring individuals, distinguished most conspicuously by differences of dress; and the chance is (and it not seldom chances) that he will give the same names to other individuals showing like differences; the real relation of male and female parent to child he comes to comprehend only much later—not to speak of the physiological mysteries involved in it, which no man yet comprehends. As little does he understand the real nature of water and milk; he knows no more than that, among the liquids (that name, to be sure, comes much later, but not till long after the child has realized the distinction of liquid and solid) constantly brought before him there are two which he readily distinguishes, by look and by taste, and to which other people give these names; and he follows their example. The names are provisional, convenient nuclei for the gathering of more knowledge about; where the liquids come from will be learned by and by: and their chemical constitution, perhaps, in due time. As for *good*, the first association of the term is probably with what has a pleasant taste; then what is otherwise agreeable comes to be comprehended under the same name; it gets applied to behavior which is agreeable to the parents, as judged by a standard which the child himself is far from understanding—and this transfer to a moral sphere is by no means an easy one; as he grows up, the child is (perhaps) all the time learning to distinguish more accurately between *good* and *bad;* but he is likely to be at the last baffled by finding that the wisest heads in the world have been and are irreconcilably at variance as to what *good* really means—whether it implies only utility, or an independent and absolute principle.

These are only typical examples, fairly illustrating the whole process of speech-getting. The child begins as a learner, and he continues such. There is continually in presence of his intellect more and better than he can grasp. By words he is made to form dim conceptions, and draw rude distinctions, which after experience shall make truer and more distinct, shall deepen, explain, correct. He has no time to be original; far more rapidly than his crude and confused impressions can crystallize independently into shape, they are, under the example and instruction of others, centred and shaped about certain definite points. So it goes on indefinitely. The young mind is always learning words, and things through words; in all other cases as really, if not so obviously, as when, by description and picture or by map and plan, it is led to form some inaccurate half-conception of the animal *lion* or the city *Peking.* The formal distinctions made by the inflectional system of even so simple a language as English, and by words of relation, are at first out of the child's reach. He can grasp and wield only the grosser elements of speech. He does not apprehend the relation of one and more than one clearly enough to use the two numbers of nouns; the singular has to do duty for both; and so also the root-form of the verb, to the neglect of persons, tenses, and moods. It is an era in his education when he first begins to employ preterits and plurals and their like. So with the pronouns. He is slow to catch the trick of those shifting names, applied to persons according as they are speaking, spoken to, or spoken of; he does not see why each should not have an own name, given alike in all situations: and he speaks of himself and others by such a name and such only, or blunders sorely in trying to do

otherwise—till time and practice set him right.[1] Thus, in every
respect, language is the expression of matured and practised
thought, and the young learner enters into the use of it as
fast as natural capacity and favoring circumstances enable
him to do so. Others have observed, and classified, and abstracted; he only reaps the fruit of their labors. It is precisely
as when the child studies mathematics; he goes over and
appropriates, step by step, what others have wrought out, by
means of word and sign and symbol; and he thus masters in
a few years what it has taken generations and ages to produce, what his unaided intellect could never have produced;
what, perhaps, he could never independently have produced
a single item of, having just mental force enough to follow
and acquire it: though also, perhaps, he has capacity to increase it by and by, adding something new for those to learn
who come after him—even as the once educated speaker may
come to add, in one way and another (as will be pointed out
later), new stores of expression to language.

In all this, now, is involved infinitely more than linguistic
science has any call to deal with and explain. Let us consider,
for example, the word *green*. Its presence in our vocabulary
implies first the physical cause of the color, wherein is involved the whole theory of optics: and this concerns the physicist; it is for him to talk of the ether and its vibrations, and
of the frequency and length of the waves which produce the
sensation of greenness. Then there is the structure of the eye:
its wondrous and mysterious sensitiveness to just this kind of
vibration, the apparatus of nerves which conveys the impression to the brain, the cerebral structure which receives the
impression: to treat of all this is the duty of the physiologic.
His domain borders and overlaps that of the psychologist,
who has to tell us what he can of the intuition and resulting
conception, considered as mode and product of mental action,
of the power of apprehension and distinction and abstrac-

---

[1] The amount of sapient philosophy which has been aimlessly expended
on this simple fact—as if it involved the metaphysical distinction of the
ego and the *non-ego*—is something truly surprising.

tion, and of the sway of consciousness over the whole. Then, in the hearing of the word *green* is involved the wonderful power of audition, closely akin with that of vision: another sensitive apparatus, which notes and reports another set of vibratory waves, in another vibrating medium: it falls, like vision, into the hands of the physicist and physiologist. They, too, have to do with the organs of utterance, which produce the audible vibration; with their obedience to the direction of the will: directions given but not executed under the review of consciousness, and implying that control of the mind over the muscular apparatus of the body which is by no means the least of mysteries. We might go on indefinitely thus, noticing what is included in the simplest linguistic act; and behind all would lie as a background the great mystery of existence and its cause, which no philosophy has yet been able to do more than recognize. Every part of this is of interest and importance to the linguistic scholar, but each in its own way and degree; and his specific and central business is with none of it, but rather with something else. This namely: there exists an uttered and audible sign, *green,* by which, in certain community, are designated a certain class of kindred shades among the infinitely varied hues of nature and of art; and every person who, by birth or by immigration or as a visitor (a bodily visitor, or only a mental one, as student of its literature), comes into the community in question, learns to associate that sign with the given group of shades, and to understand and employ it as designating them; and he learns to classify the infinity of hues under that and certain other signs, of like nature and use. About this pivotal fact all the other matters involved fall into position as more or less nearly auxiliary; from it as point of view they are judged and have their value estimated. Language, both in its single items and as a whole, is primarily the sign of the idea, the sign with its accompanying idea; and to take any other department of the questions involved as the central one is to throw the whole into a false position. distorting the propositions and relations of every part. And, as the science of language seeks after causes, endeavors to explain the facts of language, the primary inquiry respecting this fact is: how came this sign to be thus used? what is the history of its production and application? and even, what is its ultimate origin and the reason of it? provided we can reach so far.

For there is, recognizably and traceably, a time when and a reason why many of our words come into use as signs for the ideas they represent. For example, a certain other shade of color, a peculiar red, was produced (with more, of its kind) not many years ago, as result of the chemical manipulation of coal tar, and was, reflectively and artificially, called by its inventor *magenta*, after the name of a place which a great battle had recently made famous. The word *magenta* is just as real and legitimate a part of the English language as *green*, though vastly younger and less important; and those who acquire and use the latter do so in precisely the same manner as the former, and generally with equal ignorance and unconcern as to its origin. The word *gas* is of much longer standing and wider use with us, and has its respectable family of derivatives and compounds—as *gaseous, gassify, gas-pipe*—and even its colloquial figurative uses—as when we call an empty and sophistical but ready talker *gassy;* but it was the wholly arbitrary invention of a Dutch chemist (Van Helmont), about A.D. 1600. Science was at that time getting so far along as to begin to form the distinct conception of an aëriform or *gaseous* condition of existence of matter; and this name chanced to be introduced and supported in a way that commended it to general acceptance; and so it became the name, and for all Europe. The young now for the most part know it first as the title of a certain kind of *gas*, made practically useful in giving light; but by and by, if fairly educated, they are led in connection with the word to form by themselves the scientific idea of which this is the sign. To trace the history of these two vocables is to inform ourselves as to the time and the circumstances of production of the aniline colors, and as to the taking of a certain important step forward in scientific thinking. We cannot follow so clearly toward or to its source the word *green*, because it is vastly older, reaching back far beyond the period of literary record; but we do seem to arrive by inference at a connection of it with our word *grow*, and at seeing that a *green* thing was named from its being a *growing* thing; and this is a matter of no small interest as bearing on the history of the word.

It is not the place here to follow up this line of inquiries, and see what is meant by etymologizing, or tracing the history of words toward the origins; the subject is one which will occupy us more properly later. We touch it in passing merely in order to note that the reason of first attribution of a sign to its specific use is one thing, and that the reason of its after employment in that use is another and a very different thing. To the child learning to speak, all signs are in themselves equally good for all things; he could acquire and reproduce one as well as another for a given purpose. In fact, children in different communities do learn every possible variety of names for the same thing: instead of *green*, the German child learns *grün*, the Dutch *groen*, the Swedish *grön*—all related to our *green*, yet not identical with it; and the French child learns *vert*, the Spanish *verde*, the Italian *viride*—a similar group of related yet diverse names; while the Russian says *zelenüi*, the Hungarian *zöld*, the Turk *ishil*, the Arab *akhsar*, and so on. Each of these, and of hundreds of others, is obtained in the same way: the child hears it uttered by those about him under such circumstances as make plain to him what it signifies; by its aid he in part learns to abstract the quality of color from the colored object and conceive it separately; and he learns to combine in one comprehensive conception the different shades of green, distinguishing them together from the other colors, as blue and yellow, into which they pass by insensible gradations. The learner grasps the conception, at least in a measure, and then associates his own word with it by a purely external tie, having been able, if so guided, to form the same association with any other existing or possible word, and not less easily and surely. An internal and necessary tie between word and idea is absolutely non-existent for him; and whatever historical reason there may be is also non-existent to his sense. He may sometimes ask "what for?" about a word, as he does, in his childish curiosity, about everything else; but it makes no difference with the young etymologist (any more than with the older one) what answer he gets, or whether he gets an answer; to him, the sole and sufficient reason why he should use this particular sign is that it is used by those about him. In the true and proper meaning of the terms, then, every word handed down in every human language is an arbitrary and conventional sign: arbitrary, because any one of the thousand other words current among men, or of the tens of thousands which might be fabricated, could have been equally well learned and applied to this particular purpose; conventional, because the reason for the use of this rather than another lies solely in the fact that it is already used in the community to which the speaker belongs. The word exists θέσει, 'by attribution,' and not Φύσει, 'by nature,' in the sense that there is, either in the nature of things in general, or in the nature of the individual speaker who uses it, any reason that prescribes and determines it.

There is obviously mental training and shaping, as well as mental equipment, in the process of learning to speak. The mental action of the individual is schooled into certain habits, consonant with those of his community; he acquires the current classifications and abstractions and ways of looking at things. To take an example: the quality of color is so conspicuous, and our apprehension of it so urged by the infinity of its manifested differences which are ever before our eyes, that the conception of color is only quickened and rendered more distinct by acquisition of the words which denote it. But in the classification of the shades of hue the phraseology of the language acquired bears a determining part; they fall into order under and about the leading names, as *white, black, red, blue, green;* and each hue is tested in the mind by aid of these, and referred to the one or the other class. And different languages make different classifications: some of them so unlike ours, so much less elaborate and complete, that their acquisition gives the eye and mind a very inferior training in distinguishing colors. This is still more strikingly the case as regards number. There are dialects which are in a state of infantile bewilderment before the problem of numeration; they have words for 'one,' 'two,' and 'three;' but all beyond is an undivided 'many.' None of us, it is tolerably certain, would ever have gone farther than that by his own absolutely unassisted efforts; but by words—and only by words; for such is the abstractness of the relations of number that they, more than any others, are dependent for their realization and manageableness on expression—more and more intricate numerical relations have been mastered by us, until finally we are provided with a system which is extensible to every thing short of infinity—the decimal system, namely, or that which proceeds by constant additions of ten individuals of any given denomination to form the next higher. And what is the foundation of this system? Why, as every one knows, the simple fact that we have ten fingers ("digits") on our two hands; and that fingers are the handiest substitutes for figures, the most ready and natural aids to an unready reckoner. A fact as external and physical as this, and seemingly so trivial, has shaped the whole science of mathematics, and, altogether without his being aware of it, gives form to all the numerical conceptions of each new learner. It is a suggestion of general human experience in the past, translated through language into a law for the government of thought in the future.

The same, in varying way and measure, is true of every part of language. All through the world of matter and of mind, our predecessors, with such wisdom as they had at command, have gone observing, deducing, and classifying; and we inherit it and through language the results of their wisdom. So with the distinctions of *living* and *lifeless; of animal* and *vegetable* and *mineral; of fish* and *reptiles* and *bird* and *insect; of tree* and *bush* and *herb; of rock* and *pebble* and *sand* and *dust.* So with those of *body, life, mind, spirit, soul,* and their kindred. So with the qualities of objects, both physical and moral, and with their relations, through the whole round of the categories: position and succession, form and size, manner and degree: all, in their indefinite multitude, are divided and grouped, like the shades of color, and each group has its own sign, to guide the apprehension and help the discrimination of him who uses it. So, once more, with the apparatus of logical statement: the ability to put a subject and predicate closely together, and to test their correspondence by repeated comparison, comes only by language; and it is the fruitful means whereby old cognitions are corrected and new ones attained. So, in fine, with the auxiliary apparatus of inflections and form-words, wherein various tongues are most of all discordant, each making its own selection of what it will express and what it will leave for the mind to understand without expression.

Every single language has thus its own peculiar framework of established distinctions, its shapes and forms of thought, into which, for the human being who learns that language as his "mother-tongue," is cast the content and product of his mind, his store of impressions, however acquired, his experience and knowledge of the world. This is what is sometimes called the "inner form" of language—the shape and cast of thought, as fitted to a certain body of expressions. But it comes as the result of external influence; it is an accompaniment of the process by which the individual acquires the body of expression itself; it is not a product of his internal forces, in their free and undirected workings; it is something imposed from without. It amounts simply to this: that the mind which was capable of doing otherwise has been led to view things in this particular way, to group them in a certain manner, to contemplate them consciously in these and those relations.

There is thus an element of constraint in language-learning. But it is an element of which the learner is wholly unconscious. Whatever language he first acquires, this is to him the natural and necessary way of thinking and speaking; he conceives of no other as even possible. The case could not be otherwise. For even the poorest language in existence

is so much better than any one's powers could have produced unaided, that its acquisition would imply a greatly
accelerated drawing out and training of the powers of even
the most gifted being; the advantage is so great that the
disadvantage entirely disappears before it. We, to be sure,
looking on from without, can sometimes find reason for re-
gret, saying: "Here is a man of capacities far beyond the
average of the degraded community of which he is a member; in justice to those capacities, he should have had his
birth where a higher language would have developed them
into what they were able to become; only," we should have
to add, "this barbarian tongue raises him far above what
he could have become had he never learned to speak at all."
Moreover, it is far oftener the case that the individual's
linguistic lot is beyond his deserts: that he acquires a language above his level, and would have been better fitted by
a lower dialect.

It is not easy to over-estimate the advantage won by the
mind in the obtaining of a language. Its confused impressions are thus reduced to order, brought under the distinct
review of consciousness and within reach of reflection; an
apparatus is provided with which it can work, like the artisan
with his tools. There is no other parallel so close, as regards
both the kind and the degree of assistance afforded, as this
between words, the instruments of thought, and those other
instruments, the creation and the aids of man's manual
dexterity. By as much as, supplied with these, man can
traverse space, handle and shape materials, frame textures,
penetrate distance, observe the minute, beyond what he
could compass with his unequipped physical powers, by so
much is the reach and grasp, the penetration and accuracy,
of his thought increased by speech. This part of the value of
speech is by no means easy to bring to full realization, because our minds are so used to working by and through
words that they cannot even conceive of the plight they
would be in if deprived of such helps. But we may think,

for example, of what the mathematician would be without figures and symbols.

In respect to this general training and equipment of the mind for work, the first acquisition of a language does for the individual what can never be repeated later. When we first take hold of an additional language, we cannot help translating its signs into those we already know; the peculiarities of its "inner form," the non-identity and incommensurability of its shaped and grouped ideas with those of our native speech, escape our notice. As we gain familiarity with it, as our conceptions adapt themselves to its framework and operate directly through it, we come to see that our thoughts are cast by it into new shapes, that its phraseology is its own and inconvertible. Perhaps it is here that we get our most distinct hint of the elements of constraint in language-learning. Certainly, the exceptionally-gifted Polynesian or African who should learn a European language—as English, French, German—would find himself prepared for labor in departments of mental action which had before been inaccessible to him, and would realize how his powers had been balked of their best action by the possession of only the inferior instrument. The scholars of the Middle Ages, who employed the Latin for the expression of their higher thought, do so partly because the popular dialects had not yet become enriched to a capacity for aiding the production of such thought and for expressing it.

But in all other respects, the learning of a second language is precisely the same process as the learning of a first, of one's own "mother-tongue." It is the memorizing of a certain body of signs for conceptions and their relations, used in certain community, existing or extinct—signs which have no more natural and necessary connection with the conceptions they indicate than our own have, but are equally arbitrary and conventional with the latter; and of which we may make ourselves masters to a degree dependent only on our opportunities, our capacity, our industry, and the length of time devoted to the work; even coming to substitute, if circumstances favor, the second language in our constant and ready use, and to become unfamiliar with and forget its predecessor.

We realize better in the case of a second or "foreign," than in that of a first or "native" language, that the process of acquisition is a never-ending one; but it is not more true of the one than of the other. We say, to be sure, of a child who has reached a certain grade that he "has learned to speak;" but we mean by this only that he has acquired a limited number of signs, sufficient for the ordinary purposes of the childish life, together with the power, by much practice, of wielding them with adroitness and general correctness. There are, probably, only a few hundred such signs, all told; and outside their circle, the English is as much an unknown language to the child as is German, or Chinese, or Choctaw. Even ideas which he is fully able to grasp when put into his acquired phraseology are unintelligible if expressed as grown-up men would naturally write them; they must be translated into childish phrase. What he has is especially the central core of language, as we may call it: signs for the most commonly recurring conceptions, words which every speaker uses every day. As he grows older, as his powers develop and his knowledge increases, he acquires more and more; and in different departments, according to circumstances. He who has to turn at once to the hard work of life may add to the first childish store little besides the technical expressions belonging to his own narrow vocation; he, on the other hand, who devotes years to the sole work of getting himself educated, and continues to draw in knowledge through the rest of his life, appropriates constantly larger stores, and rises to higher styles of expression. The ordinary vocabulary of the educated, including a great variety of the technical terms of special branches of knowledge with which the educated man must have at least a degree of acquaintance, he may come to understand and to use with intelligence; but there

will be whole bodies of English expressions which he cannot wield, as well as styles to which he does not attain. The
vocabulary of a rich and long-cultivated language like the
English may be roughly estimated at about 100,000 words
(although this excludes a great deal which, if "English"
were understood in its widest sense, would have to be
counted in); but thirty thousand is a very large estimate
for the number ever used, in writing or speaking, by a well-
educated man; three to five thousand, it has been carefully
estimated, cover the ordinary needs of cultivated intercourse;
and the number acquired by persons of lowest training and
narrowest information is considerably less than this. Nowhere more clearly than here does it appear that one gets
his language by a process of learning, and only thus; for
all this gradual increase of one's linguistic resources goes on
in the most openly external fashion, by dint of hearing and
reading and study; and it is obviously only a continuation,
under somewhat changed circumstances, of the process of
acquisition of the first nucleus; while the whole is parallel
to the beginning and growth of one's command of a "for
eign" tongue.

The same thing, however, appears clearly enough, if we
consider more narrowly the somewhat shifting relations between our linguistic signs and the conceptions for which
they stand. The relation is established at first by a tentative
process, liable to error and subject to amendment. The child
finds out very soon that names do not in general belong to
single objects alone, but rather to classes of related objects;
and his power of noting resemblances and differences, the
most fundamental activity of intellect, is from the first called
into lively action and trained by the constant necessity of
applying names rightly. But the classes are of every variety
of extent, and in part determined by obscure and perplex-
ing criteria. We have noted already the natural and frequent childish error of using *papa* and *mamma* in the sense
of 'man and 'woman;' the child is puzzled, by and by, by
finding that there are other *papas* and *mammas*, though he
must not call them so. An older child he learns to call, for

example, *George;* but he finds that he must not say *George* of other kindred beings; there is another word, *boy,* for that use. But then, again, he makes acquaintances with still other *Georges;* and to find the tie that binds them into a class together is a problem quite beyond his powers. A variety of creatures of very diverse appearance he learns to call *dog;* but he may not take the same liberty with *horse;* though mules and donkeys are much more like horses than greyhounds and lapdogs are like terriers, they must be carefully distinguished in appellation. A sun in a picture is still a *sun;* and in a cultivated community the child soon gets his imagination trained to recognize the pictured representations of things, and to call them by the same names, while still distinctly aware of the relation between things and picture; while a grown-up untutored savage is completely baffled by such a counterfeit, seeing in it only a confusion of lines and scratches. A toy house or tree is to have the title *house* or *tree;* but a kind of toy human being has the specific name of *doll.* The words of degree have their peculiarities of application; *new* is sometimes at an inch of distance, sometimes at a rod; a *big* apple is not nearly so big as a *little* house; a *long* time means a few minutes or a few years. The inconsistencies of expression are numberless; and till added experience explains them, there is room for misapprehensions and blunders. Moreover, there are cases in which the difficulty is much more persistent, or is never wholly removed. *Fish* even adult apprehension makes to include whales and dolphins, till scientific knowledge points out a fundamental difference as underlying the superficial resemblance.

But it is especially in regard to matters of which the knowledge is won in a more artificial way, that the beginner's ideas are vague and insufficient. For example, children are apt to be taught the names and definitions of geographical objects and relations without gaining any real comprehension of what it all means; a map, a more unintelligible kind of picture, is little better than a puzzle; and even older children, or grown men, have defective concep-

tions which are only rectified by exceptional experience in
after-life. Localities, of course, are most incorrectly imagined
by those who have not seen them. Of Sedan, Peking, Hawaii,
Chimborazo, every well-instructed person knows enough to
be able to talk about them; but how imperfectly do we
conceive them, as compared with one who has lived at or
near them! We have to be extremely careful, in teaching the
young, not to push them on too rapidly, lest we prove to
have been building up a mere artificial and empty structure
of names, without real enlightenment. And yet, something
of this is unavoidable, a necessary incident of instruction.
A host of grand conceptions are put before the youthful
mind, and kept there by a paltry association or two, while
it is left for after-development to fill them out to more
nearly their true value. The child is ludicrously unable at
first to know what is meant by *God,* or *good,* or *duty,* or
conscience, or the *world,* even as *sun* and *moon, weight* and
color, involve infinity more than he has an inkling of; but
the word, in each case, gives him a definite nucleus, about
which more and ever more knowledge may be grouped; he
makes a constant approach toward the right conception,
even if it be one to which no human wisdom has yet attained. For the condition of the child, after all, differs only
in degree from that of the man, and in no very great degree.
Our words are too often signs for crude and hasty, for indefinite and indefinable, generalizations. We use them accurately enough for the ordinary practical purposes of life; and
most of mankind go through life content with that, letting
instruction and experience bring what improvement they
may; few have the independence, even if they had the time
and ability, to test every name to the bottom, drawing precise limits about each. For the most part, we are loose thinkers and loose talkers, misled into error in an infinity of cases
by our ignorance of the terms we glibly use. But even the
wisest and most thorough of us is met by the impossibility
of giving to speech a preciseness of definition which should
exclude misunderstanding and unsound reasoning—especially as to matters of subjective import, where it is hard to

bring conceptions to a sharp test. And so the differences of view, even of philosophers, take on the form of verbal questions, controversies hinge on the interpretation of a term, and every writer who aims at exactness has to begin with definitions—to which, then, he finds it impossible to be faithful; some antagonist or successor, perhaps, shows him to have failed of exactness at a critical point, and tumbles into ruins the whole magnificent structure of fancied truth which he had erected.

We see from all this, it may be observed, how far language is from being identical with thought. It is so just as much as the mathematician's figures and symbols are identical with his conceptions of mathematical quantities and relations; and not one whit more. It is, as we noticed at the outset, the means of expression of thought, an instrumentality auxiliary to the processes of thought. An acquired language is something imposed from without upon the methods and results of mental action. It does, indeed, as a frame-work imposed upon a growing and developing, body, give shape to that which underlies it, determining the "inner form;" and yet it is everywhere loose and adjustable. While working by it, the mind also works under it, shifting and adapting, changing and improving its classifications, working in new knowledge and better insight. Thus far we have emphasized the passive receptive work of the mind in dealing with language, because that is, especially at the outset, the bulk of its work; in the following chapters we have to take account of its more independent and creative activity.

But nothing that has been said is to be misconstrued into meaning that the mind is not, in all its work, essentially an active and creative force, or that it gets by instruction a faculty which it did not before possess. All that is implied in the power to speak belongs indefeasibly to man, as a part of his natural endowment; but this power is guided in its development, and determined in the result it attains, by the example and instruction of other minds, already developed. It does nothing which it might not have done alone, under favoring circumstances, and with sufficient time—the life-time, namely, of a few score or hundred generations; but for what it actually does, both as regards the how much and the how, it has to thank those about it. Its acquisition of language is a part of its education, in just the same manner and degree as the other parts of education.

"How To Make Our Ideas Clear"

Charles S. Peirce

Born in Cambridge, Massachusetts, in 1839, Charles S. Peirce was the son of the great mathematician Benjamin Peirce, who taught at Harvard for nearly fifty years. Charles was educated at Harvard, graduating in 1859. He is the acknowledged author of the philosophy of pragmatism. For years Peirce was associated with the Geodetic Society and wrote many articles on chemistry, logic, psychology, mathematics, and other scientific subjects. He was also a principal contributor to the Century Dictionary. He lectured for several years at Harvard and at Johns Hopkins. However, it was not until William James that the philosophy of pragmatism came to be widely known. Peirce died in 1914. The article used here was the second paper in a series published in *Popular Science Monthly*, January 1878.

WIIOEVER has looked into a modern treatise on logic of the common sort, will doubtless remember the two distinctions between *clear* and *obscure* conceptions, and between *distinct* and *confused* conceptions. They have lain in the books now for nigh two centuries, unimproved and unmodified, and are generally reckoned by logicians as among the gems of their doctrine.

A clear idea is defined as one which is so apprehended that it will be recognized wherever it is met with, and so that no other will be mistaken for it. If it fails of this clearness, it is said to be obscure.

This is rather a neat bit of philosophical terminology; yet, since it is clearness that they were defining, I wish the logicians had made their definition a little more plain. Never to fail to recognize an idea, and under no circumstances to mistake another for it, let it come in how recondite a form it may, would indeed imply such prodigious force and clearness of intellect as is seldom met with in this world. On the other hand, merely to have such an acquaintance with the idea as to have become familiar with it, and to have lost all hesitancy in recognizing it in ordinary cases, hardly seems to deserve the name of clearness of apprehension, since after all it only amounts to a subjective feeling of mastery which may be entirely mistaken. I take it, however, that when the logicians speak of "clearness," they mean nothing more than such a familiarity with an idea, since they regard the quality as but a small merit, which needs to be supplemented by another, which they call *distinctness*.

A distinct idea is defined as one which contains nothing which is not clear. This is technical language; by the *contents* of an idea logicians understand whatever is contained in its definition. So that an idea is *distinctly* apprehended, according to them, when we can give a precise definition of it, in abstract terms. Here the professional logicians leave the subject; and I would not have troubled the reader with what they have to say, if it were not such a striking example of how they have been slumbering through ages of intellectual activity, listlessly disregarding the enginery of modern thought, and never dreaming of applying its lessons to the improvement of logic. It is easy to show that the doctrine that familiar use and abstract distinctness make the perfection of apprehension, has its only true place in philosophies which have long been extinct; and it is now time to formulate the method of attaining to a more perfect clearness of thought, such as we see and admire in the thinkers of our own time.

When Descartes set about the reconstruction of philosophy, his first step was to (theoretically) permit skepticism and to discard the practice of the schoolmen of looking to

authority as the ultimate source of truth. That done, he
sought a more natural fountain of true principles, and professed to find it in the human mind; thus passing, in the
directest way, from the method of authority to that of
apriority, as described in my first paper. Self-consciousness
was to furnish us with our fundamental truths, and to decide what was agreeable to reason. But since, evidently, not
all ideas are true, he was led to note, as the first condition
of infallibility, that they must be clear. The distinction between an idea *seeming* clear and really being so, never occurred to him. Trusting to introspection, as he did, even for
a knowledge of external things, why should he question its
testimony in respect to the contents of our own minds? But
then, I suppose, seeing men, who seemed to be quite clear
and positive, holding opposite opinions upon fundamental
principles, he was further led to say that clearness of ideas is
not sufficient, but that they need also to be distinct, i.e., to
have nothing unclear about them. What he probably meant
by this (for he did not explain himself with precision) was,
that they must sustain the test of dialectical examination;
that they must not only seem clear at the outset, but that
discussion must never be able to bring to light points of obscurity connected with them.

Such was the distinction of Descartes, and one sees that
it was precisely on the level of his philosophy. It was somewhat developed by Leibnitz. This great and singular genius
was as remarkable for what he failed to see as for what he
saw. That a piece of mechanism could not do work perpetu-
ally without being fed with power in some form, was a thing
perfectly apparent to him; yet he did not understand that
the machinery of the mind can only transform knowledge,
but never originate it, unless it be fed with facts of observation. He thus missed the most essential point of the Carte-
sian philosophy, which is, that to accept propositions which
seem perfectly evident to us is a thing which, whether it be
logical or illogical, we cannot help doing. Instead of regarding the matter in this way, he sought to reduce the first principles of science to formulas which cannot be denied with-

out self-contradiction, and was apparently unaware of the great difference between his position and that of Descartes. So he reverted to the old formalities of logic, and, above all, abstract definitions played a great part in his philosophy. It was quite natural, therefore, that on observing that the method of Descartes labored under the difficulty that we may seem to ourselves to have clear apprehensions of ideas which in truth are very hazy, no better remedy occurred to him than to require an abstract definition of every important term. Accordingly, in adopting the distinction of *clear* and *distinct* notions, he described the latter quality as the clear apprehension of everything contained in the definition; and the books have ever since copied his words. There is no danger that his chimerical scheme will ever again be over-valued. Nothing new can ever be learned by analyzing def-initions. Nevertheless, our existing beliefs can be set in order by this process, and order is an essential element of intellec-tual economy, as of every other. It may be acknowledged, therefore, that the books are right in making familiarity with a notion the first step toward clearness of apprehen-sion, and the defining of it the second. But in omitting all mention of any higher perspicuity of thought, they simply mirror a philosophy which was exploded a hundred years ago. That much-admired "ornament of logic"—the doctrine of clearness and distinctness—may be pretty enough, but it is high time to relegate to our cabinet of curiosities the antique *bijou,* and to wear about us something better adapt-ed to modern uses.

The very first lesson that we have a right to demand that logic shall teach us is, how to make our ideas clear; and a most important one it is, depreciated only by minds who stand in need of it. To know what we think, to be masters of our own meaning, will make a solid foundation for great and weighty thought. It is most easily learned by those whose ideas are meagre and restricted; and far happier they than such as wallow helplessly in a rich mud of conceptions. A nation, it is true, may, in the course of generations, over-come the disadvantage of an excess wealth of language and its natural concomitant, a vast, unfathomable deep of ideas. We may see it in history, slowly perfecting its literary forms, sloughing at length its metaphysics, and, by virtue of the untirable patience which is often a compensation, attaining great excellence in every branch of mental acquirement. The page of history is not yet unrolled which is to tell us whether such a people will or will not in the long run prevail over one whose ideas (like the words of their language) are few, but which possesses a wonderful mastery over those which it has. For an individual, however, there can be no question that a few clear ideas are worth more than many confused ones. A young man would hardly be persuaded to sacrifice the greater part of his thoughts to save the rest; and the muddled head is the least apt to see the necessity of such a sacrifice. Him we can usually only commiserate, as a person with a congenital defect. Time will help him, but intellectual maturity with regard to clearness comes rather late, an unfortunate arrangement of Nature, inasmuch as clearness is of less use to a man settled in life, whose errors have in great measure had their effect, than it would be to one whose path lies before him. It is terrible to see how a single unclear idea, a single formula without meaning, lurking in a young man's head, will sometimes act like an obstruction of inert matter in an artery, hindering the nutrition of the brain, and condemning its victim to pine away in the fullness of his intellectual vigor and in the midst of intellectual plenty. Many a man has cherished for years as his hobby some vague shadow of an idea, too meaningless to be positively false; he has, nevertheless, passionately loved it, had made it his companion by day and by night, and has given to it his strength and his life, leaving all other occupations for its sake, and in short has lived with it and for it, until it has become, as it were, flesh of his flesh and bone of his bone; and then he has waked up some bright morning to find it gone, clean vanished away like the beautiful Melusina of the fable, and the essence of his life gone with it. I have myself known such a man; and who can tell how many histories of circle-squarers, metaphysicians, astrologers, and what not, may not be told in the old German story?

The principles set forth in the first of these papers lead, at once, to a method of reaching a clearness of thought of a far higher grade than the "distinctness" of the logicians. We have there found that the action of thought is excited by the irritation of doubt, and ceases when belief is attained; so that the production of belief is the sole function of thought. All these words, however, are too strong for my purpose. It is as if I had described the phenomena as they appear under a mental microscope. Doubt and Belief, as the words are commonly employed, relate to religious or other grave discussions. But here I use them to designate the starting of any question, no matter how small or how great, and the resolution of it. If, for instance, in a horse-car, I pull out my purse and find a five-cent nickel and five coppers, I decide, while my hand is going to the purse, in which way I will pay my fare. To call such a question Doubt, and my decision Belief, is certainly to use words very disproportionate to the occasion. To speak of such a doubt as causing an irritation which needs to be appeased, suggests a temper which is uncomfortable to the verge of insanity. Yet, looking at the matter minutely, it must be admitted that, if there is the least hesitation as to wheher I shall pay the five coppers or the nickel (as there will be sure to be, unless I act from some previously contracted habit in the matter), though irritation is too strong a word, yet I am excited to such small mental activity as may be necessary to deciding how I shall act. Most frequently doubts arise from some indecision, however momentary, in our action. Sometimes it is not so. I have, for example, to wait in a railway-station, and to pass the time I read the advertisements on the walls, I compare the advantages of different trains and different routes which I never expect to take, merely fancying myself to be in a state of hesitancy, because I am bored with having nothing to trouble me. Feigned hesitancy, whether feigned for mere amusement or with a lofty purpose, plays a great part in the production of scientific inquiry. However the doubt may originate, it stimulates the mind to an activity which may be slight or energetic, calm or turbulent. Images pass rapidly through consciousness, one incessantly melting into another, until at last, when all is over—it may be in a fraction of a second, in an hour, or after long years—we find ourselves decided as to how we should act under such circumstances as those which occasioned our hesitation. In other words, we have attained belief.

In this process we observe two sorts of elements of consciousness, the distinction between which may best be made clear by means of an illustration. In a piece of music there are the separate notes, and there is the air. A single tone may be prolonged for an hour or a day, and it exists as perfectly in each second of that time as in the whole taken together; so that, as long as it is sounding, it might be present to a sense from which everything in the past was as completely absent as the future itself. But it is different with the air, the performance of which occupies a certain time, during the portions of which only portions of it are played. It consists in an orderliness in the succession of sounds which strike the ear at different times; and to perceive it there must be some continuity of consciousness which makes the events of a lapse of time present to us. We certainly only perceive the air by hearing the separate notes; yet we cannot be said to directly hear it, for we hear only what is present at the instant, and an orderliness of succession cannot exist in an instant. These two sorts of objects, what we are *immediately* conscious of and what we are *mediately* conscious of, are found in all consciousness. Some elements (the sensations) are completely present at every instant so long as they last, while others (like thought) are actions having beginning, middle, and end, and consist in a congruence in the succession of sensations which flow through the mind. They cannot be immediately present to us, but must cover some portion of the past or future. Thought is a thread of melody running through the succession of our sensations.

We may add that just as a piece of music may be written in parts, each part having its own air, so various systems of relationship of succession subsist together between the same sensations. These different systems are distinguished by having different motive, ideas, or functions. Thought is only one such system; for its sole motive, idea, and function is to produce belief, and whatever does not concern that purpose belongs to some other system of relations. The action of thinking may incidentally have other results. It may serve to amuse us, for example, and among *dilettanti* it is not rare to find those who have so perverted thought to the purposes of pleasure that it seems to vex them to think that the questions upon which they delight to exercise it may ever get finally settled; and a positive discovery which takes a favorite subject out of the arena of literary debate is met with ill-concealed dislike. This disposition is the very debauchery of thought. But the soul and meaning of thought, abstracted from the other elements which accompany it, though it may be voluntarily thwarted, can never be made to direct itself toward anything but the production of belief. Thought in action has for its only possible motive the attainment of thought at rest; and whatever does not refer to belief is no part of the thought itself.

And what, then, is belief? It is the demi-cadence which closes a musical phrase in the symphony of our intellectual life. We have seen that it has just three properties: First, it is something that we are aware of; second, it appeases the irritation of doubt; and, third, it involves the establishment in our nature of a rule of action, or, say for short, a *habit*. As it appeases the irritation of doubt, which is the motive for thinking, thought relaxes, and comes to rest for a moment when belief is reached. But, since belief is a rule for action, the application of which involves further doubt and further thought, at the same time that it is a stopping-place, it is also a new starting-place for thought. That is why I have permitted myself to call it thought at rest, although thought is essentially an action. The *final* upshot of thinking is the exercise of volition, and of this thought no longer forms a part; but belief is only a stadium of mental action, an effect upon our nature due to thought, which will influence future thinking.

The essence of belief is the establishment of a habit, and different beliefs are distinguished by the different modes of action to which they give rise. If beliefs do not differ in this respect, if they appease the same doubt by producing the same rule of action, then no mere differences in the manner of consciousness of them can make them different beliefs, any more than playing a tune in different keys is playing different tunes. Imaginary distinctions are often drawn between beliefs which differ only in their mode of expression; —the wrangling which ensues is real enough, however. To believe that any objects are arranged as in Fig. 1, and to be-

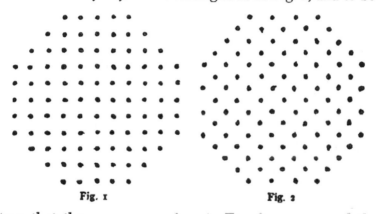

Fig. 1   Fig. 2

lieve that they are arranged as in Fig. 2, are one and the same belief; yet it is conceivable that a man should assert one proposition and deny the other. Such false distinctions do as much harm as the confusion of beliefs really different, and are among the pitfalls of which we ought constantly to beware, especially when we are upon metaphysical ground. One singular deception of this sort, which often occurs, is to mistake the sensation produced by our own unclearness of thought for a character of the object we are thinking. Instead of perceiving that the obscurity is purely subjective, we fancy that we contemplate a quality of the object which is essentially mysterious; and if our conception be afterward presented to us in a clear form we do not recognize it as the same, owing to the absence of the feeling of unintelligibility.

So long as this deception lasts, it obviously puts an impassable barrier in the way of perspicuous thinking; so that it equally interests the opponents of rational thought to perpetuate it, and its adherents to guard against it.

Another such deception is to mistake a mere difference in the grammatical construction of two words for a distinction between the ideas they express. In this pedantic age, when the general mob of writers attend so much more to words than to things, this error is common enough. When I just said that thought is an *action,* and that it consists in a *relation,* although a person performs an action but not a relation, which can only be the result of an action, yet there was no inconsistency in what I said, but only a grammatical vagueness.

From all these sophisms we shall be perfectly safe so long as we reflect that the whole function of thought is to produce habits of action; and that whatever there is connected with a thought, but irrelevant to its purpose, is an accretion to it, but no part of it. If there be a unity among our sensations which has no reference to how we shall act on a given occasion, as when we listen to a piece of music, why we do not call that thinking. To develop its meaning, we have, therefore, simply to determine what habits it produces, for what a thing means is simply what habits it involves. Now, the identity of a habit depends on how it might lead us to act, not merely under such circumstances as are likely to arise, but under such as might possibly occur, no matter how improbable they may be. What the habit is depends on *when* and *how* it causes us to act. As for the *when,* every stimulus to action is derived from perception; as for the *how,* every purpose of action is to produce some sensible result. Thus, we come down to what is tangible and practical, as the root of every real distinction of thought, no matter how subtle it may be; and there is no distinction of meaning so fine as to consist in anything but a possible difference of practice.

To see what this principle leads to, consider in the light of it such a doctrine as that of transubstantiation. The Pro-

testant churches generally hold that the elements of the
sacrament are flesh and blood only in a tropical sense; they
nourish our souls as meat and the juice of it would our bodies. But the Catholics maintain that they are literally just
that; although they possess all the sensible qualities of wafer-
cakes and diluted wine. But we can have no conception of
wine except what may enter into a belief, either—

1. That this, that, or the other, is wine; or,
2. That wine possesses certain properties.

Such beliefs are nothing but self-notifications that we
should, upon occasion, act in regard to such things as we
believe to be wine according to the qualities which we believe wine to possess. The occasion of such action would
be some sensible perception, the motive of it to produce
some sensible result. Thus our action has exclusive reference to what affects the senses, our habit has the same bearing as our action, our belief the same as our habit, our conception the same as our belief; and we can consequently
mean nothing by wine but what has certain effects, direct
or indirect, upon our senses; and to talk of something as having all the sensible characters of wine, yet being in reality
blood, is senseless jargon. Now, it is not my object to pursue
the theological question; and having used it as a logical
example I drop it, without caring to anticipate the theolo-
gian's reply. I only desire to point out how impossible it is
that we should have an idea in our minds which relates to
anything but conceived sensible effects of things. Our idea
of anything *is* our idea of its sensible effects; and if we fancy
that we have any other we deceive ourselves, and mistake
a mere sensation accompanying the thought for a part of the
thought itself. It is absurd to say that thought has any
meaning unrelated to its only function. It is foolish for Catholics and Protestants to fancy themselves in disagreement
about the elements of the sacrament, if they agree in regard
to all their sensible effects, here or hereafter.

It appears, then, that the rule for attaining the third grade
of clearness of apprehension is as follows: Consider what
effects, which might conceivably have practical bearings,

we conceive the object of our conception to have. Then, our conception of these effects is the whole of our conception of the object.

Let us illustrate this rule by some examples; and, to begin with the simplest one possible, let us ask what we mean by calling a thing *hard*. Evidently that it will not be scratched by many other substances. The whole conception of this quality, as of every other, lies in its conceived effects. There is absolutely no difference between a hard thing and a soft thing so long as they are not brought to the test. Suppose, then, that a diamond could be crystallized in the midst of a cushion of soft cotton, and should remain there until it was finally burned up. Would it be false to say that that diamond was soft? This seems a foolish question, and would be so, in fact, except in the realm of logic. There such questions are often of the greatest utility as serving to bring logical principles into sharper relief than real discussions ever could. In studying logic we must not put them aside with hasty answers, but must consider them with attentive care, in order to make out the principles involved. We may, in the present case, modify our question, and ask what prevents us from saying that all hard bodies remain perfectly soft until they are touched, when their hardness increases with the pressure until they are scratched. Reflection will show that the reply is this: there would be no *falsity* in such modes of speech. They would involve a modification of our present usage of speech with regard to the words hard and soft, but not of their meanings. For they represent no fact to be different from what it is; only they involve arrangements of facts which would be exceedingly maladroit. This leads us to remark that the question of what would occur under circumstances which do not actually arise is not a question of fact, but only of the most perspicuous arrangement of them. For example, the question of free-will and fate in its simplest form, stripped of verbiage, is something like this: I have done something of which I am ashamed; could I, by an effort of the will, have resisted the temptation, and done otherwise? The philosophical reply is, that this is not a question of

fact, but only of the arrangement of facts. Arranging them
so as to exhibit what is particularly pertinent to my question
—namely, that I ought to blame myself for having done
wrong—it is perfectly true to say that, if I had willed to do
otherwise than I did, I should have done otherwise. On the
other hand, arranging the facts so as to exhibit another important consideration, it is equally true that, when a temptation has once been allowed to work, it will, if it has a certain force, produce its effect, let me struggle how I may.
There is no objection to a contradiction in what would result from a false supposition. The *reductio ad absurdum* consists in showing that contradictory results would follow from
a hypothesis which is consequently judged to be false. Many
questions are involved in the free-will discussion, and I am
far from desiring to say that both sides are equally right.
On the contrary, I am of opinion that one side denies important facts, and that the other does not. But what I do
say is, that the above single question was the origin of the
whole doubt; that, had it not been for this question, the controversy would never have arisen; and that this question is
perfectly solved in the manner which I have indicated.

Let us next seek a clear idea of Weight. This is another
very easy case. To say that a body is heavy means simply
that, in the absence of opposing force, it will fall. This
(neglecting certain specifications of how it will fall, etc.,
which exist in the mind of the physicist who uses the word)
is evidently the whole conception of weight. It is a fair question whether some particular facts may not *account* for gravity; but what we mean by the force itself is completely involved in its effects.

This leads us to undertake an account of the idea of Force
in general. This is the great conception which, developed in
the early part of the seventeenth century from the rude idea
of a cause, and constantly improved upon since, has shown
us how to explain all the changes of motion which bodies
experience, and how to think about all physical phenomena;
which has given birth to modern science, and changed the
face of the globe; and which, aside from its more special
uses, has played a principal part in directing the course of

modern thought, and in furthering modern social development. It is, therefore, worth some pains to comprehend it. According to our rule, we must begin by asking what is the immediate use of thinking about force; and the answer is, that we thus account for changes of motion. If bodies were left to themselves, without the intervention of forces, every motion would continue unchanged both in velocity and in direction. Furthermore, change of motion never takes place abruptly; if its direction is changed, it is always through a curve without angles; if its velocity alters, it is by degrees. The gradual changes which are constantly taking place are conceived by geometers to be compounded together according to the rules of the parallelogram of forces. If the reader does not already know what this is, he will find it, I hope, to his advantage to endeavor to follow the following explanation; but if mathematics are insupportable to him, pray let him skip three paragraphs rather than that we should part company here.

A *path* is a line whose beginning and end are distinguished. Two paths are considered to be equivalent, which, beginning at the same point, lead to the same point. Thus the two paths, *A B C D E* and *A F G H E* (Fig. 3), are equivalent. Paths which do *not* begin at the same point are considered to be equivalent, provided that, on moving either of them without turning it, but keeping it always parallel to its original position, [so that] when its beginning coincides with that of the other path, the ends also coincide. Paths are considered as geometrically added together, when one be-

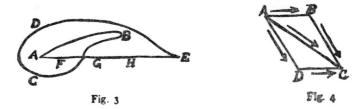

Fig. 3   Fig. 4

gins where the other ends; thus the path *A E* is conceived to be a sum of *A B*, *B C*, *C D*, and *D E*. In the parallelogram of Fig. 4 the diagonal *A C* is the sum of *A B* and *B C;* or since *A D* is geometrically equivalent to *B C,* *A C* is the geometrical sum of *A B* and *A D.*

All this is purely conventional. It simply amounts to this: that we choose to call paths having the relations I have described equal or added. But, though it is a convention, it is a convention with a good reason. The rule for geometrical addition may be applied not only to paths, but to any other things which can be represented by paths. Now, as a path is determined by the varying direction and distance of the point which moves over it from the startingpoint, it follows that anything which from its beginning to its end is determined by a varying direction and a varying magnitude is capable of being represented by a line. Accordingly, *velocities* may be represented by lines, for they have only directions and rates. The same thing is true of *accelerations,* or changes of velocities. This is evident enough in the case of velocities; and it becomes evident for accelerations if we consider that precisely what velocities are to positions—namely, states or change of them—that accelerations are to velocities.

The so-called "parallelogram of forces" is simply a rule for compounding accelerations. The rule is, to represent the accelerations by paths, and then to geometrically add the paths. The geometers, however, not only use the "parallelogram of forces" to compound different accelerations, but also to resolve one acceleration into a sum of several. Let *A B*

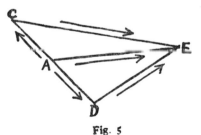

Fig. 5

(Fig. 5) be the path which represents a certain acceleration — say, such a change in the motion of a body that at the end of one second the body will, under the influence of that change, be in a position different from what it would have had if its motion had continued unchanged, such that a path equivalent to *A B* would lead from the latter position to the former.

This acceleration may be considered as the sum of the accelerations represented by $A\,C$ and $C\,B$. It may also be considered as the sum of the very different accelerations represented by $A\,D$ and $D\,B$, where $A\,D$ is almost the opposite of $A\,C$. And it is clear that there is an immense variety of ways in which $A\,B$ might be resolved into the sum of two accelerations.

After this tedious explanation, which I hope, in view of the extraordinary interest of the conception of force, may not have exhausted the reader's patience, we are prepared at last to state the grand fact which this conception embodies. This fact is that if the actual changes of motion which the different particles of bodies experience are each resolved in its appropriate way, each component acceleration is precisely such as is prescribed by a certain law of Nature according to which the bodies in the relative positions which the bodies in question actually have at the moment, always receive certain accelerations, which, being compounded by geometrical addition, give the acceleration which the body actually experiences.

This is the only fact which the idea of force represents, and whoever will take the trouble clearly to apprehend what this fact is, perfectly comprehends what force is. Whether we ought to say that a force *is* an acceleration, or that it *causes* an acceleration, is a mere question of propriety of language, which has no more to do with our real meaning than the difference between the French idiom *"Il fait froid"* and its English equivalent *"It is cold."* Yet it is surprising to see how this simple affair has muddled men's minds. In how many profound treatises is not force spoken of as a "mysterious entity," which seems to be only a way of confessing that the author despairs of ever getting a clear notion of what the word means! In a recent admired work on *Analytic Mechanics* it is stated that we understand precisely the effect of force, but what force itself is we do not understand! This is simply a self-contradiction. The idea which the word force excites in our minds has no other function than to affect our actions, and these actions can have no reference to force otherwise than through its effects. Consequently, if we know what the effects of force are, we are acquainted with every fact which is implied in saying that a force exists, and there is nothing more to know. The truth is, there is some vague notion afloat that a question may mean something which the mind cannot conceive; and when some hair-splitting philosophers have been confronted with the absurdity of such a view, they have invented an empty distinction between positive and negative conceptions, in the attempt to give their non-idea a form not obviously nonsensical. The nullity of it is sufficiently plain from the consideration given a few pages back; and, apart from those considerations, the quibbling character of the distinction must have struck every mind accustomed to real thinking.

Let us now approach the subject of logic, and consider a conception which particularly concerns it, that of *reality*. Taking clearness in the sense of familiarity, no idea could be clearer than this. Every child uses it with perfect confidence, never dreaming that he does not understand it. As for clearness in its second grade, however, it would probably puzzle most men, even among those of a reflective turn of mind, to give an abstract definition of the real. Yet such a definition may perhaps be reached by considering the points of difference between reality and its opposite, fiction. A figment is a product of somebody's imagination; it has such characters as his thought impresses upon it. That those characters are independent of how you or I think is an external reality. There are, however, phenomena within our own minds, dependent upon our thought, which are at the same time real in the sense that we really think them. But though their characters depend on how we think, they do not depend on what we think those characters to be. Thus, a dream has a real existence as a mental phenomenon, if somebody has really dreamt it; that he dreamt so and so, does not depend on what anybody thinks was dreamt, but is completely independent of all opinion on the subject. On the other hand, considering, not the fact of dreaming, but the thing dreamt, it retains its peculiarities by virtue of no other fact than that it was dreamt to possess them. Thus we may define the real as that whose characters are independent of what anybody may think them to be.

But, however satisfactory such a definition may be found, it would be a great mistake to suppose that it makes the idea of reality perfectly clear. Here, then, let us apply our rules. According to them, reality, like every other quality, consists in the peculiar sensible effects which things partaking of it produce. The only effect which real things have is to cause belief, for all the sensations which they excite emerge into consciousness in the form of beliefs. The question, therefore, is, how is true belief (or belief in the real) distinguished from false belief (or belief in fiction). Now, as we have seen in the former paper, the ideas of truth and falsehood, in their full development, appertain exclusively to the scientific method of settling opinion. A person who arbitrarily chooses the propositions which he will adopt can use the word truth only to emphasize the expression of his determination to hold on to his choice. Of course, the method of tenacity never prevailed exclusively; reason is too natural to men for that. But in the literature of the dark ages we find some fine examples of it. When Scotus Erigena is commenting upon a poetical passage in which Helleborus is spoken of as having caused the death of Socrates, he does not hesitate to inform the inquiring reader that Helleborus and Socrates were two eminent Greek philosophers, and that the latter having been overcome in argument by the former took the matter to heart and died of it! What sort of an idea of truth could a man have who could adopt and teach, without the qualification of a perhaps, an opinion taken so entirely at random? The real spirit of Socrates, who I hope would have been delighted to have been "overcome in argument," because he would have learned something by it, is in curious contrast with the naïve idea of the glossist, for whom discussion would seem to have been simply a struggle. When philosophy began to awake from its long slumber, and before theology completely dominated it, the practice seems to have for each professor to seize upon any philosophical position he found unoccupied and which seemed a strong one, to intrench himself in it, and to sally forth from time to time to give battle to the others. Thus, even the scanty records we possess of those disputes enable us to make out a dozen or more opinions held by different teachers at one time concerning the question of nominalism and realism. Read the opening part of the *Historia Calamitatum* of Abelard, who was certainly as philosophical as any of his contemporaries, and see the spirit of combat which it breathes. For him, the truth is simply his particular stronghold. When the method of authority prevailed, the truth meant little more than the Catholic faith. All the efforts of the scholastic doctors are directed toward harmonizing their faith in Aristotle and their faith in the Church, and one may search their ponderous folios through without finding an argument which goes any further. It is noticeable that where different faiths flourish side by side, renegades are looked upon with contempt even by the party whose belief they adopt; so completely has the idea of loyalty replaced that of truth-seeking. Since the time of Descartes, the defect in the conception of truth has been less apparent. Still, it will sometimes strike a scientific man that the philosophers have been less intent on finding out what the facts are, than on inquiring what belief is most in harmony with their system. It is hard to convince a follower of the *a priori* method by adducing facts; but show him that an opinion he is defending is inconsistent with what he has laid down elsewhere, and he will be very apt to retract it. These minds do not seem to believe that disputation is ever to cease; they seem to think that the opinion which is natural for one man is not so for another, and that belief will, consequently, never be settled. In contenting themselves with fixing their own opinions by a method which would lead another man to a different result, they betray their feeble hold of the conception of what truth is.

On the other hand, all the followers of science are fully persuaded that the processes of investigation, if only pushed far enough, will give one certain solution to every question to which they can be applied. One man may investigate the velocity of light by studying the transits of Venus and the aberration of the stars; another by the oppositions of Mars and the eclipses of Jupiter's satellites; a third by the method of Fizeau; a fourth by that of Foucault; a fifth by the motions of the curves of Lissajoux; a sixth, a seventh, an eighth and a ninth, may follow the different methods of comparing the measures of statical and dynamical electricity. They may at first obtain different results, but, as each perfects his method and his processes, the results will move steadily together toward a destined center. So with all scientific research. Different minds may set out with the most antagonistic views, but the progress of investigation carries them by a force outside of themselves to one and the same conclusion. This activity of thought by which we are carried, not where we wish, but to a foreordained goal, is like the operation of destiny. No modification of the point of view taken, no selection of other facts for study, no natural bent of mind even, can enable a man to escape the predestinate opinion. This great law is embodied in the conception of truth and reality. The opinion which is fated to be ultimately agreed to by all who investigate, is what we mean by the truth, and the object represented in this opinion is the real. That is the way I would explain reality.

But it may be said that this view is directly opposed to the abstract definition which we have given of reality, inasmuch as it makes the characters of the real depend on what is ultimately thought about them. But the answer to this is that, on the one hand, reality is independent, not necessarily of thought in general, but only of what you or I or any finite number of men may think about it; and that, on the other hand, though the object of the final opinion depends on what that opinion is, yet what that opinion is does not depend on what you or I or any man thinks. Our perversity and that of others may indefinitely postpone the settlement of opinion; it might even conceivably cause an arbitrary proposition to be universally accepted as long as the human race should last. Yet even that would not change the nature of the belief, which alone could be the result of investigation carried sufficiently far; and if, after the extinction of our race, another should arise with faculties and disposition for investigation, that true opinion must be the one which they would ultimately come to. "Truth crushed to earth shall rise again," and the opinion which would finally result from investigation does not depend on how anybody may actually think. But the reality of that which is real does depend on the real fact that investigation is destined to lead, at last, if continued long enough, to a belief in it.

But I may be asked what I have to say to all the minute facts of history, forgotten never to be recovered, to the lost books of the ancients, to the buried secrets.

> "Full many a gem of purest ray serene
> The dark, unfathomed caves of ocean bear;
> Full many a flower is born to blush unseen,
> And waste its sweetness on the desert air."

Do these things not really exist because they are hopelessly beyond the reach of our knowledge? And then, after the universe is dead (according to the prediction of some scientists), and all life has ceased forever, will not the shock of atoms continue though there will be no mind to know it? To this I reply that, though in no possible state of knowledge can any number be great enough to express the relation between the amount of what rests unknown to the amount of the known, yet it is unphilosophical to suppose that, with regard to any given question (which has any clear meaning), investigation would not bring forth a solution of it, if it were carried far enough. Who would have said, a few years ago, that we could ever know of what substances stars are made whose light may have been longer in reaching us than the human race has existed? Who can be sure of what we shall not know in a few hundred years? Who can guess what would be the result of continuing the pursuit of science for ten thousand years, with the activity of the last hundred? And if it were to go on for a million, or a billion, or any number of years you please, how is it possible to say that there is any question which might not ultimately be solved?

But it may be objected, "Why make so much of these

remote considerations, especially when it is your principle that only practical distinctions have a meaning?" Well, I must confess that it makes very little difference whether we say that a stone on the bottom of the ocean, in complete darkness, is brilliant or not—that is to say, that it *probably* makes no difference, remembering always that that stone *may* be fished up to-morrow. But that there are gems at the bottom of the sea, flowers in the untraveled desert, etc., are propositions which, like that about a diamond being hard when it is not pressed, concern much more the arrangement of our language than they do the meaning of our ideas.

It seems to me, however, that we have, by the application of our rule, reached so clear an apprehension of what we mean by reality, and of the fact which the idea rests on, that we should not, perhaps, be making a pretension so presumptuous as it would be singular, if we were to offer a metaphysical theory of existence for universal acceptance among those who employ the scientific method of fixing belief. However, as metaphysics is a subject much more curious than useful, the knowledge of which, like that of a sunken reef, serves chiefly to enable us to keep clear of it, I will not trouble the reader with any more Ontology at this moment. I have already been led much further into that path than I should have desired; and I have given the reader such a dose of mathematics, psychology, and all that is most abstruse, that I fear he may already have left me, and that what I am now writing is for the compositor and proofreader exclusively. I trusted to the importance of the subject. There is no royal road to logic, and really valuable ideas can only be had at the price of close attention. But I know that in the matter of ideas the public prefer the cheap and nasty; and in my next paper I am going to return to the easily intelligible, and not wander from it again. The reader who has been at the pains of wading through this paper, shall be rewarded in the next one by seeing how beautifully what has been developed in this tedious way can be applied to the ascertainment of the rules of scientific reasoning.

We have, hitherto, not crossed the threshold of scientific

logic. It is certainly important to know how to make our ideas clear, but they may be ever so clear without being true. How to make them so, we have next to study. How to give birth to those vital and procreative ideas which multiply into a thousand forms and diffuse themselves everywhere, advancing civilization and making the dignity of man, is an art not yet reduced to rules, but of the secret of which the history of science affords some hints.

"The Higher Learning As An Expression of the Pecuniary Culture"

Thorstein B. Veblen

The son of Norwegian parents, Thorstein B. Veblen was born in Wisconsin in 1857. He grew up in farming communities in Wisconsin and Minnesota. He attended Carlton College and The Johns Hopkins University. Later he obtained his Ph.D. from Yale University. For a time he was at Cornell University, then was professor of political economy at the University of Chicago (1896-1906), at Stanford University (1906-1910), and at The University of Missouri (1911-1918). He taught at the New School for Social Research. His death came in 1929. Among his books are *The Theory of the Leisure Class; The Theory of Business Enterprise; The Higher Learning in America;* and *The Vested Interests.* The selection below is Chapter 14 of *The Theory of the Leisure Class,* published in 1899 by the Macmillan Company.

T O the end that suitable habits of thought on certain heads may be conserved in the incoming generation, a scholastic discipline is sanctioned by the common sense of the community and incorporated into the accredited scheme of life. The habits of thought which are so formed under the guidance of teachers and scholastic traditions have an economic value —a value as affecting the serviceability of the individual— no less real than the similar economic value of the habits of thought formed without such guidance under the discipline of everyday life. Whatever characteristics of the accredited scholastic scheme and discipline are traceable to the pre-

175

dilections of the leisure class or to the guidance of the canons of pecuniary merit are to be set down to the account of that institution, and whatever economic value these features of the educational scheme possess are the expression in detail of the value of that institution. It will be in place, therefore, to point out any peculiar features of the educational system which are traceable to the leisure-class scheme of life, whether as regards the aim and method of the discipline, or as regards the compass and character of the body of knowledge inculcated. It is in learning proper, and more particularly in the higher learning, that the influence of leisure-class ideals is most patent; and since the purpose here is not to make an exhaustive collation of data showing the effect of the pecuniary culture upon education, but rather to illustrate the method and trend of leisure-class influence in education, a survey of certain salient features of the higher learning, such as may serve this purpose, is all that will be attempted.

In point of derivation and early development, learning is somewhat closely related to the devotional function of the community, particularly to the body of observances in which the service rendered the supernatural leisure class expresses itself. The service by which it is sought to conciliate supernatural agencies in the primitive cults is not an industrially profitable employment of the community's time and effort. It is, therefore, in great part, to be classed as a vicarious leisure performed for the supernatural powers with whom negotiations are carried on and whose good-will the service and the professions of subservience are conceived to procure. In great part, the early learning consisted in an acquisition of knowledge and facility in the service of a supernatural agent. It was therefore closely analogous in character to the training required for the domestic service of a temporal master. To a great extent, the knowledge acquired under the priestly teachers of the primitive community was a knowledge of ritual and ceremonial; that is to say, a knowledge of the most proper, most effective, or most acceptable manner of approaching and of serving the preternatural agents. What was learned was how to make oneself indispensable to these pow-

ers, and so to put oneself in a position to ask, or even to require, their intercession in the course of events or their
abstention from interference in any given enterprise. Propi-
tiation was the end, and this end was sought, in great part,
by acquiring facility in subservience. It appears to have been
only gradually that other elements than those of efficient service of the master found their way into the stock of priestly
or shamanistic instruction.

The priestly servitor of the inscrutable powers that move
in the external world came to stand in the position of a
mediator between these powers and the common run of un-
instructed humanity; for he was possessed of a knowledge of
the supernatural etiquette which would admit him into the
presence. And as commonly happens with mediators between
the vulgar and their masters, whether the masters be natural
or preternatural, he found it expedient to have the means at
hand tangibly to impress upon the vulgar the fact that these
inscrutable powers would do what he might ask of them.
Hence, presently, a knowledge of certain natural processes
which could be turned to account for spectacular effect, together with some sleight of hand, came to be an integral part
of priestly lore. Knowledge of this kind passes for knowledge
of the "unknowable," and it owes its serviceability for the
sacerdotal purpose to its recondite character. It appears to
have been from this source that learning, as an institution,
arose, and its differentiation from this its parent stock of
magic ritual and shamanistic fraud has been slow and tedious, and is scarcely yet complete even in the most advanced
of the higher seminaries of learning.

The recondite element in learning is still, as it has been in
all ages, a very attractive and effective element for the purpose of impressing, or even imposing upon, the unlearned;
and the standing of the savant in the mind of the altogether
unlettered is in great measure rated in terms of intimacy with
the occult forces. So, for instance, as a typical case, even so
late as the middle of this century, the Norwegian peasants
have instinctively formulated their sense of the superior
erudition of such doctors of divinity as Luther, Melanch-

thon, Peder Dass, and even so late a scholar in divinity as Grundtvig, in terms of the Black Art. These, together with a very comprehensive list of minor celebrities, both living and dead, have been reputed masters in all magical arts; and a high position in the ecclesiastical personnel has carried with it, in the apprehension of these good people, an implication of profound familiarity with magical practice and the occult sciences. There is a parallel fact nearer home, similarly going to show the close relationship, in popular apprehension, between erudition and the unknowable; and it will at the same time serve to illustrate, in somewhat coarse outline, the bent which leisure-class life gives to the cognitive interest. While the belief is by no means confined to the leisure class, that class to-day comprises a disproportionately large number of believers in occult sciences of all kinds and shades. By those whose habits of thought are not shaped by contact with modern industry, the knowledge of the unknowable is still felt to be the ultimate if not the only true knowledge.

Learning, then, set out with being in some sense a by-product of the priestly vicarious leisure class; and, at least until a recent date, the higher learning has since remained in some sense a by-product or by-occupation of the priestly classes. As the body of systematised knowledge increased, there presently arose a distinction, traceable very far back in the history of education, between esoteric and exoteric knowledge, the former—so far as there is a substantial difference between the two—comprising such knowledge as is primarily of no economic or industrial effect, and the latter comprising chiefly knowledge of industrial processes and of natural phenomena which were habitually turned to account for the material purposes of life. This line of demarcation has in time become, at least in popular apprehension, the normal line between the higher learning and the lower.

It is significant, not only as an evidence of their close affiliation with the priestly craft, but also as indicating that their activity to a good extent falls under that category of conspicuous leisure known as manners and breeding, that the learned class in all primitive communities are greater sticklers for form, precedent, gradations of rank, ritual, ceremonial vestments, and learned paraphernalia generally. This is of course to be expected, and it goes to say that the higher learning, in its incipient phase, is a leisure-class occupation —more specifically an occupation of the vicarious leisure class employed in the service of the supernatural leisure class. But this predilection for the paraphernalia of learning goes also to indicate a further point of contact or of continuity between the priestly office and the office of the savant. In point of derivation, learning, as well as the priestly office, is largely an outgrowth of sympathetic magic; and this magical apparatus of form and ritual therefore finds its place with the learned class of the primitive community as a matter of course. The ritual and paraphernalia have an occult efficacy for the magical purpose; so that their presence as an integral factor in the earlier phases of the development of magic and science is a matter of expediency, quite as much as of affectionate regard for symbolism simply.

This sense of the efficacy of symbolic ritual, and of sympathetic effect to be wrought through dexterous rehearsal of the traditional accessories of the act or end to be compassed, is of course present more obviously and in larger measure in magical practice than in the discipline of the sciences, even of the occult sciences. But there are, I apprehend, few persons with a cultivated sense of scholastic merit to whom the ritualistic accessories of science are altogether an idle matter. The very great tenacity with which these ritualistic paraphernalia persist through the later course of the development is evident to any one who will reflect on what has been the history of learning in our civilisation. Even to-day there are such things in the usage of the learned community as the cap and gown, matriculation, initiation, and graduation ceremonies, and the conferring of scholastic degrees, dignities, and prerogatives in a way which suggests some sort of a scholarly apostolic succession. The usage of the priestly orders is no doubt the proximate source of all these features of learned ritual, vestments, sacramental initiation, the transmission of peculiar dignities and virtues by the imposition of hands, and the like; but their derivation is traceable back of this point, to the source from which the specialised priestly class proper received them in the course of differentiation by which the priest came to be distinguished from the sorcerer on the one hand and from the menial servant of a temporal master on the other hand. So far as regards both their derivation and their psychological content, these usages and the conceptions on which they rest belong to a stage in cultural development no later than that of the angekok and the rain-maker. Their place in the later phases of devout observance, as well as in the higher educational system, is that of a survival from a very early animistic phase of the development of human nature.

These ritualistic features of the educational system of the present and of the recent past, it is quite safe to say, have their place primarily in the higher, liberal, and classic institutions and grades of learning, rather than in the lower, technological, or practical grades and branches of the system. So far as they possess them, the lower and less reputable branches of the educational scheme have evidently borrowed these things from the higher grades; and their continued persistence among the practical schools, without the sanction of the continued example of the higher and classic grades, would be highly improbable, to say the least. With the lower and practical schools and scholars, the adoption and cultivation of these usages is a case of mimicry—due to a desire to conform as far as may be to the standards of scholastic reputability maintained by the upper grades and classes, who have come by these accessory features legitimately, by the right of lineal devolution.

The analysis may even be safely carried a step farther. Ritualistic survivals and reversions come out in fullest vigour and with the freest air of spontaneity among those seminaries of learning which have to do primarily with the education of the priestly and leisure classes. Accordingly it should appear, and it does pretty plainly appear, on a survey of recent developments in college and university life, that wherever schools founded for the instruction of the lower classes in the immediately useful branches of knowledge grow into institutions of the higher learning, the growth of ritualistic ceremonial and paraphernalia and of elaborate scholastic "functions" goes hand in hand with the transition of the schools in question from the field of homely practicality into the higher, classical sphere. The initial purpose of these schools, and the work with which they have chiefly had to do at the earlier of these two stages of their evolution, has been that of fitting the young of the industrious classes for work. On the higher, classical plane of learning to which they commonly tend, their dominant aim becomes the preparation of the youth of the priestly and the leisure classes—or of an incipient leisure class—for the consumption of goods, material and immaterial, according to a conventionally accepted, reputable scope and method. This happy issue has commonly been the fate of schools founded by "friends of the people" for the aid of struggling young men, and where this transition is made in good form there is commonly, if not invariably, a coincident change to a more ritualistic life in the schools.

In the school life of to-day, learned ritual is in a general way best at home in schools whose chief end is the cultivation of the "humanities." This correlation is shown, perhaps more neatly than anywhere else, in the life-history of the American colleges and universities of recent growth. There may be many exceptions from the rule, especially among those schools which have been founded by the typically reputable and ritualistic churches, and which, therefore, started on the conservative and classical plane or reached the classical position by a short-cut; but the general rule as regards the colleges founded in the newer American communities during the present century has been that so long as the community has remained poor, and so long as the constituency from which the colleges have drawn their pupils has been dominated by habits of industry and thrift, so long the reminiscences of the medicine-man have found but a scant and precarious acceptance in the scheme of college life. But so soon as wealth begins appreciably to accumulate in the community, and so soon as a given school begins to lean on a leisure-class constituency, there comes also a perceptibly increased insistence on scholastic ritual and on conformity to the ancient forms as regards vestments and social and scholastic solemnities. So, for instance, there has been an approximate coincidence between the growth of wealth among the constituency which supports any given college of the Middle West and the date of acceptance—first into tolerance and then into imperative vogue—of evening dress for men and of the décolleté for women, as the scholarly vestments proper to occasions of learned solemnity or to the season of social amenity within the college circle. Apart from the mechanical difficulty of so large a task, it would scarcely be a difficult matter to trace this correlation. The like is true of the vogue of the cap and gown.

Cap and gown have been adopted as learned insignia by many colleges of this section within the last few years; and it is safe to say that this could scarcely have occurred at a much earlier date, or until there had grown up a leisure-class sentiment of sufficient volume in the community to support a strong movement of reversion towards an archaic view as to the legitimate end of education. This particular item of learned ritual, it may be noted, would not only commend itself to the leisure-class sense of the fitness of things, as appealing to the archaic propensity for spectacular effect and the predilection for antique symbolism; but it at the same time fits into the leisure-class scheme of life as involving a notable element of conspicuous waste. The precise date at which the reversion to cap and gown took place, as well as the fact that it affected so large a number of schools at about the same time, seems to have been due in some measure to a wave of atavistic sense of conformity and reputability that passed over the community at that period. . . .

"Classic" always carries this connotation of wasteful and archaic, whether it is used to denote the dead languages or the obsolete or obsolescent forms of thought and diction in the living language, or to denote other items of scholarly activity or apparatus to which it is applied with less aptness. So the archaic idiom of the English language is spoken of as "classic" English. Its use is imperative in all speaking and writing upon serious topics, and a facile use of it lends dignity to even the most commonplace and trivial string of talk. The newest form of English diction is of course never written; the sense of that leisure-class propriety which requires archaism in speech is present even in the most illiterate or sensational writers in sufficient force to prevent such a lapse. On the other hand, the highest and most conventionalised style of archaic diction is—quite characteristically—properly employed only in communications between an anthropomorphic divinity and his subjects. Midway between these extremes lies the everyday speech of leisure-class conversation and literature.

Elegant diction, whether in writing or speaking, is an effective means of reputability. It is of moment to know with some precision what is the degree of archaism conventionally required in speaking on any given topic. Usage differs appreciably from the pulpit to the market-place; the latter, as might be expected, admits the use of relatively new and effective words and turns of expression, even by fastidious persons. A discriminate avoidance of neologisms is honorific, not only because it argues that time has been wasted in acquiring the obsolescent habit of speech, but also as showing that the speaker has from infancy habitually associated with persons who have been familiar with the obsolescent idiom. It thereby goes to show his leisure-class antecedents. Great purity of speech is presumptive evidence of several successive lives spent in other than vulgarly useful occupations; although its evidence is by no means entirely conclusive to this point.

As felicitous an instance of futile classicism as can well be found, outside of the Far East, is the conventional spelling of the English language. A breach of the proprieties in spelling is extremely annoying and will discredit any writer in the eyes of all persons who are possessed of a developed sense of the true and beautiful. English orthography satisfies all the requirements of the canons of reputability under the law of conspicuous waste. It is archaic, cumbrous, and ineffective;

its acquisition consumes much time and effort; failure to acquire it is easy of detection. Therefore it is the first and readiest test of reputability in learning, and conformity to its ritual is indispensable to a blameless scholastic life.

On this head of purity of speech, as at other points where a conventional usage rests on the canons of archaisms and waste, the spokesmen for the usage instinctively take an apologetic attitude. It is contended, in substance, that a punctilious use of ancient and accredited locutions will serve to convey thought more adequately and more precisely than would the straight forward use of the latest form of spoken English; whereas it is notorious that the ideas of to-day are effectively expressed in the slang of to-day. Classic speech has the honorific virtue of dignity; it commands attention and respect as being the accredited method of communication under the leisure-class scheme of life, because it carries a pointed suggestion of the industrial exemption of the speaker. The advantage of the accredited locutions lies in their reputability; they are reputable because they are cumbrous and out of date, and therefore argue waste of time and exemption from the use and the need of direct and forcible speech.

"Language the Educator of the Human Race"

Michel Bréal

Michel Bréal was born near Landau, France, in 1832. Educated in the French lycée, he attended graduate school in Germany. At the University of Berlin he studied linguistics under the direction of Professor de Bopp and Professor Weber. He returned to France and became professor of comparative grammar at the Collège de France in 1864. Later he was appointed Inspector General of Public Instruction for the French school system. One of his first scholarly works was a translation of Bopp's *Comparative Grammar of European Languages*. His original work in the field of linguistics includes *La Reforme de l'Ortographe Française*, 1890; and *Essai de Semantique*, 1897. He died in Paris in 1915. Our selection is Chapter 26 of *Semantics: Studies in the Science of Meaning*, published in 1900 by William Heinemann Company.

THERE is no reason to fear that the importance of Language in the education of the human race will ever be depreciated. We can in this matter trust to the natural instinct of mothers; their first impulse is to talk to the child, their first joy to hear it speak. Then come masters of all degrees and of all kinds, whose various arts each presuppose Language, even if not absolutely one with it. In every country, in antiquity as in our own days, in China and in India as in Athens and in Rome, Language supplies both the instrument and the matter of the first lessons.

This universal agreement has its reasons; it is not difficult to understand the great influence which is exercised over the mind by Language, if we reflect that we none of us receive it whole and intact, but are each obliged to build it afresh for ourselves. Here is an apprenticeship which, though escaping notice and ignored even by those who take part in it, forms nevertheless a kind of training-school of humanity. If it be true that the best instruction is that which gives us the most to do by ourselves, what more profitable study can be imagined for a child?

The greatest attention is needed for the mere recognition of the *word*, since it is a question of disengaging it from what precedes and from what follows, of distinguishing the permanent element from the variable elements, and of understanding that the permanent element is, to some degree, confided to us, in order that we should in our turn wield it, and submit it to the same variations. On what occasions, under what circumstances, after what models? For the most part we are told nothing: on us lies the burden of discovery. The most simple phrase invites us to analyse its thought and to note the special contributions of each word. The adjective, the verb, are the first abstractions understood by the child. The pronouns *me* and *you*, *my* and *your*, which, in changing mouths, transfer themselves from one to the other, contain its first lesson in psychology.

Teaching mounts a step higher in proportion as mankind advances in this apprenticeship.

Let us imagine the effort which must have been required in their own days to speak the ancient languages with even moderate accuracy. It was necessary in the case of the various declensions to establish different series, in which certain inflections corresponded to without resembling each other, and in which other inflections were similar, but had to be kept apart. An analogous classification was necessary for the persons, tenses, and moods.[1] Herein lies a whole chapter of inner life which began afresh with every individual. The people was therefore possessed of an unwritten grammar, into which no doubt various mistakes and errors crept, but which, since these languages have for centuries been trans-

---

[1] H. Paul, *Principien der Sprachgeschichte*, 2nd edit., p. 24. See also the studies of Steinthal and Lazarus in their Journal.

mitted from generation to generation, must nevertheless have
been endowed with a certain fixity.

When we consider the trouble which these ancient languages cost us even now, we are somewhat surprised. But we
must remember that the teaching of a mother-tongue has the
advantage of being continued at all times and in all places,
that it is spurred by the stimulus of necessity, that it has to
deal with minds in the freshness of youth, and finally, that it
possesses the unique characteristic of linking words to things,
and not the words of one language to the words of another
language. The same circumstances occur in the case of all
mother-tongues; everywhere the mind of the child triumphs
over them. I do not mean indeed that the course of time may
not produce such difficulties as to disconcert the new generations. But then, as we have seen, the popular mind extricates
itself from these in the most simple manner; it evades the
difficulty by means of analogy, of unification, and of suppres-
sion. The people being in this matter both pupil and master,
whatever it changes, unifies, or abrogates, becomes the rule
of the future.

Our modern languages, though less encumbered with a
formal apparatus, are yet by no means free. The complication
has, moreover, been diverted on to another point. The question is to know how to employ words which are almost
wholly devoid of meaning, words so abstract and "servile,"
that one may all one's life ignore their existence, while duly
placing them in their proper position. Here we may notice an
action of the mind which has passed to a condition of instinct,
similar to that which guides the fingers of the lace-worker
when she moves her distaff without looking at it.

Were all the usages of our prepositions to be enumerated
and explained, they would form a whole volume. Littré's
dictionary gives no less than twelve columns[2] to the word
à alone. Yet the people finds its way with no difficulty in this

---

[2] "By an evil chance, the alphabetical order forced me at the very outset of my labours to treat of the preposition à, that most tiresome of all
words, and one with which I did not succeed to my satisfaction."—Littré,
Comment j'ai fait mon Dictionnaire.

seeming chaos. Not, as we have seen, owing to a more or less clear notion of the import of the word: no more than the philologists, would it be able to give a definition that fitted every usage. It allows itself to be directed by a certain number of expressions which the memory retains and uses as models. In this way the turns of phrase are preserved and propagated. Invention always builds on a foundation which exists already.

Every one has at times admired the unpremeditated turns of phrase in popular language. Besides the pleasure which is felt at any discovery, these encounters have the added advantage of showing us the roads by which the mind has travelled. It is especially on occasions when some passion warms the soul and intensifies its power, that we can best observe these improvisations of the moment.

The human intellect obtains from Language, for its daily operations, the same services that it obtains from number for its calculations. One consequence of the infirmity of our understanding, an infirmity familiar to all philosophers, is that it is easier for us to work upon the signs of the ideas than upon the ideas themselves.[3] Before the invention of writing men counted by means of pebbles. The idea certainly had to come first, but this idea is vacillating, fugitive, difficult to transmit; once incorporated in a sign, we are more sure of possessing it, of handling it at will, and of communicating it to others. Such is the service rendered by Language; it makes thought objective.

Having been from the very first associated with the conception, it was not long before the words took the place of the conception; we compare, we connect, we oppose the signs, not the ideas. It is true that behind these signs there survives a partial memory, a fragmentary recollection of the

---

[3] In this lies the answer to the question why the intelligence of animals remains stationary. They have not arrived at the point of voluntarily incorporating their thought in a sign: their whole ulterior development has remained thenceforward arrested in its very first steps. The idiot child does not speak, but it is not the organs of speech which are lacking to it. The inward labour of observation and of classification which allows the idea to be affixed to the sign is beyond its strength.

idea which it represents, and we inwardly believe that we could, if we would, recall the idea in its pristine clearness.[4] But it is no less true that in the case of rather complicated operations, of operations to be effected rapidly, the signs are enough for us. Not words alone, but also those unions of words which we have called Articulated Groups, are necessary. All this goes to form Language. It at the same time renders the ideas manageable, and furnishes the framework of reasoning.

Thinkers have turned this into an occasion for reproach. "Every word represents indeed a portion of actuality, but a portion roughly hewn, as though humanity had carved according to its own convenience and its own wants, instead of following the articulations of the reality." Let us suppose for a moment that this reproach is well-founded. Even then how slight it is in comparison with the immense service rendered to the mass of mankind! However imperfect, Language yet outstrips most of us: we need time to overtake it. How few would be capable of setting to work on their own account to produce these carvings! We have seen, moreover, that the outlines are not so fixed and unyielding but that they can be bent or enlarged for insertion in new classifications. On the contrary, a philosophical language such as has often been planned, a language resulting from a system, in which each word should remain for ever delimited by its definition, and in which the affinity of words should be traced from the real or imagined connection of ideas,—such a language may indeed be suitable for a few special sciences, like chemistry, but if applied to human thought, with its fluctuations and its progressions, could not fail to become, in the course of time, a hindrance and a restraint. In proportion as the experience of the human race increases, Language, thanks to its elasticity, acquires new meaning.

Were it necessary to say wherein lies the superiority of the Indo-European languages, I should turn neither to the grammatical mechanism, nor to the compounds nor even to the

[4] Taine, *De l'Intelligence,* bk. i, chap. iii, 2 Bergson.

syntax: I believe it to lie in another direction. It consists of the facility of these languages from the most ancient periods of which we have any knowledge, in creating abstract nouns. If we examine the suffixes which serve for this usage, we shall be astonished at their number and variety. They are by no means peculiar to such and such a language, but are to be found alike in Latin, Greek, Sanscrit, Zend, and in every branch of the family. They are therefore of early date; and indeed of a date so early, that, to borrow the denominations of another science which marks the epochs by the monuments which are left of it, we might speak of a *period of suffixes*, a period which necessarily presupposes a certain power of abstraction and reflection. It is the presence of these nouns in great number, added to the possibility of making others after the same pattern, which has rendered the Indo-European languages so well fitted to all the operations of the mind.[5] Even at the present day we still make use of the same means of expression, to which hardly anything has been added by posterior ages. If we cared to examine the methods used by modern literature to renew the resources and the character of its style, we should be convinced that it still has recourse to those same abstractions, the first specimens of which were contemporaneous with the Vedas and with Homer.

It is not on this account necessary to imagine transcendent intelligences. There are divers degrees of abstraction to be distinguished. The one in question is derived more from mythology than from metaphysics. The same order of thought is there when the people talks of a reigning fashion or disease, or of electricity running along a wire. The abstraction created by the popular mind assumes for it a sort of existence. The world is full of these entities. The form of phrase, in which all subjects are represented as active, is a still sur-

---

[5] It is easy to imagine how useful these suffixes have been for the language of philosophy. Greek, in combining the two pronouns ωο οοs and ωοι οs with an abstract suffix makes ωο οσφηs "quantity," ωοισφηs, "quality." In the same way, in Latin, *qualitas, quantitas*. In Sanscrit, the pronoun *tat*, "this," gives, in combination with the abstract suffix *tvam*, the substantive *tattvam*, "reality."

viving witness of this state of mind. Language and mythology issued from one and the same conception. This, as we have already said, is the explanation of the fact that the majority of abstract nouns are feminine; they are of the same sex as the innumerable divinities which peopled sky, earth, and water. Even at the present day—so great is the continuity of things—those who discuss Matter, Force, Substance, perpetuate more or less this ancient condition of mind.

Accustomed as we are to Language, we do not easily realise the accumulation of intellectual work which it represents. But, to be convinced of this, we have only to take a page of any book, and to suppress all the words which, not corresponding to any objective reality, must be the result of an operation of the mind. Of a page so treated hardly anything will remain. The peasant who speaks of times and of seasons, the merchant who advertises his assortment of wares, the child who brings his notes of conduct or progress, all move in a world of abstractions. The words *number, form, distance, situation,* are so many concepts of the mind. Language is a translation of reality, a transposition in which objects appear already generalised and classified by the work of thought.

Are there in Europe any languages which are more favourable than others to intellectual progress? With the exception of slight differences we can answer in the negative. They are all (or nearly all) sprung from the same origin, built on the same plan, drawing from the same sources. They have been more or less nourished on the same models, perfected by the same education. They are therefore capable of expressing the same things, although within the limits of this close relationship we can already note certain special aptitudes. But if we wished to realise the help which Language gives to the mind, as well as the particular turn which it imposes, we should have to compare some language of Central Africa or some indigenous dialect of America. In Brazilian, the one word *tuba* signifies: (1) he has a father; (2) his father; (3) he is a father. Actually, *tuba* means "he the father." It is as the speech of a child. Even languages provided with a rich literature do not always form a sufficient support for the mind. In Chinese, this phrase: *sîn hī thīen* may be translated: (1) the saint aspires to heaven; (2) he is a saint to aspire to heaven; (3) he is a saint, who aspires to heaven. Chinese merely says: *Saint aspire heaven.*[6] The service rendered us by our languages is to impose upon us a form that compels precision.

Language has been called an *organism,* a hollow deceptive word too freely lavished at the present day, and used every time that we want to dispense with the trouble of seeking for true causes. Since certain illustrious philologists have declared that man counted for nothing in the evolution of Language, that he was incapable of modifying anything, or of adding anything, and that one might as well try to change the laws of the circulation of the blood; since others have compared this evolution to the trajectory of a shell or to the orbit of a planet; since this is to-day currently accepted as a truth and passed on from book to book: it has seemed to me useful to have it out with these assertions, and once for all to make an end of this phantasmagoria.

Our forefathers of the school of Condillac, those ideologists who for fifty years served as target to a certain school of criticisms, were less far from the truth when they said, in simple and honest fashion, that words are signs. Where they went wrong was when they referred everything to a reasoning reason, and when they took Latin for the type of all Language. Words are signs: they have no more existence than the signals of the semaphore, or than the dots and dashes of Morse telegraphy. To say that Language is an organism is but to darken counsel and to sow a seed of error in the minds of men. It might be said, with an equal degree of truth, that writing is also an organism, since we see it evolving throughout the ages, without any one in particular having a very perceptible influence on its development. It might be said that song, religion, law, all the component parts of human life, are each an organism.

---

[6] Misteli, in Techmer's *Zeitschrift,* vol. ii.

If we take nature in its widest sense, it evidently comprises man and the production of man. The history of morals, of customs, of habitation, of dress, of the arts, as well as social and political history, will, together with Language, form part of natural history. But if we admit a difference between the historical sciences and the natural sciences, if we consider man as furnishing the material for a separate chapter in our study of the universe, Language, which is the work of man, cannot remain on the other side, and the Science of Language, by a necessary consequence, will form part of the historical sciences. If, on the other hand, on account of phonetics, which study the sounds of language produced by the larynx and the mouth, it were necessary to transfer the Science of Language back to the natural sciences, all the rest, man and all his works, must inevitably accompany it, since human productions, of whatever kind, come after all from the organs of mankind and are directed to those organs.

With still more reason will Semantics belong to the class of historical investigations. There is not a single change of meaning, a single modification of grammar, a single peculiarity of syntax which should not be counted as a small historical event. Will it be said that there is no free will in this domain, because I am not free to change the meaning of words, nor to construct a phrase according to a grammar of my own? We have shown that this limitation of freedom arises from the desire for comprehension, that is to say, it is of the same kind as the other laws which govern our social life. To speak here of natural law is to create confusion.

I have come to the end of my labours. Warned by example, I have avoided comparisons drawn from botany, from physiology, from geology, with the same zeal which others have shown in seeking them out. The exposition of my argument is in the consequence more abstract but, I think I am justified in saying, more true.

I have no wish to be unjust towards the theory which, with a certain show of brilliancy, has classed the Science of Language among the sciences of nature. At a time when these sciences rightly enjoyed the favour of the public, it was a clever and politic act. It also imposed on philologists the duty of prosecuting their observations with a redoubled accuracy. Finally this idea contained just the amount of paradox necessary to excite curiosity. If the phrase had been: *regular development, constant progress,* nobody would have cared. But at the words: *blind laws, astronomical precision,* general attention was aroused.

I think, however, that I am right in saying that the history of Language, when referred to intellectual laws, is not only more true, but also more interesting: it cannot be a matter of indifference to us to note, above the seeming chance which governs the destiny of the words and forms of Language, the appearance of laws corresponding in each case to an advance of the mind. For the philosopher, for the historian, for every man who watches the progress of humanity, there is a certain pleasure in verifying this ascent of the intelligence which is perceptible in the slow renewal of languages.

"Fashion In Language"

James B. Greenough

and George L. Kittredge

One of America's great scholars, George L. Kittredge, was born in Boston on February 28, 1860. He graduated from Harvard University in 1882. In 1888 he became an instructor at Harvard and during the next 48 years rose successively in academic rank to professorial status. Although he never took an advanced degree, Kittredge became one of the outstanding scholars of his time. He collaborated with James B. Greenough in publishing *Words and Their Ways in English Speech.* His major works include *Essays on Chaucer,* 1914; *Witchcraft in Old and New England,* 1929; he also edited *The Complete Works of William Shakespeare,* 1936. Kittredge died in Barnstable, Massachusetts, on July 23, 1941. James B. Greenough was born in Portland, Maine, in 1833. After graduating from Harvard in 1856, he practiced law in Michigan. Later he returned to Harvard as Professor of Latin and in 1872 instituted the study of Sanskrit and comparative literature there. Greatly interested in the education of women, Greenough was active in the founding of Radcliffe College. He died in Cambridge in 1901. Our selection is Chapter nine from *Words and Their Ways in English Speech* and is used by permission of The Macmillan Company.

A POWERFUL influence in bringing in new words or reviving old ones, as well as in changing the use and meaning of established expressions, is what may be called, in a broad way, 'fashion,'—a term under which we include not

merely the fads and whimsicalities of the moment, but
certain larger and more impressive movements and tendencies. The sway of fashion is easily detected both in literature
and in our common talk. In the case of literature, we dignify
such habits of expression by calling them stylistic tendencies.
When they attract our attention in colloquial speech, we
stigmatize them as slang or affectation. In the uncontrolled
utterances of the street boy, these tendencies result in the
rapid propagation of every new phrase that falls upon his
ear, till there grows up a language so grotesquely vulgar
as to acquire a kind of humorous right to existence. In the
domain of letters, they result in those large differences of
style which characterize particular schools of writing or
even distinct 'epochs' or 'ages' in literary history. Yet the
underlying principles are the same both in literature and in
the individual,—fondness for novelty, the desire to be original, and finally, the wish of every man to be as wise as his
neighbor, which results in a general imitation of whatever
is striking or distinctive.

The effect of fashion in introducing new words into our
vocabulary, in bringing certain words already existent into
peculiar prominence for the time being, and in banishing
some old words altogether, may be observed by contrasting
the language of different individuals who, though frequent-
ing much each other's society, are nevertheless brought under the control of different modes of expression. Thus, a law
student, a medical student, and a young 'sport,' will be sure
to have widely different vocabularies, even if they are personal friends. This is true not only when they are 'talking
shop,' but when they are discussing subjects quite outside
of their professional interests. The young lawyer will be sure
to interlard his conversation with fragments of legal lore
and with figures of speech derived from his text-books. The
physician will find it difficult to avoid allusions to the clinic
or the dissecting-room. The sporting man will speak a
dialect compounded of the race-track, the prize-ring, and
the foot-ball field. And all this may be quite without affectation. The words that we hear oftenest and that are as-

sociated with our dearest interests must come to our lips most readily. That a physician should speak of 'dissecting' a subject, a chemist of 'analyzing' it, a preacher of 'expounding' it, is as natural as that an ordinary man should speak of 'explaining' it or 'making it clear.' A calamity may be called 'a cropper' by the horsey man, 'a knock-out' by the amateur of pugilism, 'a lost case' by a lawyer. Such differences will be perceptible both in the colloquial dialect and in more dignified speech.

Another fashion is the knack of literary allusion. It is akin to the habit of quotation,—itself a fashion in language that comes and goes; but it shows itself in a less formal and tangible way. The use of scraps of French, much commoner fifty years ago than at present, and the trick of using big words on slight occasion, whether for humorous effect or for the sake of 'talking like a book,' are other examples of individual peculiarities which may at any moment become general.

But the sway of fashion may be observed not merely in the several vocabularies of speakers whose professions are different, but also in the changes that come over one's own vocabulary as it is subjected to successive influences in the course of a lifetime. School or the university produces a marked effect on the speech of a young man. Another immediate change comes about when he begins the study of his profession, or enters upon the business of his life. Even after one's vocabulary seems definitely established, current events of general interest will always modify it strongly for the time being. During the heat of a political campaign everybody talks political jargon, even when politics are not under discussion. The Spanish War filled American ears with hitherto unheard-of words of Spanish origin, and the war in South Africa has familiarized all of us with an odd corner of the Dutch vocabulary, hitherto known only to South African colonists. For a time it was easy to call any difficult barrier a *trocha,* and the policy of *reconcentration* often appeared in strange company. So every little hill was a *kopje,* a lodging-place of any kind was a *laager,* all sorts of things were *commandeered,* and the suggestion that this or that might 'stagger humanity' was on every lip. Similarly, intense religious excitement may charge the language of an individual or a community with biblical or theological terms or phrases. Within a century the progress of scientific discovery and invention, and the rise of the economic and social sciences, have profoundly affected our speech. 'Society' and 'social' have taken on new senses. The 'social problem' means much more than it ever did before. 'Unproductive consumer,' 'unearned increment,' 'the law of supply and demand,' 'medium of exchange,' 'standard of living,' 'wages fund,' 'pauper labor,' 'coöperative association,' are commonly heard, even from persons who have never read a chapter of political economy. 'Evolution,' 'the struggle for existence,' 'the survival of the fittest,' have become so vague in their common application that one hardly dares to employ them in serious discussion for fear of begging the question. *Force* is regularly used to explain everything, as if it were not in itself a word that assumes the very point which it attempts to prove. Indeed, it has become one of the vague terms which language requires to express indefinite and indefinable conceptions.

These are some of the fashions that every grown-up man can remember, as having from time to time increased his vocabulary, and either enriched or impoverished his thought.

If we broaden our scope, we shall find that what happens to the individual in a single lifetime, applies also to a whole people in the lifetime of their language. New interests assert themselves from age to age, and induce new forms of expression. The fashion changes and language must 'follow the style.' Let us consider some of the movements that have affected the English language from time to time.

We may begin with a simple, but sufficiently curious, illustration. The style of the Anglo-Saxon translator of Bede's Ecclesiastical History is marked by a peculiar trick of repetition. Again and again he uses two synonymous nouns or verbs or adjectives, where one would suffice to convey his whole meaning. This may be called, then, an English literary habit of the ninth century. It came, perhaps, from an unskilful imitation of the Latin, or it may be due to some uncertainty as to the exact scope of the English words, then first applied to the finer shades of thought. At all events, the habit survived in English prose until the end of the eighteenth century. And, though out of favor at the moment, it has left a number of idiomatic or colloquial phrases in the language: as, 'end and aim,' 'lord and master,' 'without let or hindrance,' 'act and deed,' 'pure and simple,' 'in deed and truth,' 'really and truly,' 'bright and shining,' 'honest and true,' 'proud and haughty,' 'weak and feeble,' 'race and run,' 'grunt and groan,' 'pull and tug,' 'holla and bawl,' 'cry and scream,' 'clean and neat,' 'toil and delve.'[1]

Such double phrases occur very frequently in the Book of Common Prayer, where we find, for instance, 'sins and wickedness,' 'dissemble nor cloak,' 'assemble and meet together,' 'requisite and necessary,' 'erred and strayed,' 'declare and pronounce,' 'pardoneth and absolveth,' 'bless and sanctify,' 'offer and present,' 'rule and govern,' 'knowledge and understanding,' 'religiously and devoutly,' 'food and sustenance,' 'search and examine your consciences,' 'prayers and supplications,' 'to try and examine themselves,' 'confirm and strengthen.'

In several of these instances, one word is native and the other foreign. Hence many have supposed that the repetition came from a wish to be intelligible both to the Saxon and the Norman element in the population, or, at all events, both to the uneducated and to the educated classes. But this is pure assumption, and it is contradicted by the habits of English speech. Remembering the composite character of our vocabulary, we are not surprised that in a pair of synonyms one should be of native stock and the other bor-

---

[1] It is not meant that these particular phrases come down from King Alfred's time, nor that they originated in tautology pure and simple, but merely that they owe their currency to a habit of the language which we may observe in full swing in the formal prose of the ninth century. On the whole matter see Emerson, Modern Language Notes, 1893, pp. 202 ff.; J. M. Hart, in An English Miscellany presented to Dr. Furnivall, pp. 150 ff.

rowed. Besides, the examples from the prayer-book show every kind of combination: sometimes both words are native (as was of course always the case in Anglo-Saxon), sometimes both are foreign, and sometimes the pair includes one word of each kind. Most of our older writers illustrate the same stylistic habit. Lord Bacon, for instance, writes 'donatives and largesses,' 'pageants or gaudery,' 'amplitude and greatness,' 'to forsake or destitute a plantation,' 'he runs and is swift of foot,' 'good and fair dealing,' 'putrefy and corrupt,' 'the spreading or publishing of them,' 'to stay and arrest nature,' 'look sharply and attentively,' 'honored and respected.' The *rationale* of such phrases is evident enough. A single noun or verb seldom expresses the full scope of an idea. The pair of words covers the whole meaning intended by the writer, since the synonyms that he chooses have somewhat different senses. To be sure, some repetition is involved, since the second word repeats a large part of the meaning of the first, though adding some meaning of its own. Yet the author prefers to express his thought say one-and-a-quarter times to the opposite method of expressing three-quarters of it and leaving the rest to be inferred. In Modern English we take the latter course, though not uniformly. The older fashion conduces to dignity and copiousness of style, but easily betrays one into tiresome verbiage.

In the Middle Ages, the English language was a good deal affected by the allegorical treatment of love. This followed various conventions, drawing its figures especially from warfare, chivalry, the law, and religion. Thus the lady's heart was a castle to which the knight laid siege. The metaphor was elaborately developed and even acted, as a kind of pantomimic tableau. Hence our phrases, 'to take one's heart by storm,' 'to surrender at discretion.' Or the lover was the lady's vassal, her 'man,' bound to unquestioning obedience, her 'servant,' her 'thrall' or slave. Love was a monarch whose courtiers were Pity, Disdain, Fair Welcoming, False Semblant, and the like; he sat in judgment and heard the complaints of suitors against their hard-hearted mistresses. Strangest of all, to our thinking, is the religious convention. The lady was the 'saint' to whom one prayed. The God or Goddess of Love was addressed in terms appropriate to the Deity. Faithful lovers were Cupid's 'saints.' Dido and Phyllis, who died for Love, were Love's 'martyrs.' As the Church recognized seven deadly sins and seven principal virtues, so there were sins and virtues in the worship of Love. Hence came many figurative expressions which to us sound blasphemous or, at least, in very bad taste. But the religion of the Middle Ages was not remote from life. It was a matter of course, which nobody hesitated to talk about, and consequently such figures conveyed no hint of irreverence. One of the first and best effects of intelligent linguistic study is to emancipate us from that form of provincialism which erects the present fashions in language into eternal canons of criticism.

The Elizabethan age was marked rather by the prevalence of every possible kind of literary mannerism than by the predominance of any. Euphuism was only one of several fashions in speech and writing. The language of the Euphuist was not, as has often been thought, full of strange and affected words. So far as mere vocabulary is concerned, it was usually pure and dignified. But it resorted to excessive antithesis; it balanced itself so nicely from clause to clause as to make monotony into a fine art; and it heightened false point by puerile tricks of alliteration and jingle. Besides all this, it was overloaded with far-fetched similes from what passed for natural history. These peculiarities are all illustrated in the following passage from Lyly's Euphues, a kind of moral romance, from which the style in question takes its name:[2]—

It fareth with me, Psellus, as with the ostrich, who pricketh none but herself, which causeth her to run when she would rest; or as with the pelican, who striketh blood out of her own body to do others good; or with the wood-culver, who plucketh off her feathers in winter to keep others from the cold; or as with the stork, who, when she is

---

[2] *Euphues* is the hero's name. It is Gr. ενΦυης, 'of an excellent nature,' from ευ, 'well,' and φνω, 'to be born.' Eν is familiar to us in *eu-phony* (φωνς, 'sound'), and *euphemism* (φηνι, 'to say'); φνω we have in *physics, physician, physiology,* and so on.

least able, carrieth the greatest burthen. So I practise all things that may hurt me, to do her good that never regardeth my pains, so far is she from rewarding them.

The coinage of strange words, the borrowing of new terms from the classic languages, and excessive Latinization, were also characteristics of the Elizabethans. Hence the contemporary satire on 'ink-horn terms.' A rough-and-ready caricature is Rowlands' 'Signieur Word-Monger, the Ape of Eloquence' (1600):—

> As on the way I itinerated,
> A rural person I obviated,
> Interrogating time's transitation
>
> And of the passage demonstration.
> My apprehension did ingenious scan
> That he was merely a simplician;
> So when I saw he was extravagant,
> Unto the obscure vulgar consonant,
> I bade him vanish most promiscuously,
> And not contaminate my company.

Translated into plain English, this farrago means merely: 'As I was walking in the road, I met a countryman, who asked me the time and the way. When I saw he was a vagabond, and belonged to the common people, I told him to begone and not disgrace me by his company.'

Another trick of Elizabethan writers was to archaize. Chaucer was much read and 'Chaucerisms' were abundant. The most eminent of all archaizers is Spenser, only a small part of whose poetry is written in the language of his time. The influence of France, in which a remarkable literary movement was then in progress, has been traced in some of the Elizabethan whimsicalities.[3] Spain and Italy were also potent forces. Euphuism itself is commonly referred to Spanish influence, and certainly shows much likeness to the celebrated Guevara.

Sometimes sham antiques have slipped in. Spenser, the most distinguished of all our archaizers, made many mis-

---

[3] See J. B. Fletcher, Aeropagus and Pleiade, in Journal of Germanic Philology, II, 429-53.

takes, and his imitators in the eighteenth and nineteenth centuries were not better instructed. Thus the strange compound noun *derring-do*, which he introduced, and which has had some currency in the sense of 'courage,' 'valorous achievement,' is due to a headlong misunderstanding of a passage in Chaucer, 'in derring do that longeth to a knight,' *i.e.* 'in daring to do what belongs to a knight.' So *iwis*, an adverb meaning 'certainly' (cognate with Ger. *gewiss*), has usually been treated by archaizing writers as if it were a pronoun and a verb,—*I wis*, 'I know,'—though this is an impossible form,—the present tense being really *I wot*, and the preterite *I wistë* (cf. the biblical, 'he wist not what he said'). *Trow* really means 'to think,' but it has often been used as a synonym for 'I know.' *Gramarye* is set down in all the dictionaries as meaning 'magic' (like Fr. *grimoire*, which has the same origin), but the only old sense of this word that can be discovered in English is 'grammar,'—its original and proper meaning. It looks as if the sense of 'magic' were a coinage of Bishop Percy's,—a clever coinage, it must be admitted, or a happy blunder, for nothing ever had more the air of a fine old word.[4] The connection between the idea of 'grammar' (*i.e.* 'learning') and 'magic' is also close, and the Fr. *grimoire*, 'a conjuring book,' shows how natural the development is.

Finally, we may mention the universal Elizabethan habit of punning, which pervaded conversation and literature alike. Every kind of play on words was common, from the merest jingle in sound to the most elaborate calembour. Puns are now out of favor, probably because we think that the punster wishes us to laugh at them.[5] We should be careful, however, not to take the punning habit of the Elizabethans so seriously. Clearly the Elizabethans did not laugh at

---

[4] See Child, *English and Scottish Popular Ballads*, V, 340.

[5] *Pun* is of uncertain etymology, and was doubtless a slang word at the outset. It is commonly referred to *pound* (of which there is a clipped form *pun*, 'to beat,' occurring in Shakspere). An older word is *clench* or *clinch*, either from the twist in the meaning of the words punned on or from the sense of 'repartee,'—something that clinches the argument. *Quirk* (a 'turn' or 'flourish') and *quip* (from *quid pro quo*) are synonyms.

puns, unless they were peculiarly amusing. They got merely a certain intellectual titillation out of the grotesque association of ideas which punning induced. The pun became for the first and last time in our literary history a definite feature of the language. Some of the commonest puns became idiomatic, and attracted no attention whatever. Our own speech always seems familiar to us, however odd it may sound to our neighbors over the border, in space or in time.

In general, the Elizabethans handled the language with the greatest freedom. It was an age of novelty. The English people was at last awake to its importance as a power in the world at large. It was ceasing to be isolated, and was becoming conscious of a great political destiny. Discoveries, as of the New World, Utopian schemes, and phantom commonwealths were in the air. Men's minds were stimulated in the highest degree, and the mental temper was alert and ready. Fantastic imitation of foreign ways was inevitable. Each Elizabethan felt that he was an individual, and burned to distinguish himself, if only by the cut of his coat. It was the age of Pericles, without the restaints of Greek taste,—which, however, were not so binding on the actual Athenians as they have become in the tradition of retrospective critics. The stage reproduces for us almost every trick of Elizabethan speech and manners. The mere vocabulary of a single dramatist would wreck his reputation with the purists if he were a modern.

In the next age, thought, literature, and language were influenced by those complex causes which we sum up rather vaguely as 'Puritanism.' The most obvious effect on our language was to bring theology and biblical turns of phrase into the common speech to a degree unknown before. Yet it would be a serious mistake to suppose that any great number of the religious words that are now a part of our ordinary vocabulary are derived from this movement. Most of them had been in the language for a long time, and many had gone through a development which had obscured their origin, so that they were no longer felt as religious allusions. The religious vocabulary was not the invention of the Puri-

tans, nor was its common use in everyday dialogue a specifically Puritan fashion. What the Puritans did was to carry
the habit out to its ultimate limits in use. They also made
constant appeal to the legislation of the Old Testament,
and thus filled the language, for a time, with allusions to
Hebrew law and ritual, as well as to the poets and prophets
of the Old Dispensation. In short, they focussed their minds
on biblical phraseology, with results that permanently affected our stock of words and idioms. In New England these
forces worked with peculiar power. Congregationalism was
long established by law, and all who refused to conform to
that system were 'dissenters.'[6] The intellectual history of
Massachusetts, for example, was practically unaffected by
the Restoration.

The reaction from Puritanism in the life of the nation
is mirrored in the language of the eighteenth century. Writers were in constant dread of 'enthusiasm' (which was a
synonym for 'fanaticism') and 'the romantic' (by which was
meant anything fanciful or imaginative or emotional that
was not instantly reducible to common sense). Their ideal
was the easy elegance of language which befits a cultivated
man of fashion. Polish, wit, and epigram were the mode.
Imagination was repressed. Warmth of feeling was not to be
uttered without suspicion of vulgarity. The good writer, it
was held, should steer his course between exaltation, on the
one hand, and dulness on the other. Above all, he should be
clear and logical, or at all events, should have the semblance
of being so. To preserve one's self-control under all circumstances, without appearing to be self-conscious, was to reach
the acme of the kind of excellence then most admired. The
model was France, the polite nation.

There can be no doubt that the eighteenth century had
a beneficial effect on our language. In particular, it made
for what we now call 'grammatical correctness.' The regularity of English syntax is mainly due to the tendencies
which we have been describing. Many constructions, freely

---

[6] See A. C. Goodell, in the Publications of The Colonial Society of Massachusetts, I, 140 ff.

used in the Elizabethan age, were gradually discarded in the eighteenth century because they seemed to be irregular, or because they tended to ambiguity. Similarly, the meanings of words became more limited, with a manifest gain in exactness. And finally, our literary vocabulary was subjected to a purifying process. The Elizabethans, as we have seen, were very free in coining new words or in reviving old ones, and the learned times had brought in many sesquipedalian terms from the Latin. This gave a peculiar richness to Elizabethan phraseology, and a fine dignity to that of the seventeenth century; but such processes cannot go on indefinitely without removing the language of literature too far from that of common life. A period of rest has to intervene, that the language may, so to speak, take account of stock, or, to change the figure, may digest what it has somewhat indiscriminately devoured. The eighteenth century was such a period. No better standard can be found than the easy language of cultivated men who are neither specialists nor pedants, and this was the standard which the eighteenth century used in codifying 'good English.' Many blunders were made in matters of detail, but the general movement was sound, and its results were good. Of course, this schoolmastering tendency could not last forever. Long before the end of the century there were revolts against the repressive canons of what was called good taste, and the language began once more to go on in its free course of development. There is such a thing as pedantic dread of pedantry, and as soon as the eighteenth century reached that stage, its work had been done, and another readjustment began.

What is called the 'Romantic Revival,' toward the end of the eighteenth century, is the next great influence which our language felt. This is a vague term for a very complicated group of causes, and the literary historians find some trouble in defining it. The effect upon our language, however, is a much simpler matter to study. There was a revolt against French neatness and 'correctness' of style, a return to the older models of English,—to Spenser, and Shakspere, and Milton. Obsolete and half-obsolete words were revived, not always with an accurate knowledge of their sense. Variety and striking effects were sought after. Metaphor became bolder, and versification was freed from some of its more recent shackles. Poetry showed this first; and in the nineteenth century the reaction extended itself to prose. The easiest catchword for the revolt is 'individualism,' as opposed to the view that a man must conform his language to that of everybody else, or that all must follow some definite model or models, ancient or modern. We have a feeling that 'the style is the man,' and that every author is therefore entitled to use that form of language which best expresses his individuality. Thus it is impossible to say that there is any prevailing style that marks the nineteenth century. A hundred years hence, when the small men have sunk out of sight, and only a few great authors emerge from the level of forgotten mediocrity, the future historian may be able to characterize nineteenth-century English, but it cannot be done by a contemporary. In one and the same author, we often find marked preciosity of phrase cheek by jowl with the baldest colloquialism. Affected brutality of diction associates itself on the same page with equally affected sentimental refinement. In some particulars, however, we can hardly go wrong. It is certain, as we have already remarked, that the progress of science and mechanics, and the widespread popular interest in discovery and invention, have profoundly modified our vocabulary. Another influence, of a widely different kind, has come from the almost passionate study of literature as a fine art, and from the consequent development of literary criticism. And, finally, there has never been a time in the history of our language when 'syntactical correctness' has ruled with so capricious and tyrannical a sway. The proof-reader has become a court of last resort for many of us.

We have now considered not only the great movements which brought the English language to pass, but some of the modifying influences or 'fashions' to which it has been subjected from age to age. Among the fashions, we have counted mere tricks of style, like the Anglo-Saxon tautology,

and such far-reaching social and religious forces as Puritanism. Despite all these modifying influences, we observe that
the English tongue is still the English tongue. It has changed
much since the East Midland became the literary language
five hundred years ago, yet all the changes have not essentially modified its character. The 'genius of the language' is
still the same.

Such persistence of uniformity in the face of chance and
change challenges our attention. Words, as we know, are but
the signs of thought. They do nothing of themselves, and
have only such senses as the mind of the speaker and the
hearer gives them. Yet, when we observe their conduct in the
presence of various forces that act upon them, they almost
seem to have an independent life, apart from the mind of the
man who uses them.

And, indeed, this is in a manner true. For no sooner has
an idea been expressed in words than the form of expression
reacts on the speaker and influences his subsequent thought.
If this happens in the case of a casual utterance, phrased in
a conventional way, how much more powerful must have
been the reaction in the minds of those whose first acquaintance with that idea was associated with the particular form
of language in which it was couched! Every one knows how
a peculiar or striking phrase, embodying a certain thought,
may recur to the memory whenever the thought comes back
to us, and thus, by a kind of haunting persistence, make it
difficult to phrase the thought otherwise. We all have our
favorite catchwords, which, originating in this way, have
become as much a part of our individuality as our tricks of
gait or gesture or facial expression.

Now, in long lapses of time the continuance of similar
impressions produces in one speaker a mode or habit of
thought consonant with that of others. The several impressions in the mind as a particular word is constantly used
act somewhat like objects in a composite photograph: all
that is alike is constantly accumulating, while that which is
individual or peculiar is as rapidly dissipated. Thus there
arises a regular and persistent mode of thought and conse-

quently of expression, which more or less dominates the form of the language in the mouths of all its speakers, whether they mean to be guided by it or not. To this tendency the Germans have given the expressive name *Sprachgefühl*, or 'speech-feeling.' We have no settled term for it in English, —that is, no name which our *Sprachgefühl* has accepted,—so that we are more or less in the habit of employing the German word.

It is of course absurd to ascribe feeling to language, except in a metaphorical way. Fortunately, however, the vague syntax of composition allows the German word to mean a 'feeling *for* speech' as well as 'feeling *of* speech,' and by-and-by we shall either adopt the term as an English word, or the *feeling* itself will accept some other suitable phrase to express the idea. For the *Sprachgefühl* is a very real thing in a long-cultivated language like our own. It affects every word that we utter, though we may think that we are speaking as the whim of the moment dictates; and thus it is the strongest and most pervasive of all conservative forces, and has kept our language true to itself through all the vicissitudes which we have been describing.

The writer has a thousand times had occasion to notice the difference in this *Sprachgefühl* in the use of Latin, French, and English, and has constantly been surprised at the way in which the language insisted upon writing itself almost in spite of him. Thus a monumental simplicity of style and a single point of view are almost inseparable from a Latin essay; French must make itself scintillating and epigrammatic; and it is almost impossible not to be copious and diffuse in writing English.

No author, however eminent, can disregard this subtle and pervasive law. Men of genius may take great liberties with their mother tongue without offence; but let them once run counter to its characteristic tendencies, let them violate the English *Sprachgefühl*, and their mannerism becomes, as it were, a foreign language. They are writing not English, but—say Carlylese.

"What Is Meaning?"

Lady V. Welby

Lady V. Welby, God-daughter of Queen Victoria and later her Maid of Honour, was named Victoria Alexandrina Stuart-Worley, daughter of the Honorable Charles Stuart-Worley and his wife, Lady Emmeline. In her youth she travelled much in the Far East. She married Sir William Earle Welby-Gregory in 1863; their two children were Sir Charles Welby and Mrs. Henry Cust (who, incidentally, translated Bréal's *Semantics*). In later years men of letters frequently visited with her at Harrow, where she died in 1912. Her books include *Grains of Sense*, 1897; *What Is Meaning?* 1903; and *Significs and Language*, 1911. She also wrote the article on "Significs" for the eleventh edition of the *Encyclopedia Britannica*. Our selection is Chapter I from *What Is Meaning?* published in 1903 by the Macmillan Company. Sub-title of the book is "Studies in the Development of Significance."

Attention has already been called in an article in *Mind* (New Series, vol. v., Nos. 17, 18)[1] to the strange fact that the very condition on which all forms of study and knowledge depend, that which is vaguely called their 'meaning,'—that very meaning which to intelligence is the cardinal quality of fact,—remains for us a virtually unstudied subject.

It may be well briefly to summarise the line then taken. It was pointed out that the conception of Meaning, its significance and its interpretation, have so far been practically

[1] It should be noted that Interpretation was here used instead of Significance, because the point of view taken was mainly psychological, and the present trend had not at the time been fully thought out.

ignored, and that this curious neglect leads to the loss of distinctions valuable for thought, and to a low average of interpreting power. Attention was then called (1) to the absence, especially in education, of any careful study of the conditions of meaning and its interpretation, much being lost by the present dearth of means of expression and of training in their use, and (2) to the advantages which must accrue from such study. Works on philosophy and science too, and especially on logic and psychology, supply ample witness, both conscious and unconscious, to the need for a special study of meaning which might be called Significs, as no term already in use covers enough ground. It was claimed that such a study, so far from being impossible, seems indicated and called for on every side, and might be made not only practical but attractive, even to the quite young child. At present, largely from the absence of such training, language betrays a disastrous lack of power to adapt itself to the growing needs of experience. But this power would soon be acquired as the result of the training here suggested, and would even to a certain extent follow a general awakening to the importance of the question.

The idea that definition (useful enough in its own sphere) is the true remedy for defects of expression, was shown to be fallacious. Ambiguity, it was urged, is an inherent characteristic of language as of other forms of organic function. Thought may suffer from a too mechanical precision in speech. Meaning is sensitive to psychological 'climate.' But the kind of ambiguity which acts as a useful stimulant to intelligence, and enriches the field of conjecture, is very different from that which in the intellectual sphere begins and ends in confusion, or in the moral sphere begins in disingenuousness and ends in deliberate and successful imposture. We all alike, in fact, suffer and lose by these; by the endless disputation which the one entails, and the force given by the other to the specious oratory of charlatans.

The question of remedy was then dealt with. It was contended that it rests with education to initiate the needed 'fresh start.' Only those trained from the first to detect (1) the sense, (2) the meaning, and (3) the significance,—that is the tendency, the intention, and the essential interest of what is brought before their notice,—can hope to emerge from the present bondage to the plausible. It is with education as with economics; we have been told *ad nauseam* that man will not work except for food: that all else is mere play, and that the moment the economic pressure is removed he loafs. But that is false. Man inherits (as Professor Loeb tells us) the "instinct of work"; and if this is stunted or killed, it is a pathological condition: civilisation has made him ill. So in education. When that problem is solved, the difficulty will be ever to wean the young mind from its 'studies,' since these, as in the case of the babe, will share the fascination of play. Play, indeed, will be but the obverse of work, and the two will be interchangeable under the broader term of energy. Our language is admitted, even by foreigners, to have peculiar facilities for inquiries and studies of this kind;[2] and therefore it is incumbent upon English teachers and thinkers to lead the way. These considerations led to the conclusion that at least it would be well to realise more fully both the extent of the present anarchy, and the direction in which we may hope to advance.[3]

The article now summarised was of course written, under advice, with reference only to psychology and philosophy.[4]

---

[2] *E.g.* Professors Jespersen, Carl Abel, Bréal, etc. But not only these: Dr. Sweet (*A Practical Study of Languages,* 1899, p. 274) speaks of the "admitted fact that English is one of the most expressive and concise languages that have ever existed, and that ideas can be expressed in it with as much facility and accuracy as in Greek and Latin."

An American ethnologist (Mr. Powell, *Evolution of Language,* 1881, p. 15) is quoted by Professor Hanns Oertel in his *Lectures on the Study of Language* as follows: "When inflections are greatly multiplied, as they are in the (American) Indian languages alike with Greek and Latin, the speaker is compelled in the choice of his words to think of a multiplicity of things which have no connection with that which he wishes to express. . . . In the development of the English, as well as the French and German, linguistic evolution has not been in vain. Judged by these criteria the English stands alone in the highest rank."

[3] See Note I. (B), Appendix.

[4] It ought perhaps here to be mentioned, that in obedience to a request made by the English and American editors of *Mind,* a prize was offered in 1896 for the best essay on "The causes of the present obscurity and

But the present studies are attempts to show, or at least to suggest, that the scope of the subject to be called Significs is, in fact, far wider than could there be claimed. There is no imaginable form of human interest and activity which it does not concern and could not raise in value. Yet it is only too plain that in education and in the practical as well as the scientific and philosophical worlds, the central importance of Expression and its interpretation are equally ignored.

I hope to make it clear that the 'sense' of any form of expression has not yet been differentiated from its 'meaning' and its 'significance'; and that this omission is of vital importance.[5] We often ask for meaning where by the nature of the case no meaning in the sense intended can be there: when we ought to ask for sense. And we often despair of meaning when we might discover not merely sense but something which includes and transforms it,—that is, significance. For example, great movements of population, great changes of political standard and aim, may not be consciously 'meant,' *i.e.* intended, by those who carry them out or even by their leaders. But they are significant: they imply some vast common impulse due to causes of which it may be we are as yet quite ignorant; and they impel us to search for these causes in order to direct, to utilise, or to counteract their effects. Our indifference to these questions is indeed nothing less than literally insensate; since it tends to fetter and cripple us both in that typical human energy

confusion in psychological and philosophical terminology, and the directions in which we may hope for efficient practical remedy." This was won by Professor Ferdinand Tönnies, whose admirable article (translated by Mrs. Bernard Bosanquet) appeared in *Mind* of July and October 1899, and January 1900. In *Mind* of April 1901 there appeared some notes upon this article (unfortunately delayed by illness and bereavement), with an answer from Professor Tönnies. Before that (in 1897) a little book of fragments and parables on the subject, called *Grains of Sense*, had been published.

5 Almost the only instance of this distinction which I have so far come across, occurs in an article on Tolstoy in the *Edinburgh Review* for July 1901: "the original Russian is often so involved that translators have had occasionally to choose between the meaning and the sense of a passage" (p. 58).

which we call expression, and in its comprehension.[6] When
we have the sense to concentrate training on sense in every
sense, we shall for the first time realise what meaning is and
can be; and rise to the highest sense,—that of Significance.[7]
This is no mere play upon the word 'sense,' but a study of its
range of meaning.[8]

There is, strictly speaking, no such thing as the Sense of
a word, but only the sense in which it is used—the circumstances, state of mind, reference, 'universe of discourse' belonging to it. The Meaning of a word is the intent which
it is desired to convey—the intention of the user. The Significance is always manifold, and intensifies its sense as well as
its meaning, by expressing its importance, its appeal to us, its
moment for us, its emotional force, its ideal value, its moral
aspect, its universal or at least social range. All science, all
logic, all philosophy, the whole controversy about aesthetics,
about ethics, about religion, ultimately concentrate upon
this: What is the sense of, What do we mean by, What is the
significance of, that is, Why do we care for, Beauty, Truth,
Goodness? Why do we value experience? And why do we
seek for Significance, and resume the value of innumerable
observed facts under formulae of significance like gravitation
or natural selection? Because we are the Expression of the
world, as it were 'expressed from' it by the commanding or
insistent pressure of natural stimuli not yet understood.

---

[6] Like Bruno, Leibnitz hoped for a science of signs, an algebra of
thought, but he aimed at a system in which to reason and to calculate
were identical, reason being literally ratio. On the other hand, Bruno
"hoped to perfect a method of connecting universal ideas with real knowledge, while furnishing rules for discussion and directions for the exercise
of thought and of speech. The pupil was to learn not only how to expound, to attack, and to defend, but to combine conceptions, to form
new ideas, to conceive all which is or can be; not to think alone, but
to use the thought of others" (Frith's *Life of Giordano Bruno*, 1887, p.
94). Surely we might share this last aim?

[7] Examples occur on all sides and abound daily. *E.g.* "The German
press is unanimous in regarding the Anglo-Japanese Agreement as a political event of exceptional significance" (*Times*, February 13, 1902). "The
far-reaching significance of the Colonial Secretary's visit to South Africa"
(*Times*, November 27, 1902).

[8] See also below, p. 48, etc.

Man questions and an answer is waiting for him. But first he must learn to speak, really to 'express' himself and the world. To do that he must learn to *signify* and to signalise. He must discover, observe, analyse, appraise, first the sense of all that he senses through touch, hearing, sight, and to realise its interest, what it practically signifies for him; then the meaning—the intention—of action, the motive of conduct, the cause of each effect. Thus at last he will see the Significance, the ultimate bearing, the central value, the vital implication—of what? of all experience, all knowledge, all fact, and all thought.

There is just now a marked tendency to confess that Experience is a concept which imperatively needs both expansion and enrichment.[9] In a wholesome dread of illusion we have narrowed its scope too much. Experience can only be enriched through the acquirement in a broad sense of fresh symbols or fresh significance: expression needs development in the same way for the same reason. Thus it follows that, as already suggested, every conceivable form of human interest is centrally touched and transformed by Significs.[10] The difficulty is not to make this plain, but to deal attempt even to show that the signific attitude is essentially

---

[9] Among other writers Ormond (Foundations of Knowledge, 1900) pleads both for this and for a critique of experience. See also Note II., Appendix.

[10] "The sign in speech and in writing thus has for man a significance unequalled by anything else. Inventions and discoveries, all the material acquisitions which the human mind has acquired control of, are based almost without exception upon the assumption of an intelligible and logically employed system of signs, which is the condition at the same time of the silent soliloquy of thought with itself, and of the intellectual intercourse of humanity generally; and the more we turn our glance from life generally to the provinces of intellectual activity, the more prominent a rôle do we observe the sign to assume: and its most important one in the sciences, particularly in the exact sciences" (*Signs and Symbols:* Professor Ernst Schroeder, "Open Court," October 27, 1892).

"In brief, a stupendous task arises before our eyes; the task of still further perfecting the sign, to which the human mind already owes so much, of freeing language of its imperfections, and, by the appropriate fashioning of the sign, of bringing the sign and the thing into perfect and law-governed correspondence (or, as Trendelenburg says, 'into an immediate connection')" (*Ibid.* Part II., November 3, 1892).

within any reasonable space with the evidence for it. The predictive, would imply a mass of illustrative reference which would swamp these Studies altogether.

The materials, however, have been collected and can always speak for themselves. Meanwhile it may be suggested that physical science—at present the dominant source of discovery by interpretation—best represents the signific attitude. But when the man of science has been, as a matter of course, trained on Signific lines, his power of seeing through facts, his mastery of their relations or corresponding points, of their applications and indirect implications, and of the fittest expression of these, must inevitably be greatly increased. He will become once more the 'natural philosopher,' but in a higher and more adequate sense of both terms.

In fact everything is and always will be 'in the line' of the Significian, since all converges upon it. Significs concerns the practical mind, e.g. in business or political life, more closely and inevitably than it does the speculative mind. For the thinker may go on through all his life turning over his own or others' thoughts and working them logically out. But the man of action must translate thought into deed as fast as ideas come to him; and he may ruin the cause he would serve by missing the significance of things. All signifies to him, 'matters' to him, interests him. As the word implies, 'Significs' sums up what for the 'man in the street' signifies; whatever does not signify, he will tell you, is nothing to him; and he well understands that the value of a sign is not that it may mean anything you like, and thus be used to confuse, bewilder, mislead, or that it means what is no concern of his, but that it means somewhat which in some sense has interest either for him or his fellows: he knows that it is his business to find out what this is. He knows also that signs of all kinds must point beyond themselves, must in that sense 'mean' something, or they would not be signs at all.

It need hardly be pointed out that the other man—the man in the study, the lecture-room, the council-chamber, the laboratory, the office—knows in a fuller sense still that whatever his work may be, it must signify somewhat and gain in significance as it rises and widens in importance. And most of all the original thinker, the greatest of human 'minds,' knows this.

The Poet is, in fact, the only man who has reached a world of enhanced expression which ought to be the common heritage. And even he confesses that

> The flowering moments of the mind
> Drop half their petals in our speech.

When we have overtaken the Poet he will be able to give us poetry more perfect than any he can yet put into words, while philosophy must enter upon a new quest, where answer and solution are no longer hopeless. We cannot raise the level of expression without raising the level of thought and imagination. For what is Mind, after all, but the moment in which the world takes on Meaning and its expression? As Jowett expressed it, the very language which mind uses is the result of the instincts of long-forgotten generations.[11]

Again, the spell which the Poet casts upon us largely depends upon the perfect rationality of the mind which can afford as his does, and as no other yet can, to handle thought and language. From that secure base he can travel at will, and take us with him into new worlds of beauty and truth. But let his mind be really 'unhinged,' let his assumptions be merely the casual driftings of a vagrant fancy, and some lowering of power must result, even though certain kinds of beauty and force may still survive.

These suggestions then may be provisionally summed up as follows:—

The function of expression and the response to expression are as yet but little developed; and if general interest could be aroused in the question, and it came to be widely realised that increased powers of mental communication were easily within our reach—only needing attention, resolution, and consensus—this increase would become ours as surely as in the case of physical communication.

Expression both may and ought to outstrip rigid Defini-

---

11 *Essay on Psychology*, Plato, vol. IV. (3rd edit. 1892).

tion: indeed it is probable that what is best worth expressing, best worth being interpreted, and best worth being acted upon, is often least capable of definition in the ordinary sense.[12]

As the sense for Sense becomes more acute and more discriminative, definition will, in fact, become less and less necessary, except in the historical form or within technical limits; while the power both of context and association will be more generally realised and more effectively utilised.

The question is one of much more than merely increased precision,[13] often the worst of pitfalls and the grave of a living language, much more also than a protest against ambiguity or obscurity.

It is also much more than a question of 'preciosity' or even of 'style'; though it is of vital concern to those who care for the beauty of linguistic form.

As life rises in scale and worth, it rises in Significance; and therefore the question of questions really is, What is Sense, or, What is Meaning, and what do we mean (that is, intend) to convey when we ask the momentous question, 'In what sense?'—an inquiry which needs to be made much oftener and more seriously than it is now, as the answer must at least define the sense intended.

The future of Literature hangs first upon this question; for literature is that which of all written words is most significant, gives us most thought and feeling, and is the truest

---

[12] But strange, indeed, is the notion that the terms in which we state or define any idea have no effect upon that idea, and that definition is independent of predicate and of character itself!

[13] In the case of scientific language, it is obvious that just because scientific knowledge is so constantly and rapidly growing, it becomes imperative that there should be increased consensus and better mutual understanding in this necessary development. Unless there is consistency and agreement in the definition of the term or phrase taken as a given starting-point for discussion, the indispensable variations in sense as knowledge grows (needing thus both wide expansions of connotation and many new terms) are themselves hampered and checked, or even baulked; and thus the whole subject is liable to become the prey of needless controversy—often wide of the mark—leading only to confusion or to a cul-de-sac. A pamphlet (*Witness of Science to Linguistic Anarchy*, 1898) aims at furnishing convenient illustrations of this.

human message. And the question appeals equally to the philosophical and scientific thinker, the politician and the man of business. The best hope lies in so arousing public interest in questions of expression—language in its widest sense—that the next generation should be trained from the first to put the subject in the forefront of all intellectual work as in that of all education.[14]

---

[14] Perhaps the most significant step towards the recognition of 'meaning' as a definite subject for study (and that on which all others depend) is taken by Dr. Stout in his *Manual of Psychology*, vol. i., 1898, where he speaks of "a process of fundamental importance which we may call the *acquirement of meaning*" (p. 34: italics his).

At present we might say with Lewis Carroll (*Life and Letters*, 1898, p. 331) that "one of the hardest things in the world is to convey a meaning accurately from one mind to another"; except that 'fully' or 'vitally' would fit some cases better than 'accurately.'

It may be well here to make definitely clear what was implied in the Preface that is, my consciousness of inability always to avoid the very inconsistencies and confusions of which I complain. In this I may appeal to those writers who have shown themselves most conscious of the drawbacks of our current terminology—*e.g.* Mr. A. E. Taylor in *The Problem of Conduct*, p. 39 (footnote).

"What Pragmatism Means"

William James

William James was born in 1842. After a varied education at Harvard, he eventually took an M.D. degree at the Harvard Medical School. He taught for many years at Harvard as instructor in physiology. His work in this field led him on to psychology and philosophy. In 1880 he entered the department of philosophy at Harvard where he worked out and expressed the philosophy of Pragmatism. His most important work, *Pragmatism*, 1907, is composed of his lectures at the Lowell Institute in Boston in 1906. James died in 1910. The selection used here is the first portion of Lecture II of *Pragmatism: New Name for Some Old Ways of Thinking*, published in 1907 by Longmans, Green and Company.

S OME years ago, being with a camping party in the mountains, I returned from a solitary ramble to find every one engaged in a ferocious metaphysical dispute. The *corpus* of the dispute was a squirrel—a live squirrel supposed to be clinging to one side of a tree-trunk; while over against the tree's opposite side a human being was imagined to stand. This human witness tries to get sight of the squirrel by moving rapidly round the tree, but no matter how fast he goes, the squirrel moves as fast in the opposite direction, and always keeps the tree between himself and the man, so that never a glimpse of him is caught. The resultant metaphysical problem now is this: *Does the man go round the squirrel or not?* He goes round the tree, sure enough, and the squirrel is on the tree; but does he go round the squirrel? In the unlimited leisure of the wilderness, discussion had been worn threadbare. Everyone had taken sides, and was obstinate; and the numbers on both sides were even. Each side, when I appeared therefore appealed to me to make it a majority. Mindful of the scholastic adage that whenever you meet a contradiction you must make a distinction, I immediately sought and found one, as follows: "Which party is right," I said, "depends on what you *practically mean* by 'going round' the squirrel. If you mean passing from the north of him to the east, then to the south, then to the west, and then to the north of him again, obviously the man does go round him, for he occupies these successive positions. But if on the contrary you mean being first in front of him, then on the right of him, then behind him, then on his left, and finally in front again, it is quite as obvious that the man fails to go round him, for by the compensating movements the squirrel makes, he keeps his belly turned towards the man all the time, and his back turned away. Make the distinction, and there is no occasion for any farther dispute. You are both right and both wrong according as you conceive the verb 'to go round' in one practical fashion or the other."

Although one or two of the hotter disputants called my speech a shuffling evasion, saying they wanted no quibbling or scholastic hair-splitting, but meant just plain honest English 'round,' the majority seemed to think that the distinction had assuaged the dispute.

I tell this trivial anecdote because it is a peculiarly simple example of what I wish now to speak of as *the pragmatic method.* The pragmatic method is primarily a method of settling metaphysical disputes that otherwise might be interminable. Is the world one or many?—fated or free?—material or spiritual?—here are notions either of which may or may not hold good of the world; and disputes over such notions are unending. The pragmatic method in such cases is to try to interpret each notion by tracing its respective practical consequences. What difference would it practically make to any one if this notion rather than that notion were true? If no practical difference whatever can be traced, then the alternatives mean practically the same thing, and all dispute is idle. Whenever a dispute is serious, we ought to be able to show some practical difference that must follow from one side or the other's being right.

A glance at the history of the idea will show you still better what pragmatism means. The term is derived from the same Greek word πραγμα, meaning action, from which our words 'practice' and 'practical' come. It was first introduced into philosophy by Mr. Charles Peirce in 1878. In an article entitled 'How to Make Our Ideas Clear,' in the 'Popular Science Monthly' for January of that year Mr. Peirce, after pointing out that our beliefs are really rules for action, said that, to develop a thought's meaning, we need only determine what conduct it is fitted to produce: that conduct is for us its sole significance. And the tangible fact at the root of all our thought-distinctions, however subtle, is that there is no one of them so fine as to consist in anything but a possible difference of practice. To attain perfect clearness in our thoughts of an object, then, we need only consider what conceivable effects of a practical kind the object may involve—what sensations we are to expect from it, and what reactions we must prepare. Our conception of these effects, whether immediate or remote, is then for us the whole of our conception of the object, so far as that conception has positive significance at all.

This is the principle of Peirce, the principle of pragmatism. It lay entirely unnoticed by any one for twenty years, until I, in an address before Professor Howison's philosophical union at the University of California, brought it forward again and made a special application of it to religion. By that date (1898) the times seemed ripe for its reception. The word 'pragmatism' spread, and at present it fairly spots the pages of the philosophic journals. On all hands we find the 'pragmatic movement' spoken of, sometimes with respect, sometimes with contumely, seldom with clear understanding. It is evident that the term applies itself conveniently to a number of tendencies that hitherto have lacked a collective name, and that it has 'come to stay.'

To take in the importance of Peirce's principle, one must

get accustomed to applying it to concrete cases. I found a few years ago that Ostwald, the illustrious Leipzig chemist, had been making perfectly distinct use of the principle of pragmatism in his lectures on the philosophy of science, though he had not called it by that name.

"All realities influence our practice," he wrote me, "and that influence is their meaning for us. I am accustomed to put questions to my classes in this way: In what respects would the world be different if this alternative or that were true? If I can find nothing that would become different, then the alternative has no sense."

That is, the rival views mean practically the same thing, and meaning, other than practical, there is for us none. Ostwald in a published lecture gives this example of what he means. Chemists have long wrangled over the inner constitution of certain bodies called 'tautomerous.' Their properties seemed equally consistent with the notion that an instable hydrogen atom oscillates inside of them, or that they are instable mixtures of two bodies. Controversy raged, but never was decided. "It would never have begun," says Ostwald, "if the combatants had asked themselves what particular experimental fact could have been made different by one or the other view being correct. For it would then have appeared that no difference of fact could possibly ensue; and the quarrel was as unreal as if, theorizing in primitive times about the raising of dough by yeast, one party should have invoked a 'brownie,' while another insisted on an 'elf' as the true cause of the phenomenon."

It is astonishing to see how many philosophical disputes collapse into insignificance the moment you subject them to this simple test of tracing a concrete consequence. There can *be* no difference anywhere that doesn't *make* a difference elsewhere—no difference in abstract truth that doesn't express itself in a difference in concrete fact and in conduct consequent upon that fact, imposed on somebody, somehow, somewhere, and somewhen. The whole function of philosophy ought to be to find out what definite difference it will make to you and me, at definite instants of our life, if this world-formula or that world-formula be the true one.

There is absolutely nothing new in the pragmatic method. Socrates was an adept at it. Aristotle used it methodically. Locke, Berkeley, and Hume made momentous contributions to truth by its means. Shadworth Hodgson keeps insisting that realities are only what they are 'known as.' But these forerunners of pragmatism used it in fragments: they were preluders only. Not until in our time has it generalized itself, become conscious of a universal mission, pretended to a conquering destiny. I believe in that destiny, and I hope I may end by inspiring you with my belief.

Pragmatism represents a perfectly familiar attitude in philosophy, the empiricist attitude, but it represents it, as it seems to me, both in a more radical and in a less objectionable form than it has ever yet assumed. A pragmatist turns his back resolutely and once for all upon a lot of inveterate habits dear to professional philosophers. He turns away from abstraction and insufficiency, from verbal solutions, from bad *a priori* reasons, from fixed principles, closed systems, and pretended absolutes and origins. He turns towards concreteness and adequacy, towards facts, towards action and towards power. That means the empiricist temper regnant and the rationalist temper sincerely given up. It means the open air and possibilities of nature, as against dogma, artificiality, and the pretence of finality in truth.

At the same time it does not stand for any special results. It is a method only. But the general triumph of that method would mean an enormous change in what I called in my last lecture the 'temperament' of philosophy. Teachers of the ultra-rationalistic type would be frozen out, much as the courtier type is frozen out in republics, as the ultramontane type of priest is frozen out in protestant lands. Science and metaphysics would come much nearer together, would in fact work absolutely hand in hand.

Metaphysics has usually followed a very primitive kind of quest. You know how men have always hankered after unlawful magic, and you know what a great part in magic *words* have always played. If you have his name, or the formula of incantation that binds him, you can control the spirit, genie, afrite, or whatever the power may be. Solomon knew the names of all the spirits, and having their names, he held them subject to his will. So the universe has always appeared to the natural mind as a kind of enigma, of which the key must be sought in the shape of some illuminating or power-bringing word or name. The word names the universe's *principle,* and to possess it is after a fashion to possess the universe itself. 'God,' 'Matter,' 'Reason,' 'the Absolute,' 'Energy,' are so many solving names. You can rest when you have them. You are at the end of your metaphysical quest.

But if you follow the pragmatic method, you cannot look on any such word as closing your quest. You must bring out of each word its practical cash-value, set it at work within the stream of your experience. It appears less as a solution, then, than as a program for more work, and more particularly as an indication of the ways in which existing realities may be *changed.*

Theories thus become instruments, not answers to enigmas, in which we can rest. We don't lie back upon them, we move forward, and, on occasion, make nature over again by their aid. Pragmatism unstiffens all our theories, limbers them up and sets each one at work. Being nothing essentially new, it harmonizes with many ancient philosophic tendencies. It agrees with nominalism for instance, in always appealing to particulars; with utilitarianism in emphasizing practical aspects; with positivism in its disdain for verbal solutions, useless questions and metaphysical abstractions.

All these, you see, are *anti-intellectualist* tendencies. Against rationalism as a pretension and a method pragmatism is fully armed and militant. But, at the outset, at least, it stands for no particular results. It has no dogmas, and no doctrines save its method. As the young Italian pragmatist Papini has well said, it lies in the midst of our theories, like a corridor in a hotel. Innumerable chambers open out of it. In one you may find a man writing an atheistic volume; in the next some one on his knees praying for faith and strength; in a third a chemist investigating a body's properties. In a fourth a system of idealistic metaphysics is being excogitated; in a fifth the impossibility of metaphysics is being shown. But they all own the corridor, and all must pass through it if they want a practicable way of getting into or out of their respective rooms.

No particular results then, so far, but only an attitude of orientation, is what the pragmatic method means. *The attitude of looking away from first things, principles, 'categories,' supposed necessities; and of looking towards last things, fruits, consequences, facts.*

So much for the pragmatic method! You may say that I have been praising it rather than explaining it to you, but I shall presently explain it abundantly enough by showing how it works on some familiar problems. Meanwhile the word pragmatism has come to be used in a still wider sense, as meaning also a certain *theory of truth.* I mean to give a whole lecture to the statement of that theory, after first paving the way, so I can be very brief now. But brevity is hard to follow, so I ask for your redoubled attention for a quarter of an hour. If much remains obscure, I hope to make it clearer in the later lectures.

One of the most successfully cultivated branches of philosophy in our time is what is called inductive logic, the study of the conditions under which our sciences have evolved. Writers on this subject have begun to show a singular unanimity as to what the laws of nature and elements of fact mean, when formulated by mathematicians, physicists and chemists. When the first mathematical, logical, and natural uniformities, the first *laws*, were discovered, men were so carried away by the clearness, beauty and simplification that resulted, that they believed themselves to have deciphered authentically the eternal thoughts of the Almighty. His mind also thundered and reverberated in syllogisms. He also thought in conic sections, squares and roots and ratios, and geometrized like Euclid. He made Kepler's laws for the planets to follow; he made velocity increase proportionally to the time in falling bodies; he made the law of the sines for light to obey when refracted; he established the classes, orders, families and genera of plants and animals, and fixed the distances between them. He thought the archetypes of all things, and devised their variations; and when we rediscover any one of these his wondrous institutions, we seize his mind in its very literal intention.

But as the sciences have developed farther the notion has gained ground that most, perhaps all, of our laws are only approximations. The laws themselves, moreover, have grown so numerous that there is no counting them; and so many rival formulations are proposed in all the branches of science that investigators have become accustomed to the notion that no theory is absolutely a transcript of reality, but that any one of them may from some point of view be useful. Their great use is to summarize old facts and to lead to new ones. They are only a man-made language, a conceptual shorthand, as some one calls them, in which we write our reports of nature; and languages, as is well known, tolerate much choice of expression and many dialects. . . .

"The Object of Linguistics"

Ferdinand de Saussure

Ferdinand de Saussure was born in Geneva, Switzerland, in 1857. He was the son of Henri de Saussure, the great Swiss naturalist. He attended the University of Leipzig and the University of Berlin, where he developed an interest in linguistics. In 1880 he received his doctorate from the University of Leipzig. He returned to the University of Geneva as a professor of language. De Saussure was one of the early pioneers of linguistic studies. His first work in 1879, *Mémoire sur le système primitif des voyelles dans les langues indo-européennes*, was the first of a long series of publications on linguistic science. His best known work, *Cours de linguistique générale*, appeared posthumously. De Saussure died in Vaud in 1913. The following selection is Chapter III from *Course in General Linguistics*, published by Philosophical Library, 1959.

THE OBJECT OF LINGUISTICS

1. *Definition of Language*

What is both the integral and concrete object of linguistics? The question is especially difficult; later we shall see why; here I wish merely to point up the difficulty.

Other sciences work with objects that are given in advance and that can then be considered from different viewpoints; but not linguistics. Someone pronounces the French word *nu* 'bare': a superficial observer would be tempted to call the word a concrete linguistic object; but a more careful examination would reveal successively three or four quite different things, depending on whether the word is considered as a sound, as the expression of an idea, as the equivalent of Latin *nudum,* etc. Far from it being the object that antedates the viewpoint, it would seem that it is the viewpoint that creates the object; besides, nothing tells us in advance that one way of considering the fact in question takes precedence over the others or is in any way superior to them.

Moreover, regardless of the viewpoint that we adopt, the linguistic phenomenon always has two related sides, each deriving its values from the other. For example:

1) Articulated syllables are acoustical impressions perceived by the ear, but the sounds would not exist without the vocal organs; an *n,* for example, exists only by virtue of the relation between the two sides. We simply cannot reduce language to sound or detach sound from oral articulation; reciprocally, we cannot define the movements of the vocal organs without taking into account the acoustical impression.

2) But suppose that sound were a simple thing: would it constitute speech? No, it is only the instrument of thought; by itself, it has no existence. At this point a new and redoubtable relationship arises: a sound, a complex acoustical-vocal unit, combines in turn with an idea to form a complex physiological-psychological unit. But that is still not the complete picture.

3) Speech has both an individual and a social side, and we cannot conceive of one without the other. Besides:

4) Speech always implies both an established system and an evolution; at every moment it is an existing institution and a product of the past. To distinguish between the system and its history, between what it is and what it was, seems very simple at first glance; actually the two things are so closely related that we can scarcely keep them apart. Would we simplify the question by studying the linguistic phenomenon in its earliest stages—if we began, for example, by studying th speech of children? No, for in dealing with speech, it is completely misleading to assume that the problem of early characteristics differs from the problem of

permanent characteristics. We are left inside the vicious circle.

From whatever direction we approach the question, nowhere do we find the integral object of linguistics. Everywhere we are confronted with a dilemma: if we fix our attention on only one side of each problem, we run the risk of failing to perceive the dualities pointed out above; on the other hand, if we study speech from several viewpoints simultaneously, the object of linguistics appears to us as a confused mass of heterogeneous and unrelated things. Either procedure opens the door to several sciences—psychology, anthropology, normative grammar, philology, etc. —which are distinct from linguistics, but which might claim speech, in view of the faulty method of linguistics, as one of their objects.

As I see it there is only one solution to all the foregoing difficulties: *from the very outset we must put both feet on the ground of language and use language as the norm of all other manifestations of speech.* Actually, among so many dualities, language alone seems to lend itself to independent definition and provide a fulcrum that satisfies the mind.

But what is language [*langue*]? It is not to be confused with human speech [*langage*], of which it is only a definite part, though certainly an essential one. It is both a social product of the faculty of speech and a collection of necessary conventions that have been adopted by a social body to permit individuals to exercise that faculty. Taken as a whole, speech is many-sided and heterogeneous; straddling several areas simultaneously—physical, physiological, and psychological—it belongs both to the individual and to society; we cannot put it into any category of human facts, for we cannot discover its unity.

Language, on the contrary, is a self-contained whole and a principle of classification. As soon as we give language first place among the facts of speech, we introduce a natural order into a mass that lends itself to no other classification.

One might object to that principle of classification on the ground since the use of speech is based on a natural faculty whereas language is something acquired and conventional, language should not take first place but should be subordinated to the natural instinct.

That objection is easily refuted.

First, no one has proved that speech, as it manifests itself when we speak, is entirely natural, i.e. that our vocal apparatus was designed for speaking just as our legs were designed for walking. Linguists are far from agreement on this point. For instance Whitney, to whom language is one of several social institutions, thinks that we use the vocal apparatus as the instrument of language purely through luck, for the sake of convenience: men might just as well have chosen gestures and used visual symbols instead of acoustical symbols. Doubtless his thesis is too dogmatic; language is not similar in all respects to other social institutions; moreover, Whitney goes too far in saying that our choice happened to fall on the vocal organs; the choice was more or less imposed by nature. But on the essential point the American linguist is right: language is a convention, and the nature of the sign that is agreed upon does not matter. The question of the vocal apparatus obviously takes a secondary place in the problem of speech.

One definition of *articulated speech* might confirm that conclusion. In Latin, *articulus* means a member, part, or subdivision of a sequence; applied to speech, articulation designates either the subdivision of a spoken chain into syllables or the subdivision of the chain of meanings into significant units; *gegliederte Sprache* is used in the second sense in German. Using the second definition, we can say that what is natural to mankind is not oral speech but the faculty of constructing a language, i.e. a system of distinct signs corresponding to distinct ideas.

Broca discovered that the faculty of speech is localized in the third left frontal convolution; his discovery has been used to substantiate the attribution of a natural quality to speech. But we know that the same part of the brain is the center of *everything* that has to do with speech, including writing. The preceding statements, together with observations that have been made in different cases of aphasia resulting from lesion of the centers of localization, seem to indicate: (1) that the various disorders of oral speech are bound up in a hundred ways with those of written speech; and (2) that what is lost in all cases of aphasia or agraphia is less the faculty of producing a given sound or writing a given sign than the ability to evoke by means of an instrument, regardless of what it is, the signs of a regular system of speech. The obvious implication is that beyond the functioning of the various organs there exists a more general faculty which governs signs and which would be the linguistic faculty proper. And this brings us to the same conclusion as above.

To give language first place in the study of speech, we can advance a final argument: the faculty of articulating words—whether it is natural or not—is exercised only with the help of the instrument created by a collectivity and provided for its use; therefore, to say that language gives unity to speech is not fanciful.

2. *Place of Language in the Facts of Speech*

In order to separate from the whole speech the part that belongs to language, we must examine the individual act from which the speaking-circuit can be reconstructed. The act requires the presence of at least two persons; that is the minimum number necessary to complete the circuit. Suppose that two people, A and B, are conversing with each other.

A   B

Suppose that the opening of the circuit is in A's brain, where mental facts (concepts) are associated with representations of the linguistic sounds (sound-images) that are used for their expression. A given concept unlocks a corresponding sound-image in the brain; this purely *psychological* phenomenon is followed in turn by a *physiological* process: the brain transmits an impulse corresponding to the image to the organs used in producing sounds. Then the sound waves travel from the mouth of A to the ear of B: a purely *physical process*. Next, the circuit continues in B, but the order is reversed: from the ear to the brain, the physiological transmission of the sound-image; in the brain, the psychological association of the image with the corresponding concept. If B then speaks, the new act will follow—from his brain to A's—exactly the same course as the first act and pass through the same successive phases, which I shall diagram as follows:

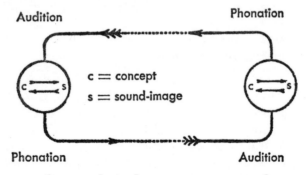

The preceding analysis does not purport to be complete. We might also single out the pure acoustical sensation, the identification of that sensation with the latent sound-image, the muscular image of phonation, etc. I have included only the elements thought to be essential, but the drawing brings out at a glance the distinction between the physical (sound waves), physiological (phonation and audition), and psychological parts (word-images and concepts). Indeed, we should not fail to note that the word-image stands apart from the sound itself and that it is just as psychological as the concept which is associated with it.

The circuit that I have outlined can be further divided into:

a) an outer part that includes the vibrations of the sounds which travel from the mouth to the ear, and an inner part that includes everything else;

b) a psychological and a nonpsychological part, the second including the physiological productions of the vocal organs as well as the physical facts that are outside the individual;

c) an active and a passive part: everything that goes from the associative center of the speaker to the ear of the listener is active, and everything that goes from the ear of the listener to his associative center is passive;

d) finally, everything that is active in the psychological part of the circuit is executive ($c \rightarrow s$), and everything that is passive is receptive ($s \rightarrow c$),

We should also add the associative and co-ordinating faculty that we find as soon as we leave isolated signs; this faculty plays the dominant role in the organization of language as a system.

But to understand clearly the role of the associative and coordinating faculty, we must leave the individual act, which is only the embryo of speech, and approach the social fact.

Among all the individuals that are linked together by speech, some sort of average will be set up: all will reproduce—not exactly of course, but approximately—the same signs united with the same concepts.

How does the social crystallization of language come about? Which parts of the circuit are involved? For all parts probably do not participate equally in it.

The nonpsychological part can be rejected from the outset. When we hear people speaking a language that we do not know, we perceive the sounds but remain outside the social fact because we do not understand them.

Neither is the psychological part of the circuit wholly responsible: the executive side is missing, for execution is never carried out by the collectivity. Execution is always individual, and the individual is always its master: I shall call the executive side *speaking* [*parole*].

Through the functioning of the receptive and co-ordinating faculties, impressions that are perceptibly the same for all are made on the minds of speakers. How can that social product be pictured in such a way that language will stand apart from everything else? If we could embrace the sum of word-images stored in the minds of all individuals, we could identify the social bond that constitutes language. It is a storehouse filled by the members of a given community through their active use of speaking, a grammatical system that has a potential existence in each brain, or, more specifically, in the brains of a group of individuals. For language is not complete in any speaker; it exists perfectly only within a collectivity.

In separating language from speaking we are at the same time separating: (1) what is social from what is individual; and (2) what is essential from what is accessory and more or less accidental.

Language is not a function of the speaker; it is a product that is passively assimilated by the individual. It never requires premeditation, and reflection enters in only for the purpose of classification, which we shall take up later.

Speaking, on the contrary, is an individual act. It is wilful and intellectual. Within the act, we should distinguish between: (1) the combinations by which the speaker uses the language code for expressing his own thought; and (2) the psychophysical mechanism that allows him to exteriorize those combinations.

Note that I have defined things rather than words; these definitions are not endangered by certain ambiguous words that do not have identical meanings in different languages. For instance, German *Sprache* means both "language" and "speech"; *Rede* almost corresponds to "speaking" but adds the special connotation of "discourse." Latin *sermo* designates both "speech" and "speaking," while *lingua* means "language," etc. No word corresponds exactly to any of the notions specified above; that is why all definitions of words are made in vain; starting from words in defining things is a bad procedure.

To summarize, these are the characteristics of language:

1) Language is a well-defined object in the heterogeneous mass of speech facts. It can be localized in the limited segment of the speaking-circuit where an auditory image becomes associated with a concept. It is the social side of speech, outside the individual who can never create nor modify it by himself; it exists only by virtue of a sort of contract signed by the members of a community. Moreover, the individual must always serve an apprenticeship in order to learn the functioning of language; a child assimilates it only gradually. It is such a distinct thing that a man deprived of the use of speaking retains it provided that he understands the vocal signs that he hears.

2) Language, unlike speaking, is something that we can study separately. Although dead languages are no longer spoken, we can easily assimilate their linguistic organisms. We can dispense with the other elements of speech; indeed, the science of language is possible only if the other elements are excluded.

3) Whereas speech is heterogeneous, language, as defined, is homogeneous. It is a system of signs in which the only essential thing is the union of meanings and sound-images, and in which both parts of the sign are psychological.

4) Language is concrete, no less so than speaking; and this is a help in our study of it. Linguistic signs, though basically psychological, are not abstractions; associations which bear the stamp of collective approval—and which added together constitute language—are realities that have their seat in the brain. Besides, linguistic signs are tangible; it is possible to reduce them to conventional written symbols, whereas it would be impossible to provide detailed photographs of acts of speaking [*actes de parole*]; the pronunciation of even the smallest word represents an infinite number of muscular movements that could be identified

and put into graphic form only with great difficulty. In language, on the contrary, there is only the sound-image, and the latter can be translated into a fixed visual image. For if we disregard the vast number of movements necessary for the realization of sound-images in speaking, we see that each sound-image is nothing more than the sum of a limited number of elements or phonemes that can in turn be called up by a corresponding number of written symbols. The very possibility of putting the things that relate to language into graphic form allows dictionaries and grammars to represent it accurately, for language is a storehouse of sound-images, and writing is the tangible form of those images.

3. *Place of Language in Human Facts: Semiology*

The foregoing characteristics of language reveal an even more important characteristic. Language, once its boundaries have been marked off within the speech data, can be classified among human phenomena, whereas speech cannot.

We have just seen that language is a social institution; but several features set it apart from other political, legal, etc. institutions. We must call in a new type of facts in order to illuminate the special nature of language.

Language is a system of signs that express ideas, and is therefore comparable to a system of writing, the alphabet of deaf-mutes, symbolic rites, polite formulas, military signals, etc. But it is the most important of all these systems.

A *science that studies the life of signs within society* is conceivable; it would be a part of social psychology and consequently of general psychology; I shall call it *semiology*[1] (from Greek *sēmeîon* 'sign'). Semiology would show what constitutes signs, what laws govern them. Since the science does not yet exist, no one can say what it would be; but it has a right to existence, a place staked out in ad-

---

[1] *Semiology* should not be confused with *semantics*, which changes in meaning, and which Saussure did not treat methodically; the fundamental principle of semantics is formulated on page 75. [Ed.]

vance. Linguistics is only a part of the general science of semiology; the laws discovered by semiology will be applicable to linguistics, and the latter will circumscribe a well-defined area within the mass of anthropological facts.

To determine the exact place of semiology is the task of the psychologist.[2] The task of the linguist is to find out what makes language a special system within the mass of semiological data. This issue will be taken up again later; here I wish merely to call attention to one thing: if I have succeeded in assigning linguistics a place among the sciences, it is because I have related it to semiology.

Why has semiology not yet been recognized as an independent science with its own object like all the other sciences? Linguists have been going around in circles: language, better than anything else, offers a basis for understanding the semiological problem; but language must, to put it correctly, be studied in itself; heretofore language has almost always been studied in connection with something else, from other viewpoints.

There is first of all the superficial notion of the general public: people see nothing more than a name-giving system in language, thereby prohibiting any research into its true nature.

Then there is the viewpoint of the psychologist, who studies the sign-mechanism in the individual; this is the easiest method, but it does not lead beyond individual execution and does not reach the sign, which is social.

Or even when signs are studied from a social viewpoint, only the traits that attach language to the other social institutions—those that are more or less voluntary—are emphasized; as a result, the goal is by-passed and the specific characteristics of semiological systems in general and of language in particular are completely ignored. For the distinguishing characteristic of the sign—but the one that

---

[2] Cf. A. Naville, *Classification des Sciences*, (2nd. ed.), p. 104. [Ed.] The scope of semiology (or semiotics) is treated at length in Charles Morris' *Signs, Language and Behavior* (New York: Prentice-Hall, 1946). [Tr.]

is least apparent at first sight—is that in some way it always eludes the individual or social will.

In short, the characteristic that distinguishes semiological systems from all other institutions shows up clearly only in language where it manifests itself in the things which are studied least, and the necessity or specific value of a semiological science is therefore not clearly recognized. But to me the language problem is mainly semiological, and all developments derive their significance from that important fact. If we are to discover the true nature of language we must learn what it has in common with all other semiological systems; linguistic forces that seem very important at first glance (e.g., the role of the vocal apparatus) will receive only secondary consideration if they serve only to set language apart from the other systems. This procedure will do more than to clarify the linguistic problem. By studying rites, customs, etc. as signs, I believe that we shall throw new light on the facts and point up the need for including them in a science of semiology and explaining them by its laws.

"Thoughts, Words and Things"

C. K. Ogden and I. A. Richards

Born in 1899, Charles Kay Ogden attended Magdalene
College, Cambridge University, where he achieved first class
honors in the classical tripos in 1910. While at Cambridge he
founded and served as editor of the *Cambridge Magazine*. He
soon became interested in language study and traveled in
Europe to increase his knowledge. The fruits of this interest
appeared in 1923 when he published, in collaboration with
I. A. Richards, *The Meaning of Meaning*. Ogden became
interested in the problem of communication with emphasis
on the simplification of language. In 1928 he published
Basic English, which was a limited collection of English
words and phrases designed to fit ordinary communication
needs. Up until the time he died in 1957, Ogden continued
his investigation of the problems of basic English. I. A.
Richards was born in 1893. He attended Magdalene College, Cambridge University, where he took first honors in
the moral science tripos in 1915. Since that time he has
served as a professor and visiting lecturer on language, literature, and criticism at universities in England, the United
States, and the Far East. His major works also include
*Principles of Literary Criticism; Practical Criticism; Coler-
idge on the Imagination;* and *Basic English and Uses.* The
selection here is Chapter I of *The Meaning of Meaning* and
is reprinted by permission of Harcourt, Brace, & World, Inc.

T HE influence of Language upon Thought has attracted
the attention of the wise and foolish alike, since Lao Tse
came long ago to the conclusion—

"He who knows does not speak, he who speaks does not
know."

Sometimes, in fact, the wise have in this field proved themselves the most foolish. Was it not the great Bentley, Master of Trinity College, Cambridge, Archdeacon of Bristol, and holder of two other livings besides, who declared: "We are sure, from the names of persons and places mentioned in Scripture before the Deluge, not to insist upon other arguments, that Hebrew was the primitive language of mankind"? On the opposite page are collected other remarks on the subject of language and its Meaning, and whether wise or foolish, they at least raise questions to which, sooner or later, an answer is desirable. In recent years, indeed, the existence and importance of this problem of Meaning have been generally admitted, but by some sad chance those who have attempted a solution have too often been forced to relinquish their ambition—whether through old age, like Leibnitz, or penury, like C. S. Peirce, or both. Even the methods by which it is to be attacked have remained in doubt. Each science has tended to delegate the unpleasant task to another. With the errors and omissions of metaphysicians we shall be much concerned in the sequel, and philologists must bear their share of the guilt. Yet it is a philologist who, of recent years, has, perhaps, realized most clearly the necessity of a broader treatment.

"Throughout the whole history of the human race," wrote the late Dr. Postgate, "there have been no questions which have caused more heart-searchings, tumults, and devastation than questions of the correspondence of words to facts. The mere mention of such words as 'religion,' 'patriotism,' and 'property' is sufficient to demonstrate this truth. Now, it is the investigation of the nature of the correspondence between word and fact, to use these terms in the widest sense, which is the proper and the highest problem of the science of meaning. That every living word is rooted in facts of our mental consciousness and history it would be impossible to gainsay; but it is a very different matter to determine what these facts may be. The primitive conception is undoubtedly that the name is indicative, or descriptive, of the thing. From which it would follow at once that from the presence of the name you could argue to the existence of the thing. This is the simple conception of the savage."

In thus stressing the need for a clear analysis of the relation between words and facts as the essential of a theory of Meaning, Dr. Postgate himself was fully aware that at some point the philosophical and psychological aspects of that theory cannot be avoided. When he wrote (1896), the hope was not unreasonable that the science of Semantics would do something to bridge the gulf. But, although M. Bréal's researches drew attention to a number of fascinating phenomena in the history of language, and awakened a fresh interest in the educational possibilities of etymology, the net result was disappointing. That such disappointment was inevitable may be seen, if we consider the attitude to language implied by such a passage as the following. The use of words as though their meaning were fixed, the constant resort to loose metaphor, the hypostatization of leading terms, all indicate an unsuitable attitude in which to approach the question.

"Substantives are signs attached to things: they contain exactly that amount of truth which can be contained by a name, an amount which is of necessity small in proportion to the reality of the object. That which is most adequate to its object is the abstract noun, since it represents a simple operation of the mind. When I use the two words *compressibility, immortality,* all that is to be found in the idea is to be found also in the word. But if I take a real entity, an object existing in nature, it will be impossible for language to introduce into the word all the ideas which this entity or object awakens in the mind. Language is therefore compelled to choose. Out of all the ideas it can choose one only; it thus creates a name which is not long in becoming a mere sign.

"For this name to be accepted it must, no doubt, originally possess some true and striking characteristic on one side or another; it must satisfy the minds of those to whom it is first submitted. But this condition is imperative only at the outset. Once accepted, it rids itself rapidly of its etymological signification; otherwise this signification might become an embarrassment. Many objects are inaccurately named, whether through the ignorance of the original authors, or by some intervening change which disturbs the harmony between the sign and the thing signified. Nevertheless, words answer the same purpose as though they were of faultless accuracy. No one dreams of revising them. They are accepted by a tacit consent of which we are not even conscious" (Bréal's *Semantics,* pp. 171-2).

What exactly is to be made of substantives which "contain" truth, "that amount of truth which can be contained by a name"? How can "all that is found in the idea be also found in the word"? The conception of language as "compelled to choose an idea," and thereby creating "a name which is not long in becoming a sign," is an odd one; while 'accuracy' and 'harmony' are sadly in need of elucidation when applied to naming and to the relation between sign and thing signified respectively. This is not mere captious criticism. The locutions objected to conceal the very facts which the science of language is concerned to elucidate. The real task before that science cannot be successfully attempted without a far more critical consciousness of the dangers of such loose verbiage. It is impossible to handle a scientific matter in such metaphorical terms, and the training of philologists has not, as a rule, been such as to increase their command of analytic and abstract language. The logician would be far better equipped in this respect were it not that his command of language tends to conceal from him what he is talking about and renders him prone to accept purely linguistic constructions, which serve well enough for his special purposes, as ultimates.

How great is the tyranny of language over those who propose to inquire into its workings is well shown in the speculations of the late F. de Saussure, a writer regarded by perhaps a majority of French and Swiss students as having for the first time placed linguistic upon a scientific basis. This author begins by inquiring, "What is the object at once integral and concrete of linguistic?" He does not ask whether it has one, he obeys blindly the primitive impulse to infer from a word some object for which it stands, and sets out determined to find it. But, he continues, speech (*le langage*), though concrete enough, as a set of events is not integral. Its sounds imply movements of speech, and both, as instruments of thought, imply ideas. Ideas, he adds, have a social as well as an individual side, and at each instant language implies both an established system and an evolution. "Thus, from whatever side we approach the question, we nowhere find the integral object of linguistic." De Saussure does not pause at this point to ask himself what he is looking for, on whether there is any reason why there should be such a thing. He proceeds instead in a fashion familiar in the beginnings of all sciences, and concocts a suitable object—'*la langue*,' the language, as opposed to speech. "What is *la langue*? For us, it is not to be confounded with speech (*le langage*); it is only a determinate part of this, an essential part, it is true. It is at once a social product of the faculty of speech, and a collection of necessary conventions adopted by the social body to allow the exercise of this faculty by individuals. . . . It is a whole in itself and a principle of classification. As soon as we give it the first place among the facts of speech we introduce a natural order in a whole which does not lend itself to any other classification." *La langue* is further "the sum of the verbal images stored up in all the individuals, a treasure deposited by the practice of speaking in the members of a given community; a grammatical system, virtually existing in each brain, or more exactly in the brains of a body of individuals; for *la langue* is not complete in any one of them, it exists in perfection only in the mass."[1]

Such an elaborate construction as *la langue* might, no doubt, be arrived at by some Method of Intensive Distraction analogous to that with which Dr. Whitehead's name is associated, but as a guiding principle for a young science it is fantastic. Moreover, the same device of inventing verbal entities outside the range of possible investigation proved

---

[1] *Cours de Linguistique Générale*, pp. 23-31.

fatal to the theory of signs which followed.[2]

As a philologist with an inordinate respect for linguistic convention, de Saussure could not bear to tamper with what he imagined to be a fixed meaning, a part of *la langue*. This scrupulous regard for fictitious 'accepted' uses of words is a frequent trait in philologists. Its roots go down very deep into human nature, as we shall see in the two chapters which follow. It is especially regrettable that a technical equipment, otherwise excellent, should have been so weak at this point, for the initial recognition of a general science of signs, 'semiology,' of which linguistic would be a branch, and the most important branch, was a very notable attempt in the right direction. Unfortunately this theory of signs, by neglecting entirely the things for which signs stand, was from the beginning cut off from any contact with scientific methods of verification. De Saussure, however, does not appear to have pursued the matter far enough for this defect to become obvious. The same neglect also renders the more recent treatise of Professor Delacroix, *Le Langage et la Pensée*, ineffective as a study of the influence of language upon thought.

---

[2] A sign for de Saussure is twofold, made up of a concept (signifié) and an acoustic image (signifiant), both psychical entities. Without the concept, he says, the acoustic image would not be a sign (p. 100). The disadvantage of this account is, as we shall see, that the process of interpretation is included by definition in the sign.

De Saussure actually prided himself upon having "defined things and not words." The definitions thus established "have nothing to fear," he writes, "from certain ambiguous terms which do not coincide in one language and another. Thus in German *Sprache* means 'langue' and *langage*.' . . . In Latin *sermo* rather signifies *language et parole* while *lingua* designates 'la langue,' and so on. No word corresponds exactly to any of the notions made precise above: this is why every definition made apropos of a word is idle; it is a bad method, to start from words to define things" (*ibid,*. p. 32). The view of definition here adopted implies, as will be shown later, remarkable ignorance of the normal procedure—the substitution, namely, of better understood for obscure symbols. Another specimen of this naïveté is found in the rejection of the term 'symbol' to designate the linguistic sign (p. 103). "The symbol has the character of never being quite arbitrary. It is not empty; there is the rudiment of a natural tie between the signifying and the signified. The symbol for justice, the scales, could not be replaced by something else at random, a carriage for instance."

Philosophers and philologists alike have failed in their attempts. There remains a third group of inquirers with an interest in linguistic theory, the ethnologists, many of whom have come to their subject after a preliminary training in psychology. An adequate account of primitive peoples is impossible without an insight into the essentials of their languages, which cannot be gained through a mere transfer of current Indo-European grammatical distinctions, a procedure only too often positively misleading. In the circumstances, each field investigator might be supposed to reconstruct the grammar of a primitive tongue from his own observations of the behaviour of a speaker in a given situation. Unfortunately this is rarely done, since the difficulties are very great; and perhaps owing to accidents of psychological terminology, the worker tends to neglect the concrete environment of the speaker and to consider only the 'ideas' which are regarded as 'expressed.' Thus Dr. Boas, the most suggestive and influential of the group of ethnologists which is dealing with the vast subject-matter provided by the American-Indian languages, formulates as the three points to be considered in the objective discussion of languages—

First, the constituent phonetic elements of the language;

Second, the groups of ideas expressed by phonetic groups;

Third, the method of combining and modifying phonetic groups.

"All speech," says Dr. Boas explicitly, "is intended to serve for the communication of ideas." Ideas, however, are only remotely accessible to outside inquirers, and we need a theory which connects words with things through the ideas, if any, which they symbolize. We require, that is to say, separate analyses of the relations of words to ideas and of ideas to things. Further, much language, especially primitive language, is not primarily concerned with ideas at all, unless under 'ideas' are included emotions and attitudes—a procedure which would involve terminological inconveniences. The omission of all separate treatment of the ways in which speech, besides conveying ideas, also expresses attitudes, desires and intentions,[3] is another point at which the work of this active school is at present defective.

In yet another respect all these specialists fail to realize the deficiencies of current linguistic theory. Preoccupied as they are—ethnologists with recording the details of fast vanishing languages; philologists with an elaborate technique of phonetic laws and principles of derivation; philosophers with 'philosophy'—all have overlooked the pressing need for a better understanding of what actually occurs in discussion. The analysis of the process of communication is partly psychological, and psychology has now reached a stage at which this part may be successfully undertaken. Until this had happened the science of Symbolism necessarily remained in abeyance, but there is no longer any excuse for vague talk about Meaning, and ignorance of the ways in which words deceive us.

Throughout the Western world it is agreed that people

------

[3] Not that definitions are lacking which include more than ideas. Thus in one of the ablest and most interesting of modern linguistic studies, that of E. Sapir, Chief of the Anthropological Section, Geological Survey of Canada, an ethnologist closely connected with the American school, language is defined as "a purely human and non-instinctive method of communicating ideas, emotions and desires by means of a system of voluntarily produced symbols" (*Language*, 1922, p. 7). But so little is the emotive element considered that in a discussion of grammatical form, as shown by the great variation of word-order in Latin, we find it stated that the change from 'hominem femina videt' to 'videt femina hominem' makes "little or no difference beyond, *possibly*, a rhetorical or a *stylistic* one" (p. 65). The italics are ours; and the same writer sums up his discussion of the complex symbol 'The farmer kills the duckling,' with the remark: "In this short sentence of five words there are expressed thirteen distinct concepts" (p. 93). As will be noted at a later stage, the use of the term 'concept' is particularly unfortunate in such an analysis, and a vocabulary so infested with current metaphysical confusions leads unavoidably to incompleteness of treatment.

By being forced to include under 'concepts' both 'concrete concepts'— material objects, and 'Pure relational concepts' (abstract ways of referring). Sapir is unable in this work—which was unfortunately never followed by his projected volume on Linguistics—to make even the distinctions which are essential inside symbolic language (cf. Chapter V., p. 101 *infra*); and when we come to deal with translation (Chapter X., p. 228) we shall find that this vocabulary has proved equally unserviceable to him.

must meet frequently, and that it is not only agreeable to talk, but that it is a matter of common courtesy to say something even when there is hardly anything to say. "Every civilized man," continues the late Professor Mahaffy, to whose *Principles of the Art of Conversation* we owe this observation, "feels, or ought to feel, this duty; it is the universal accomplishment which all must practise"; those who fail are punished by the dislike or neglect of society.

There is no doubt an Art in saying something when there is nothing to be said, but it is equally certain that there is an Art no less important of saying clearly what one wishes to say when there is an abundance of material; and conversation will seldom attain even the level of an intellectual pastime if adequate methods of Interpretation are not also available.

Symbolism is the study of the part played in human affairs by language and symbols of all kinds, and especially of their influence on Thought. It singles out for special inquiry the ways in which symbols help us and hinder us in reflecting on things.

Symbols direct and organize, record and communicate. In stating what they direct and organize, record and communicate we have to distinguish as always between Thoughts and Things.[4] It is Thought (or, as we shall usually say, *reference*) which is directed and organized, and it is also Thought which is recorded and communicated. But just as we say that the gardener mows the lawn when we know that it is the lawn-mower which actually does the cutting, so, though we

---

[4] The word 'thing' is unsuitable for the analysis here undertaken, because in popular usage it is restricted to material substances—a fact which has led philosophers to favour the terms 'entity,' 'ens' or 'object' as the general name for whatever is. It has seemed desirable, therefore, to introduce a technical term to stand for whatever we may be thinking of or referring to. 'Object,' though this is its original use, has had an unfortunate history. The word 'referent,' therefore, has been adopted, though its etymological form is open to question when considered in relation to other participial derivatives, such as agent or reagent. But even in Latin the present participle occasionally (e.g. *vehens* in equo) admitted of variation in use: and in English an analogy with substantives, such as 'reagent,' 'extent,' and 'incident' may be urged. Thus the fact that 'referent' in what follows stands for a thing and not an active person, should cause no confusion.

know that the direct relation of symbols is with thought, we also say that symbols record events and communicate facts.

By leaving out essential elements in the language situation we easily raise problems and difficulties which vanish when the whole transaction is considered in greater detail. Words, as every one now knows, 'mean' nothing by themselves, although the belief that they did, as we shall see in the next chapter, was once equally universal. It is only when a thinker makes use of them that they stand for anything, or, in one sense, have 'meaning.' They are instruments. But besides this referential use which for all reflective, intellectual use of language should be paramount, words have other functions which may be grouped together as emotive. These can best be examined when the framework of the problem of strict statement and intellectual communication has been set up. The importance of the emotive aspects of language is not thereby minimized, and anyone chiefly concerned with popular or primitive speech might well be led to reverse this order of approach. Many difficulties, indeed, arising through the behaviour of words in discussion, even amongst scientists, force us at an early stage to take into account these 'non-symbolic' influences. But for the analysis of the senses of 'meaning' with which we are here chiefly concerned, it is desirable to begin with the relations of thoughts, words and things as they are found in cases of reflective speech uncomplicated by emotional, diplomatic, or other disturbances; and with regard to these, the indirectness of the relations between words and things is the feature which first deserves attention.

This may be simply illustrated by a diagram, in which the three factors involved whenever any statement is made, or understood, are placed at the corners of the triangle, the relations which hold between them being represented by the sides. The point just made can be restated by saying that in this respect the base of the triangle is quite different in composition from either of the other sides.

Between a thought and a symbol causal relations hold. When we speak, the symbolism we employ is caused partly by the reference we are making and partly by social and psychological factors—the purpose for which we are making the reference, the proposed effect of our symbols on other persons, and our own attitude. When we hear what is said, the symbols both cause us to perform an act of reference and to assume an attitude which will, according to circumstances, be more or less similar to the act and the attitude of the speaker.

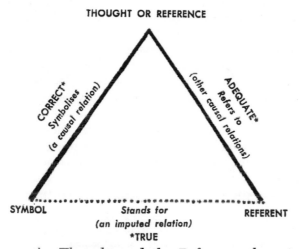

THOUGHT OR REFERENCE

CORRECT* Symbolises (a causal relation)

ADEQUATE* Refers to (other causal relations)

SYMBOL — Stands for (an imputed relation) — REFERENT

*TRUE

Between the Thought and the Reference there is also a relation; more or less direct (as when we think about or attend to a coloured surface we see), or indirect (as when we 'think of' or 'refer to' Napoleon), in which case there may be a very long chain of sign-situations intervening between the act and its referent: word—historian—contemporary record—eye-witness—referent (Napoleon).

Between the symbol and the referent there is no relevant relation other than the indirect one, which consists in its being used by someone to stand for a referent. Symbol and Referent, that is to say, are not connected directly (and when, for grammatical reasons, we imply such a relation, it will merely be an imputed,[6] as opposed to a real rela-

* Cf. Chapter V., pp. 101-2.
[6] See Chapter VI., p. 116.

tion) but only indirectly round the two sides of the triangle.[7]

It may appear unnecessary to insist that there is no direct connection between say 'dog,' the word, and certain common objects in our streets, and that the only connection which holds is that which consists in our using the word when we refer to the animal. We shall find, however, that the kind of simplification typified by this once universal theory of direct meaning relations between words and things is the source of almost all the difficulties which thought encounters. As will appear at a later stage, the power to confuse and obstruct, which such simplifications possess, is largely due to the conditions of communication. Language if it is to be used must be a *ready* instrument. The handiness and ease of a phrase is always more important in deciding whether it will be extensively used than its accuracy. Thus such shorthand as the word 'means' is constantly used so as to imply a direct simple relation between words and things, phrases and situations. If such relations could be admitted then there would of course be no problem as to the nature of Meaning, and the

---

[7] An exceptional case occurs when the symbol used is more or less directly like the referent for which it is used, as for instance, it may be when it is an onomatopoeic word, or an image, or a gesture, or a drawing. In this case the triangle is completed; its base is supplied, and a great simplification of the problem involved appears to result. For this reason many attempts have been made to reduce the normal language situation to this possibly more primitive form. Its greater completeness does no doubt account for the immense superiority in efficiency of gesture languages, within their appropriate field, to other languages not supportable by gesture within *their* fields. Hence we know far more perfectly what has occurred if a scene is well re-enacted than if it be merely described. But in the normal situation we have to recognize that our triangle is without its base, that between Symbol and Referent no direct relation holds; and, further, that it is through this lack that most of the problems of language arise. Simulative and non-simulative languages are entirely distinct in principle. Standing for and representing are different relations. It is, however, convenient to speak at times as though there were some direct relation holding between Symbol and Referent. We then say, on the analogy of the lawn-mower, that a Symbol refers to a Referent. Provided that the telescopic nature of the phrase is not forgotten, confusion need not arise. In Supplement I., Part V, *infra*, Dr. Malinowski gives a valuable account of the development of the speech situation in relation to the above diagram.

vast majority of those who have been concerned with it would have been right in their refusal to discuss it. But too many interesting developments have been occurring in the sciences, through the rejection of everyday symbolizations and the endeavour to replace them by more accurate accounts, for any naïve theory that 'meaning' is just 'meaning' to be popular at the moment. As a rule new facts in startling disagreement with accepted explanations of other facts are required before such critical analyses of what are generally regarded as simple satisfactory notions are undertaken. This has been the case with the recent revolutions in physics. But in addition great reluctance to postulate anything *sui generis* and of necessity undetectable[8] was needed before the simple natural notion of simultaneity, for instance, as a two-termed relation came to be questioned. Yet to such questionings the theory of Relativity was due. The same two motives, new discrepant facts, and distaste for the use of obscure kinds of entities in eking out explanations, have led to disturbances in psychology, though here the required restatements have not yet been provided. No Copernican revolution has yet occurred, although several are due if psychology is to be brought into line with its fellow sciences.

It is noteworthy, however, that recent stirrings in psychology have been mainly if not altogether concerned with feeling and volition. The popular success of the Psycho-analysis has tended to divert attention from the older problem of thinking. Yet in so far as progress here has consequence for all the other sciences and for the whole technique of investigation in psychology itself, this central problem of knowing or of 'meaning' is perhaps better worth scrutiny and more likely to promote fresh orientations than any other that can be suggested. As the Behaviorists have also very properly pointed out, this question is closely connected with the use of words.

But the approach to Meaning, far more than the approach to such problems as those of physics, requires a thorough-

---

[8] Places and instants are very typical entities of verbal origin.

going investigation of language. Every great advance in physics has been at the expense of some generally accepted piece of metaphysical explanation which has enshrined itself in a convenient, universally practised, symbolic shorthand. But the confusion and obstruction due to such shorthand expressions and to the naive theories they protect and keep alive, is greater in psychology, and especially in the theory of knowledge, than elsewhere; because no problem is so infected with so-called metaphysical difficulties—due here, as always, to an approach to a question through symbols without an initial investigation of their functions.

We have now to consider more closely what the causes and effects of symbols are[9]. Whatever may be the services, other than conservative and retentive, of symbolization, all experience shows that there are also disservices. The grosser forms of verbal confusion have long been recognized; but less attention has been paid to those that are more subtle and more frequent. In the following chapters many examples of these will be given, chosen in great part from philosophical fields, for it is here that such confusions become, with the passage of time, most apparent. The root of the trouble will be traced to the superstition that words are in some way parts of things or always imply things corresponding to them, historical instances of this still potent instinctive belief being given from many sources. The fundamental and most prolific fallacy is, in other words, that the base of the triangle given above is filled in.

The completeness of any reference varies; it is more or less close and clear, it 'grasps' its object in greater or less degree. Such symbolization as accompanies it—images of

---

[9] Whether symbols in some form or other are necessary to thought itself is a difficult problem, and is discussed in *The Meaning of Psychology* (Chapter XIII.) as well as in Chapter X, of the present work. But certainly the recording and the communication of thought (telepathy apart) require symbols. It seems that thought, so far as it is transitive and not in the form of an internal dialogue, can dispense with symbols, and that they only appear when thought takes on this monologue form. In the normal case the actual development of thought is very closely bound up with the symbolization which accompanies it.

all sorts, words, sentences whole and in pieces—is in no very close observable connection with the variation in the perfection of the reference. Since, then, in any discussion we cannot immediately settle from the nature of a person's remarks what his opinion is, we need some technique to keep the parties to an argument in contact and to clear up misunderstandings—or, in other words, a Theory of Definition. Such a technique can only be provided by a theory of knowing, or of references, which will avoid, as current theories do not, the attribution to the knower of powers which it may be pleasant for him to suppose himself to possess, but which are not open to the only kind of investigation hitherto profitably pursued, the kind generally known as scientific investigation.

Normally, whenever we hear anything said we spring spontaneously to an immediate conclusion, namely, that the speaker is referring to what we should be referring to were we speaking the words ourselves. In some cases this interpretation may be correct; this will prove to be what he has referred to. But in most discussions which attempt greater subtleties than could be handled in a gesture language this will not be so. To suppose otherwise is to neglect our subsidiary gesture languages, whose accuracy within their limited provinces is "far higher than that yet reached by any system of spoken or written symbols, with the exception of the quite special and peculiar case of mathematical, scientific and musical notations. Words, whenever they cannot directly ally themselves with and support themselves upon gestures, are at present a very imperfect means of communication. Even for private thinking thought is often ready to advance, and only held back by the treachery of its natural symbolism; and for conversational purposes the latitude acquired constantly shows itself to all those who make any serious attempts to compare opinions.

We have not here in view the more familiar ways in which words may be used to deceive. In a later chapter, when the function of language as an instrument for the *promotion of purposes* rather than as a means of *symbolizing references* is fully discussed, we shall see how the intention of the speaker may complicate the situation. But the *honnête homme* may be unprepared for the lengths to which verbal ingenuity can be carried. At all times these possibilities have been exploited to the full by interpretors of Holy Writ who desire to enjoy the best of both worlds. Here, for example, is a specimen of the exegetic of the late Dr. Lyman Abbott, pastor, publicist, and editor, which, through the efforts of Mr. Upton Sinclair, has now become classic. Does Christianity condemn the methods of twentieth-century finance? Doubtless there are some awkward words in the Gospels, but a little 'interpretation' is all that is necessary.

> "Jesus did not say 'Lay not up for yourselves treasures upon earth.' He said 'Lay not up for yourselves treasures upon earth *where moth and rust doth corrupt and where thieves break through and steal.*' And no sensible American does. Moth and rust do not get at Mr. Rockefeller's oil wells, and thieves do not often break through and steal a railway. What Jesus condemned was hoarding wealth."

Each investment, therefore, every worldly acquisition, according to one of the leading divines of the New World, may be judged on its merits. There is no hard and fast rule. When moth and rust have been eliminated by science the Christian investor will presumably have no problem, but in the meantime it would seem that Camphorated Oil fulfills most nearly the synoptic requirements. Burglars are not partial to it; it is anathema to moth; and the risk of rust is completely obviated.

Another variety of verbal ingenuity closely allied to this, is the deliberate use of symbols to misdirect the listener. Apologies for such a practice in the case of the madman from whom we desire to conceal the whereabouts of his razor are well known, but a wider justification has also been attempted. In the Christian era we hear of "falsifications of documents, inventions of legends, and forgeries of every description which made the Catholic Church a veritable seat of lying."[10] A play upon words in which one sense is taken by the speaker and another sense intended by him for the hearer was permitted.[11] Indeed, three sorts of equivocations were distinguished by Alfonso de Liguori, who was beatified in the nineteenth century, which might be used with good reason,[12] a good reason being " any honest object, such as keeping our goods, spiritual or temporal."[13] In the twentieth century the intensification of militant nationalism has added further 'good reason,' for the military code includes all transactions with hostile nations or individuals as part of the process of keeping spiritual and temporal goods. In war-time words become a normal part of the mechanisms of deceit, and the ethics of the situation have been aptly summed up by Lord Wolseley: "We will keep hammering along with the conviction that 'honesty is the best policy,' and that truth always wins in the long run. These pretty sentences do well for a child's copy-book, but the man who acts upon them in war had better sheathe his sword for ever."[14]

The Greeks, as we shall see, were in many ways not far from the attitude of primitive man towards words. And it is not surprising to read that after the Peloponnesian war the verbal machinery of peace had got completely out of gear, and, says Thucydides, could not be brought back into use—"The meaning of words had no longer the same relation to things, but was changed by men as they thought proper." The Greeks were powerless to cope with such a situation. We in our wisdom seem to have created institutions which render us more powerless still.[15]

---

10 Westermarck, *The Origin and Development of Moral Ideas*, Vol. II., p. 100.

11 Alagona, *Compendium Manualis D. Navarri* XII., 88, p. 94.

12 Alfonso di Liguori, *Theologia Moralis*, III, 151, Vol. I., p. 249.

13 Meyrick, *Moral and Devotional Theology of the Church of Rome,* Vol. I., p. 3. Cf. further Westermarck, *loc. cit.*

14 *Soldier's Pocket Book for Field Service*, p. 69.

15 As the late C. E. Montague (*Disenchantment*, p. 207) well put it, "the only new thing about deception in war is modern man's more perfect means for its practice. The thing has become, in his hand, a trumpet more efficacious than Gideon's own. . . . To match the Lewis gun with

On a less gigantic scale the technique of deliberate misdirection can profitably be studied with a view to corrective
measures. In accounting for Newman's *Grammar of Assent*
Dr. E. A. Abbott had occasion to describe the process of
'lubrication,' the art of greasing the descent from the premises to the conclusion, which his namesake cited above so
aptly employs. In order to lubricate well, various qualifications are necessary:

> "First a nice discrimination of words, enabling you to
> form, easily and naturally, a great number of finely gradu-
> ated propositions, shading away, as it were, from the as-
> sertion 'x is white' to the assertion 'x is black.' Secondly an
> inward and absolute contempt for logic and for words. . . .
> And what are words but toys and sweetmeats for grown-up
> babies who call themselves men?"[16]

But even where the actual referents are not in doubt, it
is perhaps hardly realized how widespread is the habit of
using the power of words not only for *bona fide* communications, but also as a method of misdirection; and in the
world as it is to-day the naïve interpreter is likely on many
occasions to be seriously misled if the existence of this un-
pleasing trait—equally prevalent amongst the classes and the
masses without distinction of race, creed, sex, or colour—
is overlooked.

Throughout this work, however, we are treating of *bona
fide* communication only, except in so far as we shall find it
necessary in Chapter IX, to discuss that derivate use of
Meaning to which misdirection gives rise. For the rest, the
verbal treachery with which we are concerned is only that

---

which he now fires his solids, he has to his hand the newspaper Press, to
let fly at the enemy's head the thing which is not." But this was a tempor-
ary use of the modern technique of misdirections, and with the return
of peace the habit is lost? Not so, says Mr. Montague. "Any weapon you
use in a war leaves some bill to be settled in peace, and the Propaganda
arm has its cost like another." The return of the exploiters of the verbal machines to their civil posts, is a return in triumph, and its effects will be
felt for many years in all countries where the power of the word amongst
the masses remains paramount.

16 Philomythus, p. 214.

involved by the use of symbols as such. As we proceed to examine the conditions of communication we shall see why any symbolic apparatus which is in general use is liable to incompleteness and defect.

But if our linguistic outfit is treacherous, it nevertheless is indispensable, nor would another complete outfit necessarily improve matters, even if it were ten times as complete. It is not always new words that are needed, but a means of controlling them as symbols, a means of readily discovering to what in the world on any occasion they are used to refer, and this is what an adequate theory of definition should provide.

But a theory of Definition must follow, not precede, a theory of Signs, and it is little realized how large a place is taken both in abstract thought and in practical affairs by sign-situations. But if an account of sign-situations is to be scientific it must take its observations from the most suitable instances, and must not derive its general principles from an exceptional case. The person actually interpreting a sign is not well placed for observing what is happening. We should develop our theory of signs from observations of other people, and only admit evidence drawn from introspection when we know how to appraise it. The adoption of the other method, on the ground that all our knowledge of others is inferred from knowledge of our own states, can only lead to the *impasse* of solipsism from which modern speculation has yet to recoil. Those who allow beyond question that there are people like themselves also interpreting signs and open to study should not find it difficult to admit that their observation of the behaviour of others may provide at least a framework within which their own introspection, that special and deceptive case, may be fitted. That this is the practice of all the sciences need hardly be pointed out. Any sensible doctor when stricken by disease distrusts his own introspective diagnosis and calls in a colleague.

There are, indeed, good reasons why what is happening in ourselves should be partially hidden from us, and we are generally better judges of what other people are doing than of what we are doing ourselves. Before we looked carefully into other people's heads it was commonly believed that an entity called the soul resided therein, just as children commonly believe that there is a little man inside the skull who looks out at the eyes, the windows of the soul, and listens at the ears. The child has the strongest introspective evidence for this belief, which, but for scalpels and microscopes, it would be difficult to disturb. The tacitly solipsistic presumption that this naïve approach is in some way a necessity of method disqualifies the majority of philosophical and psychological discussions of Interpretation. If we restrict the subject matter of the inquiry to 'ideas' and words, *i.e.*, to the left side of our triangle, and omit all frank recognition of the world outside us, we inevitably introduce confusion on such subjects as knowledge in perception, verification and Meaning itself.[17]

If we stand in the neighbourhood of a cross road and observe a pedestrian confronted by a notice *To Grantchester* displayed on a post, we commonly distinguish three important factors in the situation. There is, we are sure, (1) a Sign which (2) refers to a Place and (3) is being interpreted by a person. All situations in which Signs are considered are similar to this. A doctor noting that his patient has a temperature and so forth is said to diagnose his disease as influenza. If we talk like this we do not make it clear that signs are here also involved. Even when we speak of symptoms we often do not think of these as closely related to other groups of signs. But if we say that the doctor interprets the temperature, etc., as a Sign of influenza, we are at any rate on the way to an inquiry as to whether there is anything in common between the manner in which the pedestrian treated the object at the cross road and that in which

---

[17] This tendency is particularly noticeable in such works as Baldwin's elaborate treatise on *Thoughts and Things,* where a psychological apparatus of 'controls' and 'contents' is hard to reconcile with the subsequent claim to discuss communication. The twist given to grammatical analysis by Aristotle's similar neglect of Reference is dealt with in Appendix A.

the doctor treated his thermometer and the flushed countenance.

On close examination it will be found that very many situations which we do not ordinarily regard as Sign-situations are essentially of the same nature. The chemist dips litmus paper in his test-tube, and interprets the sign red or the sign blue as meaning acid or base. A Hebrew prophet notes a small black cloud, and remarks "We shall have rain." Lessing scrutinizes the Laocoön, and concludes that the features of Laocoön *père* are in repose. A New Zealand school-girl looks at certain letters on a page in her *Historical Manual for the use of Lower Grades* and knows that Queen Anne is dead.

The method which recognizes the common feature of sign-interpretation[18] has its dangers, but opens the way to a fresh treatment of many widely different topics.

As an instance of an occasion in which the theory of signs is of special use, the subject dealt with in our fourth chapter may be cited. If we realize that in *all* perception, as distinguished from mere awareness, sign-situations are involved,

---

[18] In all these cases a sign has been interpreted rightly or wrongly, *i.e.*, something has been not only experienced or enjoyed, but understood as referring to something else. Anything which can be experienced can also be thus understood, *i.e.*, can also be a sign; and it is important to remember that interpretation, or what happens to (or in the mind of) an Interpreter is quite distinct both from the sign and from that for which the sign stands or to which it refers. If then we speak of the meaning of a sign we must not, as philosophers, psychologists and logicians are wont to do, confuse the (imputed) relation between a sign and that to which it refers, either with the referent (what is referred to) or with the process of interpretation (the 'goings on' in the mind of the interpreter). It is this sort of confusion which has made so much previous work on the subject of signs and their meaning unfruitful. In particular, by using the same term 'meaning' *both* for the 'Goings on' inside their heads (the images, associations, etc., which enabled them to interpret signs) and for the Referents (the things to which the signs refer) philosophers have been forced to locate Grantchester, Influenza, Queen Anne, and indeed the whole Universe equally inside their heads—or, if alarmed by the prospect of cerebral congestion, at least 'in their minds' in such wise that all these objects become conveniently 'mental.' Great care, therefore, is required in the use of the term 'meaning,' since its associations are dangerous.

we shall have a new method of approaching problems where a verbal deadlock seems to have arisen. Whenever, we 'perceive' what we name a 'chair,' we are interpreting a certain group of data (modifications of the sense-organs), and treating them as signs of a referent. Similarly, even before the interpretation of a word, there is the almost automatic interpretation of a group of successive noises or letters as a word. And in addition to the external world we can also explore with a new technique the sign-situations involved by mental events, the 'goings on' or processes of interpretation themselves. We need neither confine ourselves to arbitrary generalizations from introspection after the manner of classical psychology, nor deny the existence of images and other 'mental' occurrences to their signs with the extreme Behaviorist.[19] The Double language hypothesis, which is suggested by the theory of signs and supported by linguistic analysis, would absolve Dr. Watson and his followers from the logical necessity of affecting general anæsthesia. Images, etc., are often most useful signs of our present and future behaviour—notably in the modern interpretation of dreams.[20] An improved Behaviorism will have much to say concerning the chaotic attempts at symbolic interpretation and construction by which Psychoanalysts discredit their valuable labours.

The problems which arise in connection with any 'sign-situation' are of the same general form. The relations between the elements concerned are no doubt different, but

---

[19] That the mind-body problem is due to a duplication of symbolic machinery is maintained in Chapter IV., p. 81. *Cf.* also *The Meaning of Psychology,* by C. K. Ogden (1926), Chapter II., where this view is supported wtih reference to contemporary authorities who hold it.

[20] In the terminology of the present work, many of the analyst's 'symbols' are, of course, signs only; they are not used for purposes of communication. But in the literature of psycho-analysis there is much valuable insistence on the need of wider forms of interpretation, especially in relation to emotional overcharge. *Cf.*, e.g., the late Dr. Jelliffe's "The Symbol as an Energy Condenser" (*Journal of Nervous and Mental Diseases,* December 1919), though the metaphor, like many other psycho-analytic locutions, must not be stretched too far in view of what has been said above and of what is to follow (cf. pages 102-3 and 200 *infra*).

they are the same sort. A thorough classification of these problems in one field, such as the field of symbols, may be expected, therefore, to throw light upon analogous problems in fields at first sight of a very different order.

When we consider the various kinds of Sign-situations instanced above, we find that those signs which men use to communicate one with another and as instruments of thought, occupy a peculiar place. It is convenient to group these under a distinctive name; and for words, arrangements of words, images, gestures, and such representations as drawings or mimetic sounds we use the term *symbols*. The influence of Symbols upon human life and thought in numberless unexpected ways has never been fully recognized, and to this chapter of history we now proceed.

"Nature, Communication and Meaning"

John Dewey

John Dewey was born in Burlington, Vermont, in 1859. He received his education at the University of Vermont and at The Johns Hopkins University. He taught at the universities of Michigan, Minnesota, and Chicago before joining the faculty of Columbia University in 1904. His philosophy of pragmatism has been regarded as an extension of the work of Charles Peirce and William James. Dewey served as president of the American Psychologic Association and of the American Philosophic Association. He was also one of the founders of the American Association of University Professors, and served as the organization's first president. Motivated by a great love for democracy, he maintained that "intelligent action" mattered most of all; he saw education as vital to the survival of democracy. At his death in 1952, he was regarded as America's greatest philosopher. Among his many works are *Democracy and Education; Reconstruction in Philosophy; Human Nature and Conduct; Experience and Nature; The Quest for Certainty; Art as Experience; Logic: The Theory of Inquiry.* Our selection is Chapter five from *Experience and Nature.* Permission for its inclusion has been granted by The Open Court Publishing Company.

O F all affairs, communication is the most wonderful. That things should be able to pass from the plane of external pushing and pulling to that of revealing themselves to man, and thereby to themselves; and that the fruit of communication should be participation, sharing, is a wonder by the side of which transubstantiation pales. When communication occurs, all natural events are subject to reconsideration and revision; they are re-adapted to meet the requirements

of conversation, whether it be public discourse or that preliminary discourse termed thinking. Events turn into objects, things with a meaning. They may be referred to when
they do not exist, and thus be operative among things distant in space and time, through vicarious presence in a new
medium. Brute efficiencies and inarticulate consummations
as soon as they can be spoken of are liberated from local
and accidental contexts, and are eager for naturalization in
any non-insulated, communicating, part of the world. Events
when once they are named lead an independent and double
life. In addition to their original existence, they are subject to ideal experimentation: their meanings may be infinitely combined and re-arranged in imagination, and the
outcome of this inner experimentation—which is thought—
may issue forth in interaction with crude or raw events.
Meanings having been deflected from the rapid and roar-
ing stream of events into a calm and traversable canal, rejoin
the main stream, and color, temper and compose its course.
Where communication exists, things in acquiring meaning
thereby acquire representatives, surrogates, signs and im-
plicates, which are infinitely more amenable to management,
more permanent; and more accommodating, than events in
their first estate.

By this fashion, qualitative immediacies cease to be
dumbly rapturous, a possession that is obsessive and an
incorporation that involves submergence: conditions found
in sensations and passions. They become capable of survey,
contemplation, and ideal or logical elaboration; when something can be said of qualities they are purveyors of instruction. Learning and teaching come into being, and there is
no event which may not yield information. A directly enjoyed thing adds to itself meaning, and enjoyment is thereby
idealized. Even the dumb pang of an ache achieves a significant existence when it can be designated and descanted
upon; it ceases to be merely oppressive and becomes important; it gains importance, because it becomes representative; it has the dignity of an office.

In view of these increments and transformations, it is not

surprising that meanings, under the name of forms and essences, have often been hailed as modes of Being beyond and above spatial and temporal existence, invulnerable to vicissitude; nor that thought as their possession has been treated as a non-natural spiritual energy, disjoined from all that is empirical. Yet there is a natural bridge that joins the gap between existence and essence; namely communication, language, discourse. Failure to acknowledge the presence and operation of natural interaction in the form of communication creates the gulf between existence and essence, and that gulf is factitious and gratuitous.

The slight respect paid to larger and more pervasive kinds of empirical objects by philosophers, even by professed empiricists, is apparent in the fact that while they discoursed so fluently about many topics they have discoursed little about discourse itself. Anthropologists, philologists and psychologists have said most that has been said about saying. Nevertheless it is a fact of such distinction that its occurrence changed dumb creatures—as we so significantly call them—into thinking and knowing animals and created the realm of meanings. Speaking from the standpoint of anthropology Franz Boas says: "The two outer traits in which the distinction between the minds of animals and man finds expression are the existence of organized articulate speech in man and the use of utensils of varied application."[1] It is antecedently probable that sole external marks of difference are more than external; that they have intimate connection with such intrinsic differences as religion, art and science, industry and politics. "Utensils" were discussed in the last chapter, in connection with the useful arts and knowledge, and their indispensable relation with science pointed out. But at every point appliances and application, utensils and uses, are bound up with directions, suggestions and records made possible by speech; what has been said about the rôle of tools is subject to a condition supplied by language, the tool of tools.

Upon the whole, professed transcendentalists have been

[1] The Mind of Primitive Man, p. 98.

more aware than have professed empiricists of the fact that language makes the difference between brute and man. The trouble is that they have lacked naturalistic conception of its origin and status. Logos has been correctly identified with mind; but logos and hence mind was conceived supernaturally. Logic was thereby supposed to have its basis in what is beyond human conduct and relationships, and in consequence the separation of the physical and the rational, the actual and the ideal, received its traditional formulation.

In protest against this view empirical thinkers have rarely ventured in discussion of language beyond reference to some peculiarity of brain structure, or to some psychic peculiarity, such as tendency to "outer expression" of "inner" states. Social interaction and institutions have been treated as products of a ready-made *specific* physical or mental endowment of a self-sufficing individual, wherein language acts as a mechanical go-between to convey observations and ideas that have prior and independent existence. Speech is thus regarded as a practical convenience but not of fundamental intellectual significance. It consists of "mere words," sounds, that happen to be associated with perceptions, sentiments and thoughts which are complete prior to language. Language thus "expresses" thought as a pipe conducts water, and with even less transforming function than is exhibited when a wine-press "expresses" the juice of grapes. The office of signs in creating reflection, foresight and recollection is passed by. In consequence, the occurrence of ideas becomes a mysterious parallel addition to physical occurrences, with no community and no bridge from one to the other.

It is safe to say that psychic events, such as are anything more than reactions of a creature susceptible to pain and diffuse comfort, have language for one of their conditions. It is altogether likely that the "ideas" which Hume found in constant flux whenever he looked within himself were a succession of words silently uttered. Primary to these events there was, of course, a substratum of organic psycho-physical actions. But what made the latter identifiable objects, events with a perceptible character, was their concretion in discourse. When the introspectionist thinks he has withdrawn into a wholly private realm of events disparate in kind from other events, made out of mental stuff, he is only turning his attention to his own soliloquy. And soliloquy is the product and reflex of converse with others; social communication not an effect of soliloquy. If we had not talked with others and they with us, we should never talk to and with ourselves. Because of converse, social give and take, various organic attitudes become an assemblage of persons engaged in converse, conferring with one another, exchanging distinctive experiences, listening to one another, over-hearing unwelcome remarks, accusing and excusing. Through speech a person dramatically identifies himself with potential acts and deeds; he plays many rôles, not in successive stages of life but in a contemporaneously enacted drama. Thus mind emerges.

It is significant of the differences between Greek and modern experience, that when their respective philosophers discovered discourse, they gave such different accounts of it. the moderns made of it a world separate from spatial and material existences, a separate and private world made of sensations, images, sentiments. The Greeks were more nearly aware that it was *discourse* they had discovered. But they took the structure of discourse for the structure of things, instead of for the forms which things assume under the pressure and opportunity of social cooperation and exchange. They overlooked the fact that meaning as objects of thought are entitled to be called complete and ultimate only because they are not original but are a happy outcome of a complex history. They made them primitive and independent forms of things, intrinsically regulative of processes of becoming. They took a work of social art to be nature independent of man. They overlooked the fact that the import of logical and rational essences is the consequence of social interactions, of companionship, mutual assistance, direction and concerted action in fighting, festivity, and work. Hence they conceived of ideal meanings as the ultimate framework of events, in which a system of substances and properties corresponded to subjects and predicates of the uttered proposition. Things conformed naturally and exactly to parts of speech, some being inherently subject-matter of nouns, proper and common; others of verbs, of which some expressed self-activity, while others designated adjectival and adverbial changes to which things are exposed on account of their own defects; some being external relations in which substances stand to one another, and subject-matter of propositions.

The resulting theory of substances, essential properties, accidental qualities and relations, and the identification of Being (by means of the copula "is") with the tenses of the verb (so that the highest Being was, is now, and ever shall be, in contrast to existence now and then, occasional, wholly past, merely just now, or possibly at some passing time in the future) controlled the whole scheme of physics and metaphysics, which formed the philosophic tradition of Europe. It was a natural consequence of the insight that things, meanings, and words correspond.

The insight was perverted by the notion that the correspondence of things and meanings is prior to discourse and social intercourse. Hence, every true affirmation was an assertion of the fixed belonging to one another of two objects in nature; while every true denial was an assertion of intrinsic exclusion of one object by another. The consequence was belief in ideal essences, individually complete, and yet connected in a system of necessary subordinations and dependencies. Dialectic of their relationships, definitions, classification, division in arranging essences, constituted scientific truth about the inmost constituents of nature. Thus a discovery which is the greatest single discovery of man, putting man in potential possession of liberation and of order, became the source of an artificial physics of nature, the basis of a science, philosophy and theology in which the universe was an incarnate grammatical order constructed after the model of discourse.

The modern discovery of inner experience, of a realm of purely personal events that are always at the individual's command, and that are his exclusively as well as inexpensively for refuge, consolation and thrill is also a great and liberating discovery. It implies a new worth and sense of dignity in human individuality, a sense that an individual is not a mere property of nature, set in place according to a scheme independent of him, as an article is put in its place in a cabinet, but that he adds something, that he makes a contribution. It is the counterpart of what distinguishes modern science, experimental, hypothetical; a logic of discovery having therefore opportunity for individual temperament, ingenuity, invention. It is the counterpart of modern politics, art, religion and industry where individuality is given room and movement, in contrast to the ancient scheme of experience, which held individuals tightly within a given order subordinated to its structure and patterns. But here also distortion entered in. Failure to recognize that this world of inner experience is dependent upon an extension of language which is a social product and operation led to the subjectivistic, solipsistic and egotistic strain in modern thought. If the classic thinkers created a cosmos after the model of dialectic, giving rational distinctions power to constitute and regulate, modern thinkers composed nature after the model of personal soliloquizing.

Language considered as an experienced event enables us to interpret what really happened when rational discourse and logic were discovered by the ancients, and when 'inner' experience and its interest were discovered by moderns. Language is a natural function of human association; and its consequences react upon other events, physical and human, giving them meaning or significance. Events that are objects or significant exist in a context where they acquire new ways of operation and new properties. Words are spoken of as coins and money. Now gold, silver, and instrumentalities of credit are first of all, prior to being money, physical things with their own immediate and final qualities. But as money they are substitutes, representations, and surrogates, which embody relationships. As a substitute, money not merely facilitates exchange of such commodities as existed prior to its use, but it revolutionizes as well production and consumption of all commodities, because it brings into being new transactions, forming new histories and affairs. Exchange is not an event that can be isolated. It marks the emergence of production and consumption into a new medium and context wherein they acquire new properties.

Language is similarly not a mere agency for economizing energy in the interaction of human beings. It is a release and amplification of energies that enter into it, conferring upon them the added quality of meaning. The quality of meaning thus introduced is extended and transferred, actually and potentially, from sounds, gestures and marks, to all other things in nature. Natural events become messages to be enjoyed and administered, precisely as are song, fiction, oratory, the giving of advice and instruction. Thus events come to possess characters; they are demarcated, and noted. For character is general and distinguished.

When events have communicable meaning, they have marks, notations, and are capable of con-notation and denotation. They are more than mere occurrences; they have implications. Hence interference and reasoning are possible; these operations are reading the message of things which things utter because they are involved in human associations. When Aristotle drew a distinction between sensible things that are more noted—known—to us and rational things that are more noted—known—in themselves, he was actually drawing a distinction between things that operate in a local, restricted universe of discourse, and things whose marks are such that they readily enter into indefinitely extensive and varied discourse.

The interaction of human beings, namely, association, is not different in origin from other modes of interaction. There is a peculiar absurdity in the question of how individuals become social, if the question is taken literally. Human beings illustrate the same traits of both immediate uniqueness and connection, relationship, as do other things. No more in their case than in that of atoms and physical masses is immediacy the whole of existence and therefore an obstacle to being acted upon by and affecting other things. Everything that exists in as far as it is known and knowable is in interaction with other things. It is associated, as well as solitary, single. The catching up of human individuals into association is thus no new and unprecedented fact; it is a manifestation of a commonplace of existence. Significance resides not in the bare fact of association, therefore, but in the consequences that flow from the distinctive patterns of human association. There is, again, nothing new or unprecedented in the fact that assemblage of things confers upon the assembly and its constituents, new properties by means of unlocking energies hitherto pent in. The significant consideration is that assemblage of organic human beings transforms sequence and coexistence into participation.

Gestures and cries are not primarily expressive and communicative. They are modes of organic behavior as much as are locomotion, seizing and crunching. Language, signs and significance, came into existence not by intent and mind but by over-flow, by products, in gestures and sound. The story of language is the story of the *use* made of these occurrences; a use that is eventual, as well as eventful. Those rival accounts of the origin of language that go by the nicknames of bow-wow, pooh-pooh, and ding-dong theories are not in fact theories of the origin of *language*. They are accounts, of some plausibility, of how and why certain sounds rather than others were selected to signify objects, acts and situations. If the mere existence of sounds of these kinds constituted language, lower animals might well converse more subtly and fluently than man. But they became language only when used within a context of mutual assistance and direction. The latter are alone of prime importance in considering the transformation of organic gestures and cries into names, things with significance, or the origin of language.

Observable facts of animal experience furnish us with our starting point. "Animals respond to certain stimuli . . . by the contraction of certain muscles whose functioning is of no direct consequence to the animal itself, but affects other animals by stimulating them to act. . . . Let us call this class the signaling reflexes. A few, but very diversified examples of the signaling reflexes, are the lighting of a fire-fly, the squeezing out of a black liquid from the ink bladder of a cuttle-fish, the crowing of a rooster . . . the spreading of its tail by a peacock. These reflex activities affect other animals by stimulating them. . . . If no other animals are present, or these other animals fail to respond by their own reflexes, the former reflex actions are completely wasted."[2]

Sub-human animals thus behave in ways which have no *direct* consequences of utility to the behaving animal, but which call out certain characteristic responses, sexual, protective, food-finding (as with the cluck of a hen to her chicks), in other animals. In some cases, the act evoked in other animals has in turn an important consequence for the first agent. A sexual act or a combined protective act against danger is furthered. In other cases, the consequences turn out useful to the species, to a numerically indeterminate group including individuals not yet born. Signaling acts evidently form the basic *material* of language. Similar activities occur without intent in man; thus a babe's scream attracts the attention of an adult and evokes a response useful to the infant, although the cry itself is an organic overflow having no intent. So too a man's posture and facial changes may indicate to another things which the man himself would like to conceal, so that he "gives himself away." "Expression," or signs, communication of meaning, exists in such cases for the observer, not for the agent.

While signaling acts are a material condition of language they are not language nor yet are they its *sufficient* condition. Only from an external standpoint, is the original action even a signal; the response of other animals to it is not to a sign, but, by some preformed mechanism, to a direct stimulus. By habit, by conditioned reflex, hens run to the farmer when he makes a clucking noise, or when they hear the rattle of grain

---

2 Max Meyer, The Psychology Of The Other One, 1922, p. 195; a statement of behavioristic psychology that has hardly received the attention it intrinsically deserves.

in a pan. When the farmer raises his arms to throw the grain they scatter and fly, to return only when the movement ceases. They act as if alarmed; his movement is thus not a sign of food; it is a stimulus that evokes flight. But a human infant learns to discount such movements; to become interested in them as events preparatory to a desired consummation; he learns to treat them as signs of an ulterior event so that his response is to their meaning. He treats them as means to consequences. The hen's activity is ego-centric; that of the human being is participative. The latter puts himself at the standpoint of a situation in which two parties share. This is the essential peculiarity of language, or signs.

A requests B to bring him something, to which A points, say a flower. There is an original mechanism by which B may react to A's movement in pointing. But natively such a reaction is to the movement, not to the *pointing*, not to the object pointed out. But B learns that the movement *is* a pointing; he responds to it not in itself, but as an index of something else. His response is transferred from A's direct movement to the *object* to which A points. Thus he does not merely execute the natural acts of looking or grasping which the movement might instigate on its own account. The motion of A attracts his gaze to the thing pointed to; then, instead of just transferring his response from A's movement to the native reaction he might make to the thing as stimulus, he responds in a way which is a function of A's *relationship*, actual and potential, to the thing. The characteristic thing about B's understanding of A's movement and sounds is that he responds to the thing from the standpoint of A. He perceives the thing as it may function in A's experience, instead of just ego-centrically. Similarly, A in making the request conceives the thing not only in its direct relationship to himself, but as a thing capable of being grasped and handled by B. He sees the thing as it may function in B's experience. Such is the essence and import of communication, signs and meaning. Something is literally made common in at least two different centres of behavior. To understand is to anticipate together, it is to make a cross-reference which, when acted upon, brings about a partaking in a common, inclusive, undertaking.

Stated in greater detail: B upon hearing A, makes a preparatory reaction of his eyes, hands and legs in view of the consummatory act of A's possession; he engages in the act of grasping, carrying and tendering the flower to A. At the same time, A makes a preparatory response to B's consummatory act, that of carrying and proffering the flower. Thus neither the sounds uttered by A, his gesture of pointing, nor the sight of the thing pointed to, is the occasion and stimulus of B's act; the stimulus is B's anticipatory share in the consummation of a transaction in which both participate. The heart of language is not "expression" of something antecedent, much less expression of antecedent thought. It is communication; the establishment of cooperation in an activity in which there are partners, and in which the activity of each is modified and regulated by partnership. To fail to understand is to fail to come into agreement in action; to misunderstand is to set up action at cross purposes. Take speech as behavioristically as you will, including the elimination of all private mental states, and it remains true that it is markedly distinguished from the signaling acts of animals. Meaning is not indeed a psychic existence; it is primarily a property of behavior, and secondarily a property of objects. But the behavior of which it is a quality is a distinctive behavior; cooperative, in that response to another's act involves contemporaneous response to a thing as entering into the other's behavior, and this upon both sides. It is difficult to state the exact physiological mechanism which is involved. But about the fact there is no doubt. It constitutes the intelligibility of acts and things. Possession of the capacity to engage in such activity is intelligence. Intelligence and meaning are natural consequences of the peculiar form which interaction sometimes assumes in the case of human beings.

Primarily meaning is intent and intent is not personal in a private and exclusive sense. A proposes the consummatory possession of the flower through the medium or means of B's action; B proposes to cooperate—or act adversely—in the fulfillment of A's proposal. Secondarily, meaning is the acquisition of significance by things in their status in making possible and fulfilling shared cooperation. In the first place, it is the *motion and sounds* of A which have meaning, or are signs. Similarly the movements of B, while they are immediate to him, are signs to A of B's cooperation or refusal. But secondarily the *thing* pointed out by A to B gains meaning. It ceases to be just what it brutely is at the moment, and is responded to in its potentiality, as a means to remoter consequences. The flower pointed to, for example, *is* portable; but apart from language portability is a brute contingency waiting for its actualization upon circumstance. But when A counts upon the understanding and cooperation of B, and B responds to the intent of A, the flower *is* contemporaneously portable though not now actually in movement. Its potentiality, or conditioning of consequences, is an immediately recognized and possessed trait; the flower *means* portability instead of simply *being* portable. Animism, the attribution of desire and intent to inanimate things, is no mysterious projection of psychical traits; it is a misinterpretation of a natural fact, namely, that significant things are things actually implicated in situations of shared or social purpose and execution.

The logic of animism is simple. Since words act upon things indirectly, or as signs, and since words express the significant consequences of things (the traits for the sake of which they are used), why should not words act also directly upon things to release their latent powers? Since we "call" things by their names, why should they not answer? And if they assist us as our friends do when appealed to, is not this proof they are animated by friendly intent; or if they frustrate us, proof that they are filled with the same traits which inspirit our enemies? "Animism" is thus the consequence of a direct transfer of properties of social situation to an immediate relationship of natural things to a person. Its legitimate and constant form is poetry, in which things and events are given voice and directly communicate with us.

If we consider the *form* or scheme of the situation in which meaning and understanding occur, we find an involved simul-

taneous presence and cross-reference of immediacy and efficiency, over actuality and potentiality, the consummatory
and the instrumental. A in making the request of B, at the
same time makes the incipient and preparatory response of
receiving the thing at the hands of B; he performs in readiness the consummatory act. B's understanding of the meaning
of what A says, instead of being a mere reaction to sound, is
an anticipation of a consequence, while it is also an immediate activity of eyes, legs, and hands in getting and giving the
flower to A. The flower is the thing which it immediately is,
and it also is means of a conclusion. All of this is directly
involved in the existence of intelligible speech. No such
simultaneous presence of finality and agency is possible in
things as *purely* physical—in abstraction, that is, of potential
presence in a situation of communication. Since we have
discovered that all things have a phase of potential commu-
nicability, that is, that any conceivable thing may enter into
discourse, the retrospective imputation of meanings and
logical relationships to bare things is natural; it does no harm,
save when the imputation is dogmatic and literal. What a
physical event immediately is, and what it *can* do or its relationship are distinct and incommensurable. But when an
event has meaning, its potential consequences become its
integral and funded feature. When the potential consequences are important and repeated, they form the very
nature and essence of a thing, its defining, identifying, and
distinguishing form. To recognize the thing is to grasp its
definition. Thus we become capable of perceiving things
instead of merely feeling and having them. To *perceive* is to
acknowledge unattained possibilities; it is to refer the present
to consequences, apparition to issue, and thereby to behave
in deference to the *connections* of events. As an attitude,
perception or awareness is predictive expectancy, wariness.
Since potential consequences also *mark* the thing itself, and
form its nature, the event thus marked becomes an object of
contemplation; as meaning, future consequences already belong to the thing. The act of striving to bring them existen-

tially into the world may be commuted into esthetic enjoyed possession of form.

Essence, as has been intimated, is but a pronounced instance of meaning; to be partial, and to assign *a* meaning to a thing as *the* meaning is but to evince human subjection to bias. Since consequences differ also in their consequence and hence importance, practical good sense may attach to this one-sided partiality, for the meaning seized upon as essence may designate extensive and recurrent consequences. Thus is explained the seeming paradox of the distinction and connection of essence and existence. Essence is never existence, and yet it is the essence, the distilled import, of existence; the significant thing about it, its intellectual voucher, the means of inference and extensive transfer, and object of esthetic intuition. In it, feeling and understanding are one; the meaning of a thing is the sense it makes.

Since the consequences which are liked have an emphatic quality, it is not surprising that many consequences, even though recognized to be inevitable, are regarded as if they were accidental and alien. Thus the very essence of a thing is identified with those consummatory consequences which the thing has when conditions are felicitous. Thus *the* essence, one, immutable and constitutive, which *makes* the thing *what* it is, emerges from the various meanings which vary with varying conditions and transitory intents. When essence is then thought to contain existence as the perfect includes the imperfect, it is because a legitimate, practical measure of reality in terms of importance is illegitimately altered into a theoretical measure.

Discourse itself is both instrumental and consummatory. Communication is an exchange which procures something wanted; it involves a claim, appeal, order, direction or request, which realizes want at less cost than personal labor exacts, since its procures the cooperative assistance of others. Communication is also an immediate enhancement of life, enjoyed for its own sake. The dance is accompanied by song and becomes the drama; scenes of danger and victory are most fully savored when they are told. Greeting becomes a ceremonial with its prescribed rites. Language is always a form of action and in its instrumental use is always a means of concerted action for an end, while at the same time it finds in itself all the goods of its possible consequences. For there is no mode of action as fulfilling and as rewarding as is concerted consensus of action. It brings with it the sense of sharing and merging in a whole. Forms of language are unrivalled in ability to create this sense, at first with direct participation on the part of an audience; and then, as literary forms develop, through imaginative identification. Greek thinkers had distinguished patterns in Greek literary art of consummatory uses of speech, and the meanings that were discovered to be indispensable to communication were treated as final and ultimate in nature itself. Essences were hypostatized into original and constitutive forms of all existence.

The idea put forth about the connection of meaning with language is not to be confused with traditional nominalism. It does not imply that meaning and essence are adventitious and arbitrary. The defect of nominalism lies in its virtual denial of interaction and association. It regarded the word not as a mode of social action with which to realize the ends of association, but as an expression of a ready-made, exclusively individual, mental state; sensation, image or feeling, which, being an existence, is necessarily particular. For the sound, gesture, or written mark which is involved in language is a particular existence. But as such it is not a *word*, and it does not become a word by declaring a mental existence; it becomes a word by gaining meaning; and it gains meaning when its use establishes a genuine community of action. Interaction, operative relationship, is as much a fact about events as are particularity and immediacy. Language and its consequences are characters taken on by natural interaction and natural conjunction in specified conditions of organization. Nominalism ignores organization, and thus makes nonsense of meanings.

Language is specifically a mode of interaction of at least two beings, a speaker and a hearer; it presupposes an organized group to which these creatures belong, and from whom they have acquired their habits of speech. It is therefore a relationship, not a particularity. This consideration alone condemns traditional nominalism. The meaning of signs moreover always includes something common as between persons and an object. When we attribute meaning to the speaker as *his* intent, we take for granted another person who is to share in the execution of the intent, and also something, independent of the persons concerned, through which the intent is to be realized. Persons and thing must alike serve as means in a common, shared consequence. This community of partaking is meaning.

The invention and use of tools have played a large part in consolidating meanings, because a tool is a thing used as means to consequences, instead of being taken directly and physically. It is intrinsically relational, anticipatory, predictive. Without reference to the absent, or "transcendence," nothing is a tool. The most convincing evidence that animals do not "think" is found in the fact that they have no tools, but depend upon ther own relatively-fixed bodily structures to effect results. Because of such dependence they have no way of distinguishing the immediate existence of anything from its potential efficiencies; no way of projecting its consequences to define a nature or essence. Anything whatever used as a tool exhibits distinction and identification. Fire existentially burns; while fire which is employed in order to cook and keep warm, especially after other things, like rubbing sticks together, are used as means to generate it, is an existence having meaning and potential essence. The presence of inflammation and terror or discomfort is no longer the whole story; an occurrence is now an object; and while it is absurd to hold (as idealism virtually does) that the meaning of an existence is the real substance of the existence, it is equally absurd not to recognize the full transformative import of what has happened.

As to be a tool, or to be used as means for consequences, is to have and to endow with meaning, language, being the tool of tools, is the cherishing mother of all significance. For other instrumentalities and agencies, the things usually thought of as appliances, agencies and furnishings can originate and develop only in social groups made possible by language. Things become tools ceremonially and institutionally. The notoriously conventionalized and traditional character of primitive utensils and their attendant symbolizations demonstrate this fact. Moreover, tools and artifices of agency are always found in connection with some division of labor which depends upon some device of communication. The statement can be proved in a more theoretical way. Immediacy as such is transient to the point of evanescence, and its flux has to be fixed by some easily recoverable and recurrent act within control of the organism, like gesture and spoken sounds, before things can be intentionally utilized. A creature might accidentally warm itself by a fire or use a stick to stir the ground in a way which furthered the growth of food-plants. But the effect of comfort ceases with the fire, existentially; a stick even though once used as a lever would revert to the status of being just a stick, unless the *relationship* between it and its consequence were distinguished and retained. Only language, or some form of artificial signs, serves to register the relationship and make it fruitful in other contexts of particular existence. Spears, urns, baskets, snares may have originated accidentally in some consummatory consequence of natural events. But only repetition through concerted action accounts for their becoming institutionalized as tools, and this concert of action depends upon the use of memoranda and communication. To make another aware of the possibility of a use or objective relationship is to perpetuate what is otherwise an incident as an agency; communication is a condition of consciousness.

Thus every meaning is generic or universal. It is something common between speaker, hearer and the thing to which speech refers. It is universal also as a means of generalization. For a meaning is a method of action, a way of using things as means to a shared consummation, and method is general, though the things to which it is applied are particular. The meaning, for example, of portability is something in which two persons and an object share. But portability after it is once apprehended becomes a way of treating other things; it is extended widely. Whenever this is a chance, it is applied; application ceases only when a thing refuses to be treated in this way. And even then refusal may be only a challenge to develop the meaning of portability until the thing can be transported. Meanings are rules for using and interpreting things; interpretation being always an imputation of potentiality for some consequence.

It would be difficult to imagine any doctrine more absurd than the theory that general ideas or meanings arise by the comparison of a number of particulars, eventuating in the recognition of something common to them all. Such a comparison may be employed to check a suggested widened application of a rule. But generalization is carried spontaneously as far as it will plausibly go; usually much further than it will actually go. A newly acquired meaning is forced upon everything that does not obviously resist its application, as a child uses a new word whenever he gets a chance or as he plays with a new toy. Meanings are self-moving to new cases. In the end, conditions force a chastening of this spontaneous tendency. The scope and limits of application are ascertained experimentally in the process of application. The history of science, to say nothing of popular beliefs, is sufficient indication of the difficulty found in submitting this irrational generalizing tendency to the discipline of experience. To call it *a priori* is to express a fact; but to impute *a priori* character of the generalizing force of meanings to *reason* is to invert the facts. Rationality is acquired when the tendency becomes circumspect, based upon observation and tested by deliberate experiment.

Meaning is objective as well as universal. Originating as a concerted or combined method of using or enjoying things, it indicates a possible interaction, not a thing in separate singleness. A meaning may not of course have the particular objectivity which is imputed to it, as whistling does not actually portend wind, nor the ceremonial sprinkling of water indicate rain. But such magical imputations of external refer-

ence testify to the objectivity of meaning as such. Meanings
are naturally the meaning of something or other; difficulty
lies in discriminating the right thing. It requires the discipline of ordered and deliberate experimentation to teach us
that some meanings, delightful or horrendous as they are,
are meanings communally developed in the process of communal festivity and control, and do not represent the polities,
and ways and means of nature apart from social arts. Scientific meanings were superadded to esthetic and affectional
meanings when objects instead of being defined in terms of
their consequences in social interactions and discussion were
defined in terms of their consequences with respect to one
another. This discrimination permitted esthetic and affective
objects to be freed from magical imputations, which were
due to attributing to them *in rerum natura* the consequences
they had in the transmitted culture of the group.

Yet the truth of classic philosophy in assigning objectivity
to meanings, essences, ideas, remains unassailable. It is heresy
to conceive meanings to be private, a property of ghostly
psychic existences. Berkeley with all his nominalism, saw
that "ideas," though particular in existence, are general in
function and office. His attribution of the ideas which are
efficacious in conduct to an order established by God, while
evincing lack of perception of their naturalistic origin in communication or communal interaction, manifests a sounder
sense of the objectivity of meanings than has been shown by
those who eliminated his theology while retaining his psychology. The inconsistency of the sensationalists who, stop-
ping short of extreme scepticism, postulate that some associations of ideas correspond to conjunctions among things is
also reluctantly extorted evidence of how intimation of the
objectivity of ideas haunts the mind in spite of theory to the
contrary.

Meanings are objective because they are modes of natural
interaction; such an interaction, although primarily between
organic beings, as includes things and energies external to
living creatures. The regulative force of legal meanings affords a convenient illustration. A traffic policeman holds up

his hand or blows a whistle. His act operates as a signal to direct movements. But it is more than an episodic stimulus. It embodies a rule of social action. Its proximate meaning is its near-by consequences in coordination of movements of persons and vehicles; its ulterior and permanent meaning—essence—is its consequence in the way of security of social movements. Failure to observe the signal subjects a person to arrest, fine or imprisonment. The essence embodied in the policeman's whistle is not an occult reality superimposed upon a sensuous or physical flux and imparting form to it; a mysterious subsistence somehow housed within a psychical event. Its essence is the rule, comprehensive and persisting, the standardized habit, of social interaction, and for the sake of which the whistle is used. The pattern, archetype, that forms the essence of the whistle as a particular noise is an orderly arrangement of the movements of persons and vehicles, established by social agreement as its consequence. This meaning is independent of the psychical landscape, the sensations and imagery, of the policeman and others concerned. But it is not on that account a timeless spiritual ghost nor pale logical subsistence divorced from events.

The case is the same with the essence of any non-human event, like gravity, or virtue, or vertebrate. Some consequences of the interaction of things concern us; the consequences are not *merely* physical; they enter finally into human action and destiny. Fire burns and the burning is of moment. It enters experience; it is fascinating to watch swirling flames; it is important to avoid its dangers and to utilize its beneficial potencies. When we name an event, calling it fire, we speak proleptically; we do not name an immediate event; that is impossible. We employ a term of discourse; we invoke a meaning, namely, the potential consequences of the existence. The ultimate meaning of the noise made by the traffic officer is the total consequent system of social behavior, in which individuals are subjected, by means of noise, to social coördination; its proximate meaning is a coördination of the movements of persons and vehicles in the neighborhood and directly affected. Similarly the ultimate meaning, or essence, denominated fire, is the consequences of certain natural events within the scheme of human activities, in the experience of social intercourse, the hearth and domestic altar, shared comfort, working of metals, rapid transit, and other such affairs. "Scientifically," we ignore these ulterior meanings. And quite properly; for when a sequential order of changes is determined, the final meaning in immediate enjoyments and appreciations is capable of control.

While classic thought, and its survival in later idealisms, assumed that the ulterior human meanings, meanings of direct association in discourse, are forms of nature apart from their place in discourse, modern thought is given to marking a sharp separation between meanings determined in terms of the causal relationship of things and meanings in terms of human association. Consequently, it treats the latter as negligible or as purely private, not the meanings of natural events at all. It identifies the proximate meanings with the only valid meanings, and abstract relations become an idol. To pass over in science the human meanings of the consequences of natural interactions is legitimate; indeed it is indispensable. To ascertain and state meanings in abstraction from social or shared situations is the only way in which the latter can be intelligently modified, extended and varied. Mathematical symbols have least connection with distinctively human situations and consequences; and the finding of such terms, free from esthetic and moral significance, is a necessary part of the technique. Indeed, such elimination of ulterior meanings supplies perhaps the best possible empirical definition of mathematical relations. They are meanings without direct reference to human behavior. Thus an essence becomes wholly "intellectual" or scientific, devoid of consummatory implication; it impresses the purely instrumental without reference to the objects to which the events in question are instrumental. It then becomes the starting point of reflection that may terminate in ends or consequences in human suffering and enjoyment not previously experienced. Abstraction from any particular consequence (which is the same thing as taking instrumentality generally), opens the way to new uses and consequences.

This is what happens when the meaning of the traffic officer's signal is detached from its own context, and taken up into, say, written and published language, a topic of independent consideration by experts or by civic administrators. In being placed in a context of other meanings (theoretically and scientifically discussed), it is liberated from the contingencies of its prior use. The outcome may be the invention of a new and improved system of semaphores which exercise regulation of human interaction more effectively. Deliberate abstraction, however, from all ulterior human use and consequence is hardly likely to occur in the case of discourse about a signal system. In physical science, the abstraction or liberation is complete. Things are defined by means of symbols that convey only their consequences with respect to one another. 'Water' in ordinary experience designates an essence of something which has familiar bearings and uses in human life, drink and cleansing and the extinguishing of fire. But H_2O gets away from these connections, and embodies in its essence only instrumental efficiency in respect to things independent of human affairs.

The counterpart of classic thought which took ends, enjoyments, uses, not simply as genuine termini of natural events (which they are), but as the essence and form of things independent of human experience, is a modern philosophy which makes reality purely mechanical and which regards the consequences of things in human experience as accidental or phenomenal by-products. In truth, abstraction from human experience is but a liberation from familiar and specific enjoyments, it provides means for detecting hitherto untried consequences, for invention, for the creation of new wants, and new modes of good and evil. In any sense in which the conception of essence is legitimate, these human consequences are the essence of natural events. Water still has the meanings of water of everyday experience when it becomes the essence H_2O, or else H_2O would be totally meaningless, a mere sound, not an intelligible name.

Meaning, fixed as essence in a term of discourse, may be

imaginatively administered and manipulated, experimented with. Just as we overtly manipulated things, making new separations and combinations, thereby introducing things into new contexts and environments, so we bring together logical universals in discourse, where they copulate and breed new meanings. There is nothing surprising in the fact that dialectic (or deduction, as it is termed by moderns) generates new objects; that, in Kantian language, it is "synthetic," instead of merely explicating what is already had. All discourse, oral or written, which is more than a routine unrolling of vocal habits, says things that surprise the one that says them, often indeed more than they surprise any one else. Systematic logical discourse, or ratiocination, is the same sort of thing conducted according to stricter rules. Even under the condition of rigid rules the emergence of new meanings is much more similar to what happens in general conversation than is conventionally supposed. Rules of logical order and consistency appertain to economy and efficiency of combination and separation in generating new meanings; not to meanings as such. They are rules of a certain kind of experimentation. In trying new combinations of meanings, satisfactory consequences of new meanings are hit upon; then they may be arranged in a system. The expert in thought is one who has skill in making experiments to introduce an old meaning into different situations and who has a sensitive ear for detecting resultant harmonies and discords. The most "deductive" thought in actual occurrence is a series of trials, observations and selections. In one sense of the ambiguous word intuition, it is a "series of intuitions," and logic is *ex post facto*, expressing a wit that formulates economically the congruities and incongruities that have manifested themselves. Any "syllogism" which is such *ab initio* is performed better by a machine that manipulates symbols automatically than by any "thinker."

This capacity of essences to enter readily into any number of new combinations, and thereby generate further meanings more profound and far reaching than those from which they sprang, gives them a semblance of independent life and career, a semblance which is responsible for their elevation by some thinkers into a realm separate from that of existence and superior to it. Consider the interpretations that have been based upon such essences as four, plus, the square root of minus one. These are at once so manipulable and so fertile in consequences when conjoined with others that thinkers who are primarily interested in their performances treat them not as significant terms of discourse, but as an order of entities independent of human invention and use. The fact that we can watch them and register what happens when they come together, and that the things that happen are as independent of our volition and expectation as are the discoveries of a geographic exploration, is taken as evidence that they constitute entities having subsistent Being independently not only of us but of all natural events whatever.

Alternatives are too narrowly conceived. Because meanings and essences are not states of mind, because they are as independent of immediate sensation and imagery as are physical things, and because nevertheless they are not physical things, it is assumed that they are a peculiar kind of thing, termed metaphysical, or "logical" in a style which separates logic from nature. But there are many other things which are neither physical nor psychical existences, and which are demonstrably dependent upon human association and interaction. Such things function moreover in liberating and regulating subsequent human intercourse; their essence is their contribution to making that intercourse more significant and more immediately rewarding. Take the sort of thing exemplified in the regulation of traffic. The sound of a whistle is a particular existential event numerically separate, with its own peculiar spatial temporal position. This may not be said of the rule or method of social cooperative interaction which it manifests and makes effective. A continuous way of organized action is not a particular, and hence is not a physical or psychical existence. Yet the consequences of using the method of adjusting movements, so that they do not interfere with one another, have both a physical and a mental phase. Physically, there is modification of the changes in space which would otherwise occur. Mentally, there are enjoyments and annoyances which would not otherwise happen. But no one of these incidents nor all of them put together form the essence or ulterior meaning of the sound of the whistle; they are qualifications of a more secure concert of human activity which, as a consequence of a legal order incarnate in the whistling, forms its significance.

Discussion of meaning and essence has reached such an impasse and is barbed with such entanglements, that it is further worth while to suggest consideration of legal entities as indicative of escape from the disjunction of essence from existence. What is a Corporation, a Franchise? A corporation is neither a mental state nor a particular physical event in space and time. Yet it is an objective reality, not an ideal Realm of Being. It is an objective reality which has multitudinous physical and mental consequences. It is something to be studied as we study electrons; it exhibits as does the latter unexpected properties, and when introduced into new situations behaves with new reactions. It is something which may be conducted, facilitated and obstructed, precisely as may be a river. Nevertheless it would not exist nor have any meaning and potency apart from an interaction of human beings with one another, an interaction in which external things are implicated. As legal essence, or concerted method of regulated interaction, corporation has its own and its developing career.

Again juridical rule implies jurisdiction; a particular body of persons within a certain territory to whom it applies. The legal significance of an act depends upon *where* it takes place. Yet an act is an interaction, a transaction, not isolated, self-sufficient. The initial stage of an act and the terminating consequences which, between them, determine its meaning, may be far apart in places as well as in time. Where then is the act? What is its locus? The readiest reply is in terms of the beginning of the act. The act was performed where the agent bodily was at the time of its occurrence. Suppose,

however, that before discovery, the agent in a criminal transaction changes his abode and resides within another jurisdiction. The need of security leads to the generation, in its
union with the conception of jurisdiction, of a new conception or essence, that of extradition, of comity of jurisdic-
tions. New procedures with corresponding new technical
concepts or meanings then develop by means of which a
person charged with crime may be requisitioned and removed. The concept of jurisdiction in combination with that
of security, justice, etc., deductively generates other concepts.

The process does not stop here. An agent implies a patient.
Suppose a person in New York State shoots a bullet across
the New Jersey line, and kills some one in that State; or
sends poisoned candy by mail to some one in California who
dies from eating it. *Where* is the crime committed? The guilty person is not within the jurisdiction of the State where
the death resulted; hence, his crime by definition, was not
committed in that State. But since the death did not occur
where he was bodily present at the time, no crime occurred
in that jurisdiction, locus being defined in terms of the abode
of the agent. The essence, extradition, does not apply because there is no crime for which to extradite him. In short,
because of the accepted meaning of jurisdiction, no crime
has been committed anywhere. Such an outcome is evidently
prejudicial to the integrity and security of human association
and intercourse. Thus the element of *transaction* in an act
is noted; an act initiated within a given jurisdiction becomes
a crime when its obnoxious consequences occur outside. The
locus of the act now extends all the way from New York to
California. Thus two independent particular events capable
of direct observation, together with a connection between
them which is inferred, not directly observable, are now
included in so simple a meaning as that of the locus of an art.
In the traditional language of philosophy, the essence is now
ideal or rational, non-sensible. Furthermore a system of legal
meanings is developed by modifying different ones with a
view to consistency or logical order. Thus the meanings get

more independent of the events that led up to them; they may be taught and expounded as a logical system, whose portions are deductively connected with one another.

In civil cases, however, the concept of locus even as thus extended fails to take care of all the consequences which are found to require regulation, by attachment of rights and liabilities to certain classes of acts. A transaction may concern goods or funds which operate in a jurisdiction different to that of either of the parties directly concerned in it. Its consequences include persons living in a third jurisdiction. The ultimate result is a tendency in some case to reverse the earlier and more immediately physical (or spatially limited) concept of jurisdiction with respect to place. Jurisdiction comes to mean "power to deal legally" with a certain specific affair, rather than an "area within which action has occurred": that is, area is defined by power to act, which in turn is determined with respect to consequences found desirable, while originally a concept of fixed area had been employed to fix power of legal action. If it be asked, "where" a transaction is located, the only possible answer, on the basis of legal procedure, appears in many cases to be that it is located wherever it has consequences which it is deemed socially important to regulate.[3]

Juridical institutions everywhere embody essences which are as objective and coercive with respect to opinions, emotions and sensations of individuals as are physical objects; essences which are general, capable of independent examination; of fruitful connection with one another; and of extension to concrete phenomena not previously related to them. At the same time the origin and nature of such meanings can be empirically described by reference to social interac-

---

[3] In this respect the actual tendency of law (though not always its doctrinal formulations) is further advanced than are views current among philosophers. Compare the discussions as to "where" an illusion is; or what is the locus of past experience, and "where" unrealized possibilities exist. Some writers find satisfaction in locating them "in" the mind, although they also deny that mind is spatial. Then, realizing that the psychical existence "in" which these affairs are located is itself a present particular existence, they find it necessary to place an "essence" or meaning within the skin of the physical state.

tions and their consequences. They are means of regulating consequences, through establishing a present cross-reference to one another of the diverse acts of interacting agents. If we bear in mind the capacity to transfer such a regulative method to new and previously unconnected universes of discourse, there is nothing astonishing in the fact that a stain may mean an anatomical structure, a change in the size of a mercury column, changes in atmospheric pressure and thus probable rain. There is nothing astonishing therefore in the fact that meanings expressed in symbols are capable of yielding a vast and growing system of mathematics. An essence which is a method of procedure can be linked to other methods of procedure so as to yield new methods; to bring about a revision of old methods, and form a systematic and ordered whole—all without reference to any application of any method to any particular set of concrete existences, and in complete abstraction from any particular consequences which the methods or logical universals are to regulate. For mathematics, they are as much independent objects as is the material with which a zoologist deals. Comparison with machines like a self-binding reaper or a telephone system is useful. Machines are evolved in human experience, not prior to it or independently of it. But they are objective and compelling with respect to present particular physical and psychical processes; they are general methods of reaching consequences; they are interactions of previously existing physical existences. Moreover, they depend for their efficacy upon other and independent natural existences; they produce consequences only when used in connection with other existences which limit and test their operation. When machines have attained a certain stage of development, engineers may devote themselves to the construction of new machines and to improvements in old machines without specific reference to concrete uses and applications. That is, inventors are guided by the inherent logic of existing machines, by observation of the consistency of relationships which parts of the machine bear to one another and to the pattern of the entire machine. An invention may thus result from purely mathematical calculations. Nevertheless the machine is still a machine, an instrumental device for regulating interactions with reference to consequences.

When the "concept" of a machine, its meaning or essence embodied in a symbol, deductively generates plans of new machines, essence is fruitful because it was first devised for a purpose. Its subsequent success or failure in fulfilling its purpose, in delivering the desired consequences, together with reflection upon the reason therefore, supply a basis for revising, extending, and modifying the essence in question; thus it has a career and consequence of its own. If we follow the lead of empirically verifiable cases, it would then appear that mathematical and moral essences may be dialectically fruitful, because like other machines they have been constructed for the purpose of securing certain consequences with the minimum of waste and the maximum of economy and efficiency.

Communication is consummatory as well as instrumental. It is a means of establishing coöperation, domination and order. Shared experience is the greatest of human goods. In communication, such conjunction and contact as is characteristic of animals become endearments capable of infinite idealization; they become symbols of the very culmination of nature. That God is love is a more worthy idealization than that the divine is power. Since love at its best brings illumination and wisdom, this meaning is as worthy as that the divine is truth. Various phases of participation by one in another's joy, sorrows, sentiments and purposes, are distinguished by the scope and depth of the objects that are held in common, from a momentary caress to continued insight and loyalty. When a psychologist like Bain reduced the "tender emotions" to sensations of contact he indicated a natural organic basis. But he failed to connect even organic contact with its vital function, assimilation and fruitful union; while (what is of greater import) he failed to note the transformation that this biological function undergoes when its consequences, being noted, become an objective meaning incorporated as its essence in a natural physiological occurrence.

If scientific discourse is instrumental in function, it also is capable of becoming an enjoyed object to those concerned in it. Upon the whole, human history shows that thinking in being abstract, remote and technical has been laborious; or at least that the process of attaining such thinking has been rendered painful to most by social circumstances. In view of the importance of such activity and its objects, it is a priceless gain when it becomes an intrinsic delight. Few would philosophize if philosophic discourse did not have its own inhering fascination. Yet it is not the satisfactoriness of the activity which defines science or philosophy; the definition comes from the structure and function of subject-matter. To say that knowledge as the fruit of intellectual discourse is an end in itself is to say what is esthetically and morally true for some persons, but it conveys nothing about the structure of knowledge; and it does not even hint that its objects are not instrumental. These are questions that can be decided only by an examination of the things in question. Impartial and disinterested thinking, discourse in terms of scrutinized, tested, and related meanings, is a fine art. But it is an art as yet open to comparatively few. Letters, poetry, song, the drama, fiction, history, biography, engaging in rites and ceremonies hallowed by time and rich with the sense of the countless multitudes that share in them, are also modes of discourse that, detached from immediate instrumental consequences of assistance and coöperative action, are ends for most persons. In them discourse is both instrumental and final. No person remains unchanged and has the same future efficiencies, who shares in situations made possible by communication. Subsequent consequences may be good or bad, but they are there. The part of wisdom is not to deny the causal fact because of the intrinsic value of the immediate experience. It is to make the immediately satisfactory object the object which will also be most fertile.

The saying of Matthew Arnold that poetry is a criticism of life sounds harsh to the ears of some persons of strong esthetic bent; it seems to give poetry a moral and instrumental function. But while poetry is not a criticism of life in intent, it is in effect, and so is all art. For art fixes those standards of enjoyment and appreciation with which other things are compared; it selects the objects of future desires; it stimulates effort. This is true of the objects in which a particular person finds his immediate or esthetic values, and it is true of collective man. The level and style of the arts of literature, poetry, ceremony, amusement, and recreation which obtain in a community, furnishing the staple objects of enjoyment in that community, do more than all else to determine the current direction of ideas and endeavors in the community. They supply the meanings in terms of which life is judged, esteemed, and criticized. For an outside spectator, they supply material for a critical evaluation of the life led by that community.

Communication is uniquely instrumental and uniquely final. It is instrumental as liberating us from the otherwise overwhelming pressure of events and enabling us to live in a world of things that have meaning. It is final as a sharing in the objects and arts precious to a community, a sharing whereby meanings are enhanced, deepened and solidified in the sense of communion. Because of its characteristic agency and finality, communication and its congenial objects are objects ultimately worthy of awe, admiration, and loyal appreciation. They are worthy as means, because they are the only means that make life rich and varied in meanings. They are worthy as ends, because in such ends man is lifted from his immediate isolation and shares in a communion of meanings. Here, as in so many other things, the great evil lies in separating instrumental and final functions. Intelligence is partial and specialized, because communication and participation are limited, sectarian, provincial, confined to class, party, professional group. By the same token, our enjoyment of ends is luxurious and corrupting for some; brutal, trivial, harsh for others; exclusion from the life of free and full communication excluding both alike from full possession of meanings of the things that enter experience. When the instrumental and final functions of communication live together in experience, there exists an intelligence which is the method and reward of the common life, and a society worthy to command affection, admiration, and loyalty.

"Semantic and Poetic Meaning"

Kenneth Burke

Kenneth Burke was born in Pittsburgh, Pennsylvania, May
5, 1897. He was educated at the Ohio State University and
at Columbia. He was music critic for *The Dial* and for
The Nation. He has served as visiting professor at the University of Chicago, Bennington College, and the New School
for Social Research. He has won the Dial Award for Distinguished Service, a Guggenheim Memorial Fellowship,
and grants from the American Academy of Arts and Letters.
His books include *Counter-Statement, Permanence and
Change, Attitudes Toward History, Philosophy of Literary
Form, A Grammar of Motives, A Rhetoric of Motives, Book
of Moments* (poems), and *The Rhetoric of Religion.*

"Semantic and Poetic Meaning" first appeared in *The
Southern Review* and was later included in *The Philosophy
of Literary Form.* It is used here by special permission of
Kenneth Burke.

T HIS essay may be taken as a rhetorical defense of rhetoric. It is intended to give support, sometimes directly and
sometimes indirectly, to the thesis that the ideal of a purely
"neutral" vocabulary, free of emotional weightings, attempts
to make a totality out of a fragment, "till that which suits a
part infects the whole."

The historian Toynbee, I am told, has laid stress upon the
period of "withdrawal" undergone by founders of religious
structures. It is a period of hesitancy, brooding, or even rot,
prior to the formation of the new certainties they will subsequently evangelize and organize. Stated in secular terms,
it marks a transition from a system of social values grown
unfit for the situation they would encompass, to a new order
of values felt, correctly or not, to be a more scrupulous fit
for the situation. "Circumstances alter occasions," and for the
altered occasions they would round out a new strategy.

In the semantic ideal, we get an attenuated variant of this "withdrawal" process. It would build up a technical mode of analysis that gave us permanently and constantly a kind of mitigated withdrawal, thereby converting a transitional stage into an institution. Like the monastic orders, it would "bureaucratize" a purgatorial mood, turning a "state of evanescence" into a fixity by giving it an established routine. It would prolong a moment into a "way of life."

While attempting to uphold the thesis that there is no basic opposition between the ideals of semantic and poetic naming, that they are different rather than antithetical in their ultimate realistic aims, I do grant that there is a "dialectical process" whereby a difference becomes converted into an antithesis. You have, for example, noted that when two opponents have been arguing, though the initial difference in their position may have been slight, they tend under the "dialectical pressure" of their drama to become eventually at odds in everything. No matter what one of them happens to assert, the other (responding to the genius of the contest) takes violent exception to it—and vice versa. Thus similarly we find the *differences* between "bourgeois" and "proletarian" treated, under dialectical pressure, as an *absolute antithesis*, until critics, accustomed to thinking by this pat schematization, become almost demoralized at the suggestion that there may be a "margin of overlap" held in common between different classes. And if a man has at one time been engrossed in music, and at a later time becomes engrossed in painting, he will probably evolve an emotional economy whereby music and painting become for him the *opposite* of each other (as in Odets' *Golden Boy* violin and prizefight are filled out as antitheses, the violin signifying home and harmony, the prizefight leaving-home and competition). And likewise with the semantics-poetry issue, where semantic meaning, that may be considered as a partial aspect of poetic meaning, tends to become instead the *opposite* of poetic meaning, so that a mere graded series, comprising a more-than and a less-than, changes instead into a blunt battle between poetry and antipoetry, or "poetry vs.

science." Only by a kind of "synecdochic fallacy," mistaking a part for the whole, can this opposition appear to exist.

1. THE SEMANTIC IDEAL ILLUSTRATED. For our point of departure, let us take the address on an envelope:

> M................(name)
> ....(street and number)
> ....(city or town)
> ....(state)
> ....(nation)

By filling out those few lines, you can effectively isolate one man among two billion, quite as though each individual were identified by an automobile license, with a record kept in some central bureau, like the Bertillon measurements of known criminals.

Perhaps we have exaggerated the case. The formula wouldn't work for getting an advertisement to a mid-African chieftain. Yet it can effectively isolate one of the two billion, if he happens to be among the hundreds of millions available through postal organization. The matter to be emphasized is this: In whatever areas the postal organization prevails, this brief formula generally serves to isolate the desired individual.

The formula has no orientative value in itself. It depends for its significance upon the establishment of a postal structure, as a going concern. It is like the coin in a slot machine. Given the machine, in good order, the coin will "work." The address, as a counter, works in so far as it indicates to the postal authorities what kind of operation should be undertaken. But it *assumes* an organization. Its *meaning*, then, involves the established procedures of the mails, and is in the instructions it gives for the performance of desired operations within this going concern.

The man who writes the address on an envelope may know very little about the concreteness of these operations. Likewise, the sorter who first tosses the letter into the "state" or "nation" bin will not concretely envision the act of final delivery, after the letter has been sifted down through various sub-classifications, until it reaches the pouch of the mail-man on his route. Any single worker, handling the letter in its various stages of transit, interprets the address as instructions for a different kind of operation. Its "totality" is in the organized interlocking of these operations themselves, whereby each "specialist," performing a "partial" act, yet contributes to the performing of a "total" act, the entire arc of the letter's transit, from insertion in the mailbox at the corner to delivery at the door.

This kind of meaning I should call a *semantic* meaning. And extending from that I should state, as the semantic ideal, the aim *to evolve a vocabulary that gives the name and address of every event in the universe.*

Such naming would require the kind of "operational" test put forward in Bridgman's theory of meaning, which has recently been overzealously advocated by Stuart Chase in his *The Tyranny of Words*.[1] It is also, I think, the ideal of the logical positivists. Logical positivism would *point* to events. It would attempt to describe events after the analogy of the chart (as a map could be said to describe America). And the significance of its pointing lies in the instructions implicit in the name.

An ideal semantic definition of a chair would be such that, on the basis of the definition, people knew what you wanted when you asked for one, a carpenter knew how to make it, a furniture dealer knew how to get it, etc. An ideal definition of an electron is such that the specialist knows what to do (within the limits of his technique and equipment) to bring about the kind of manifestation called an electron.

---

[1] However, Chase's book is so much closer to scissor-work than to composition that no characterization by a summarizing proposition is wholly adequate. We might, rather, classify the work by reference to its manner, thus: "A rhetorical farewell to rhetoric—or, the tyrannicide as tyrant." And we might attempt quickly to convey the quality of his "revolt" against words (done in the extreme debunking mode) by noting such chapter headings as "Promenade with the Philosophers," "Swing Your Partners with the Economists," and "Round and Round with the Judges."

On the other hand, when you have isolated your individual by the proper utilizing of the postal process, you have not at all adequately encompassed his "meaning." He means one thing to his family, another to his boss, another to his underlings, another to his creditors, etc. All such meanings are *real* enough, since at every point people act towards him on the basis of these meanings. And at many points they impinge upon purely semantic meanings. His meaning for his creditors, for instance, may be involved in a credit report from Dun and Bradstreet's. His meaning to his underlings may lead them to adopt certain proportions of familiarity and aloofness. His wife may have found out that, as the case may be, she can get him to buy a new refrigerator either by saying that the Joneses already have one or that the Joneses do not have one. His boss may have decided that he is especially good at certain kinds of business, and especially poor at certain other kinds of business. And much of this can actually be "tested," though in a less organized way than would apply to the instructions for the filling of a medical prescription.

But though this kind of meaning *impinges* upon semantic meaning, it cannot be encompassed with perfect fidelity to the *semantic ideal*. You can't give the names and addresses of all these subtle significances. There is no organization like the postal service or the laboratory or the factory, with a set of patly interlocking functions. This kind of meaning I shall call *poetic* meaning.

Seen from this angle, poetic meaning and semantic meaning would not be absolute antitheses. Poetic meaning would not be the *opposite* of semantic meaning. It would be different from, or other than, or more than, or even, if you want, less than, but not antithetical to.

2. POETIC MEANING. Semantic meaning would be a way of pointing to a chair. It would say, "That thing is a chair." And to a carpenter it would imply, in keeping with his organized technique, "By doing such and such, I can produce this thing, a chair." Poetic pointing, on the other hand,

might take many courses, roughly summed up in these
three sentences:

> "Faugh, a chair!"
> "Ho, ho! a chair!"
> "Might I call your attention to yon chair?"

Of these, the third style of pointing obviously comes nearest
to the semantic ideal. The first two, most strongly weighted
with emotional values, with *attitudes*, would be farther off.
Meaning there would unquestionably be, since an attitude
contains an implicit program of action. An attitude may be
reasonable or unreasonable; it may contain an adequate
meaning or an inadequate meaning—but in either case, it
would contain a meaning.

In aesthetics, you find the word "art" used indetermi-
nately in two ways. Sometimes the thinker appears to mean
"art, any art, all art," and at other times, "good art." And
similarly, in theories of meaning, the concept sometimes
seems to imply "any meaning, whether right or wrong,
sound or fallacious," and at other times "correct meaning."

Meaning, when used in the sense of "correct meaning,"
leads to an either-or approach. "New York City is in Iowa"
could, by the either-or principles, promptly be ruled out.
The either-or test would represent the semantic ideal. But
I am sorry to have to admit that, by the poetic ideal, "New
York City is in Iowa" could *not* be ruled out.

Has one ever stood, for instance, in some little outlying
town, on the edge of the wilderness, and watched a train
go by? Has one perhaps suddenly felt that the train, and its
tracks, were a kind of arm of the city, reaching out across
the continent, quite as though it were simply Broadway itself extended? It is in such a sense that New York City can
be found all over the country—and I submit that one would
miss very important meanings, meanings that have much
to do with the conduct of our inhabitants, were he to proceed here by the either-or kind of test.

"New York City is in Iowa" is "poetically" true. As a
metaphor, it provides valid insight. To have ruled it out,

by strict semantic authority, would have been vandalism.

"Poetic" meanings, then, cannot be disposed of on the true-or-false basis. Rather, they are related to one another like a set of concentric circles, of wider and wider scope. Those of wider diameter do not categorically eliminate those of narrower diameter. There is, rather, a progressive *encompassment*. To say that "man is a vegetable" contains much soundness. There is a vegetative level of human response, and one can find out much about it (much more, in fact, than we now know, as more is to be learned, for instance, about the ways in which the biologic organism responds to seasonal periodicity, changes in solar radiation, and the like). Again: to say that "man is an ant" does not "refute" the vegetational metaphor. The ant may be "vegetation-plus," since it too vegetates. And to say that "man is a communicant" is more comprehensive still, including the other metaphors but not abolishing them. These are examples of progressive encompassment that does not admit of mutual exclusion—and they are examples of what we take poetic characterizations to do.

3. A DIFFERENT MODE PROPOSED FOR THE TEST OF POETIC MEANING. Hence, for the validity of "poetic" meanings, I should suggest that the "test" cannot be a formal one, as with the diagrams for testing a syllogism. Poetic characterizations do not categorically exclude each other in the either-true-or-false sense, any more than the characterizations "honest" or "tall" could categorically exclude the characterizations "learned," "unlearned," or "thin." The test of a metaphor's validity is of a much more arduous sort, requiring nothing less than the *filling-out, by concrete body, of the characterizations which one would test.* There is no formal procedure, for example, for choosing among the three metaphors:

> man a vegetable
> man an ant
> man a communicant.

One can simply ask that the contestants advocate their

choice by *filling it out*. That is: *let each say all he can* by
way of giving body to the perspective inherent in his choice.
Let each show the scope, range, relevancy, accuracy, appli-
cability of the perspective, or metaphor, he would advocate.
And only after each has been so filled out, can we evaluate
among them. Thus, though there be no *formal* basis for a
choice among the three metaphors offered above, the test
of filling-out, of embodiment in concrete application, would,
I think, demonstrate the greater value of the third for interpretative purposes. One could *do more* with it. He could
integrate wider areas of human relationship. Hence, as so
tested, it would be assigned a higher place than the other
two in a hierarchy of possible perspectives. No perspective
could be formally ruled out, but one could be shown to
include another.

Such testing would also involve more than merely expository meaning, of the "graph" sort. The third metaphor would
likewise be richer in hortatory significance. It would not
merely give the names and addresses of events, but would
also suggest exhortations for the promotion of *better* names
and addresses. The metaphor would thus serve not only a
descriptive function, but also a normative function.

4. THE MORAL ASPECT OF POETIC MEANING. Much of the
partial descriptive matter now developed, as in the behaviorists' experiments with conditioning, would still be usable.
But instead of being taken as the description of man's *essence*, it would be considered simply for its value in revealing *certain important things to look out for* in any attempt to
plead for a more satisfactory communicative or coöperative
structure. Thus, if the data on conditioning were presented
as *an admonishment* about people, rather than as *the* "low
down" on them, the interpretative enterprise would be re-
stored to its proper *moralistic* basis, in contrast with the
"neutral" or "non-moral" ideals of meaning implicit in the
attempt to get merely descriptive labels (an attempt that, if
it succeeded, would find its very success a mockery, for it
would describe social events in a way that led to no moral
exhortation, and would then have simply to let moral pur-

poses creep in as contraband, a kind of irrational weakness, or benign error).

In general, primitive magic tended to transfer an animistic perspective to the charting of physical events. And positivistic science, by antithesis, leads to an opposite ideal, the transferring of a physicalist perspective to human events. Each is the migration of a metaphor in ways that require correctives, though I am willing to admit that, of the two excesses, I consider the savages' tendency to consider natural forces as spirits less deceptive than the positivists' tendency to consider people after the analogy of physical behavior. Semantic ideas of meaning could not possibly provide a proper vocabulary in which to consider the complexities of moral growth, because there is here no pragmatic routine to be "learned by repetition," as with proficiency in a trade. There is nothing to be "practiced" in the sense that one may practice tennis or carpentry. Qualitative growth cannot be "practiced" any more than biological growth can be "practiced." Given the faculty of speech, one can by practice master a new language. But there is no way for a dumb animal to acquire this faculty itself by practice. There is no "operation" for seeing a joke—though there may be operations for removing obstructions to the seeing of the joke.

The difference between the semantic ideal and the poetic ideal of moralistic interpretation would, I think, get down to this:

The semantic ideal would attempt to *get a description* by the *elimination* of attitude. The poetic ideal would attempt to *attain a full moral act* by attaining a perspective *atop all the conflicts of attitude.*

The first would try to *cut away*, to *abstract*, all emotional factors that complicate the objective charity of meaning. The second would try to derive its vision from the maximum *heaping up* of all these emotional factors, playing them off against one another, inviting them to reinforce and contradict one another, and seeking to make this active participation itself a major ingredient of the vision.

This "poetic" meaning would contain much more than

pragmatic, positivistic, futuristic values. A fully moral act is basically an act *now*. It is not promissory, it is not "investment for future profit." It is not the learning of a technique in the hopes this technique, when learned, will enable one to make wheels go or to add a few more metallurgical alloys to the 500,000 or so that "business" and "industry" have not yet found "use" for. A fully moral act is a total assertion at the time of the assertion. Among other things, it has a *style*—and this style is an integral aspect of its meaning. If it points to the chair by saying "faugh," it pledges itself to one program—to quite another if it adopts the style of "ho, ho" or "might I?" The style selected will mold the character of the selector. Each brand of imagery contains in germ its own "logic." If he says "faugh" and deeply means it, he thereby *vows* himself to "faugh"; he must go *through* the faughness, until he has either persisted by the buttressing of his choice or has burnt it out.

But I seem to be contradicting myself, since I called a stylistic act an act *now*, whereas I have been talking about its future implications. For there is a sense in which every act involves a future—but within this generalization there is a distinction. The distinction may be suggested in this way: To name something in the style of "faugh" is symbolically to act out a present attitude towards it, in the naming. To label it "Q271-Vii" is to withhold my act as a total present expression. The value of such naming will not reside so much in the rewards at the time, but in the "uses" I may subsequently put my nomenclature to. The name "Q271-Vii," for instance, may be much more serviceable as tested by some actuarial requirement or some problem in traffic regulation. To call a man a son-of-a-bitch is symbolically to make a complete assertion of attitude towards him now; it is itself a culmination, a "total summing up." To call him "Q271-Vii," on the other hand, is to put the value of the name in its future alone. It depends solely upon what you do with it, "in our next." In this sense it is relying upon the "promissory," whether mistaken or real.

5. "BEYOND GOOD AND EVIL." The semantic ideal envisions a vocabulary that *avoids* drama. The poetic ideal envisions a vocabulary that *goes through* drama. In their ideal completion, they have a certain superficial resemblance, in that both are "beyond good and evil." But the first seeks to attain this end by the programmatic elimination of a weighted vocabulary at the start (the neutralization of names containing attitudes, emotional predisposition); and the second would attain the same end by exposure to the *maximum profusion* of weightings. The first would be aside from the battle, stressing the role of the observer, whose observations it is hoped will define situations with sufficient realistic accuracy to prepare an adequate *chart* for action; the second would contend, by implication, that true knowledge can only be attained through the battle, stressing the role of the participant, who in the course of his participation, it is hoped, will define situations with sufficient realistic accuracy to prepare an *image* for action.

The poetic ideal being obviously aesthetic, we could in contrast call the semantic ideal "anesthetic"; for though *aesthetic*, in its etymological origins, derives from a word meaning "to perceive," it has come to include the idea of emotionality in the perception, whereas the semantic ideal would aim at perception without feeling. Perhaps, in view of the etymological difficulties, we should sacrifice our pun on *aesthetic-anesthetic*, and instead offer as the semantic counterpart of aesthetic, "analgesic."

We should also point out that, although the semantic ideal would eliminate the *attitudinal* ingredient from its vocabulary (seeking a vocabulary for events equally valid for use by friends, enemies, and the indifferent) the ideal is itself an attitude, hence never wholly attainable, since it could be complete only by the abolition of itself. To the logical positivist, logical positivism is a "good" term, otherwise he would not attempt to advocate it by filling it out in all its ramifications. This observation spoils the symmetry of our case, in suggesting that semantics itself may be considered as an attenuated form of poetry, that "Q271-Vii" may itself be a gesture, secretly saying in a very mild way what "fiend" or "darling" says eagerly.

It would seem fair to take the symbols of Russell and Whitehead's *Principia Mathematica,* or the formulae of Carnap, as the nearest approach we have to the vocabulary of the semantic ideal. Or one may feel that we are stacking the cards here. Perhaps the semantic ideal does not show up at its best in ultimate over-all theories, but in the specific vocabularies of technological specializations. The vocabulary of chemistry, for instance, may be much the same for communist, fascist, and liberal. A theory of ballistics may be couched in one set of symbols, whether it is to be studied by progressives or reactionaries. A topographical survey may be as "neutral" as the situation it surveys; it needs only to be *accurate,* and the soundings that the Japs are said to be taking of our Western coast line aim at precisely the same kind of description as would the soundings taken by strategists of the U.S. navy.

So, for our purposes, you may, as you prefer, consider the semantic ideal most fully embodied in either the vocabulary of any specific technique, or in the coördinating theory designed to make a body of generalizations that would *mutatis mutandis* cover all the specific techniques. In any case, even if you do prefer to insist that the vocabularies of the physical sciences represent the semantic ideal at its best, you must concede that it is the hope of the semanticist to build a vocabulary for the discussion of human, or social, events after the same model. A vocabulary that does not *judge,* but *describes* or *places,* as the psychologists' terminology is designed simply to name *how things are,* regardless of what you *want* them to be.

The coyness of the semantic strategy might be conveyed like this: A theory of ballistics, as a physical sceince, merely tells you how to shoot ammunition. As such, it is "neutral," capable of being taken over by friends or enemies. If, however, you extended the same kind of vocabulary to describe the situations of friends and enemies also, their enmity likewise would be neutralized. Leave the process half completed, develop neutrality in the vocabulary of the physical sciences while leaving prejudice in the vocabulary of social relations, and technology as a power becomes an ominous power. But extend the technological ideal throughout the social sciences as well, and technological power becomes equated with good power. If this account of the semantic hope is fair, it would justify us in saying that the over-all semantic theorics, rather than the vocabularies of specific scientific disciplines, are to be taken as representative of the ultimate semantic ideal.[2]

6. LETTING IN AND KEEPING OUT. Plays like Shakespeare's *Tempest* or Aeschylus' *Eumenides* would represent the ideal poetic vocabulary. Lucretius' *De Rerum Natura* is a mixture of both ideals. Wedded, as a materialist ("philosophical scientist") to the aim of analgesia, Lucretius nonetheless builds up extremely emotional moments. For example, in trying to make us feel the great relief that would come to us from the abolition of the gods, Lucretius exposes himself to the full rigors of religious awe. He must make us realize *awe*, in the contemplation of heavenly distances and storms, in order to make us realize the full measure of the *relief* that would follow from the dissolution of this awe (by dissolving the gods which have become the symbols, the "charismatic vessels," of it). So he becomes somewhat an advocate against his own thesis. For in trying to build up a full realization of the awe, in order to build up a full realization of the freedom that would come of banishing this awe, he leaves us with an

---

[2] Enough has been said, incidentally, to suggest that the over-all semantic chart is itself the riding of a metaphor, quite as the poet may carry some underlying metaphor, as a theme with variations, throughout his sonnet or his play. In logical positivism, according to one expositor (Julius Rudolph Weinberg: *An Examination of Logical Positivism*), "propositions are pictures of possible empirical facts." Thus the controversy does not resolve itself into an opposition between poetry as metaphorical and semantics as non-metaphorical. Every perspective requires a metaphor, implicit or explicit, for its organisational base (as I tried to make clear in the section on "Perspective by Incongruity" in *Permanence and Change*)—and semantics as a perspective cannot shift this necessity. This point may well be borne in mind at those places where I would ask to have the semantic perspective encompassed within the poetic perspective (considering semantics as a kind of special "poetic school" that would seek to erect its *partial* truth into a *whole* truth).

unforgettable image of the awe itself. We are left with the suspicion that he has never really freed himself of awe, but that he has been fighting valiantly to repress it (thereby indirectly reinforcing our sense of its pressure). He has tried, by the magic of his incantations, to get analgesia (perception without emotion); but he builds up, aesthetically, the motivation behind his anesthetic incantatory enterprise, thereby making us tremble all over again at the lines in which he reconstructs the sublimity of natural vastnesses and power, a vision reinforced by the tonal suggestiveness of his sentences (that contribute in their musicality to violate the genius of "Q271-Vii").

The pure semantic ideal, on the other hand, would have avoided this strategic difficulty at the start. For one thing, it would never discuss awe in words that, by their incantatory power, themselves suggested awe. It would spare itself Lucretius' losing task of refutation by never once giving aesthetic embodiment to the sense of awe. By never letting awe in, it would skirt the embarrassing problem of trying to get it out again. From the very start, its mode of naming "simply wouldn't give awe a chance." This feeling might possibly be lying there, in the background, as a motive in the semanticist's enterprise, but only by highly dubious detective work, by modes of metaphorical analysis that the semanticist himself would question as science, could you disclose such a motive. What the semanticist would put out, he never lets in.

7. AESCHYLUS' *Eumenides* TO ILLUSTRATE FULL POETIC MEANING. In the *Eumenides*, I think, we see the poetic method in its completeness. Where the semanticist does not fight, and Lucretius fights while stacking the odds against himself, Aeschylus completely gives himself to aesthetic exposure, and surmounts the risk. Here, to be sure, is the ideal of analgesia—but it appears at the *end* of a most painful trilogy, devoted to an aesthetic reconstruction of struggle, horror, and the tortures of remorse. And to comfort us, the dramatist undertakes nothing less than the *conversion of the gods themselves.*

In this respect the play parallels explicitly the change we

get as we turn from the wrathful Jehovah of the Old Testament (a warrior god, like warrior gods partaking of the rage that is in the Grecian Furies and the Norse Valkyries) to the Living Logos of the New Testament. Here is a ritual for the conversion of the Furies from a malign identity (named the Erinyes, from *erinyo*, to be wrathful towards) to a benign identity (named the Eumenides, from *eumeneo*, to feel kindly towards). Henceforth, we are informed, the emphasis of their function will be radically altered. No longer will they devote their ingenuity and enterprise to the *punishment of evil*, but the stress henceforth will be upon the *protection of good*. Logically, the two functions are certainly not at odds, but psychologically they are in far different realms. Fittingly, for our analysis, the Furies are characterized as *older* gods; and their conversion from malign to benign emphasis was done under the persuasion of such *younger* gods as Apollo and Athena. (Incidentally, I am indebted, for the form of this thought, to John Crowe Ransom's *God Without Thunder*, a work that has not generally been given the recognition it deserves. Unfortunately, I also have a responsibility to bear in this matter, as I was assigned *God Without Thunder* for review, but became so tangled in various ramifications of the critic's thesis that my review was never finished. In particular, as I see it now, I was struggling between a desire to salute his basic observation and a muddled disagreement with the uses he made of it. In any case, the incident has been on my conscience, for works of such incision are too rare for us to afford their neglect, and I shall feel better in so far as I have here belatedly made amends.)

What went on, in this play? Recently I caught a glimpse, or at least thought I caught a glimpse, of the exhilaration that must have lifted up the Athenian audience when it first felt the medicinal action of this ritual. On the personal plane, we have the redemption of Orestes, with whose suffering the audience had presumably been profoundly identified, so that they would also profoundly take part in his release. On the religious plane, this personal redemption is contrived by nothing less important than a reordering of divinity itself, as

the persecutional gods of wrath relinquish their torture of
Orestes only after they have been persuaded to change their
very office, taking a new temple in Athens where, under-
ground, they will zealously and jealously do well by Athenian virtue, if any. And to round out the pattern for this polis-
minded people (one of the names of Zeus was Zeus Agoraios,
Zeus the forensic) Orestes' restoration from division to unity
is the occasion for the solemnizing of a pact between Athens
and Argos. When all this had been put together (the personal, the religious, and the social—while the quick convergence
towards the close must have been breath-taking), there is one
final stroke still to be delivered:

> *Attendants.*   Then come, ye dread powers, kind and
> faithful to Athens, nor waken to wrath;
> Come hither, be cheered by the flame, pine-
> consuming, that lightens your path.
>
> *Herald.*   Shout, ye folk, a new age hath begun!
>
> *Attendants.*   Torch-illumined libations henceforward
> the people of Pallas shall bring
> To your dwelling—so Fate hath made compact
> with Zeus the Olympian King.
>
> *Herald.*   South, ye people, the chanting is done!

"A new age!" Thus had the cornerstone been grandilo-
quently laid for an ancient structure of "modernity." May
one not also discern even a certain playwright's cunning
here? For is not the final exhortation of the Herald an invita-
tion to let the stage flow over into the audience, making
participation between actors and audience complete, as they
are asked to weld their shout of approval *for* the play with
a shout that has meaning *within* the play? Could they know
quite what their applause would signify: whether it was
applause for Aeschylus, or stage applause, or applause for
the slogan that so deftly put the coming era of enlightenment
under good auspices, thereby "filling a civic need"? Thomas
Mann, in his letter to the official of Bonn University, who

had notified him of the retraction of his honorary degree, begins by taking up this matter—but before he has finished, the issue has been subtly transformed into something of much broader implications. It is hard to remember, in retrospect, just when we shifted from a point of controversy between Mann and the subservient official to a discussion of cultural trends in their most sweeping aspects. Such are the persuasive ambiguities of identification. And might we note something similar, as we cannot tell whether the shout is within the play, for the play, for Athens or for Aeschylus, for the tactics of the ritualistic compliment whereby the "new age" is evangelically announced, or for the "new age" itself? Such complexity is what I glimpsed, or thought I glimpsed, when this firm architecture of action was first unveiled before the Athenian audience. The play itself had offered its audience ample grounds to shout—and in its closing line it gives them explicitly a cue to shout.

8. "THROUGH" AND "AROUND." The particular "curve" of Aeschylus' development is to be caught perhaps as we contrast the Orestes trilogy with an earlier drama, *The Persae*, a "factional" drama where the crime is committed by "the enemy," the foreigner Xerxes, in contrast with the later work in the mode of "universal" tragedy, where the crime is committed by Everyman.

But, like or dislike this whole mode of assuagement, as you prefer: the important point to be stressed for our purposes is that it is accomplished by going *through* drama, not by going *around* drama, or perhaps more accurately, *forestalling* drama. Similarly in Socrates, both the man and the protagonist formalized by Plato, there is a "dialectical" approach (through the dramas of conflict) to the ultimate philosophic vision. With Aristotle, however, you move towards something different. Here there is somewhat the tendency "to take up where Plato left off," as though Plato were still living and were making a definitive revision of his own first draft. Aristotle's *Rhetoric* and *Poetics* are evidence that he still retained a strong appreciation of the dramatic experience. But the risk of attenuation, successfully weathered by him, becomes progressively greater as we move towards disciples who would, in turn, "take up where Aristotle left off." Such development operates to perfection in the quantitative realm, as in the successive improvements made atop a mechanical invention. But one may question whether it applies to the qualitative realm, as with some recent young composers who, impressed with the tonal inventions of Beethoven's last quartets, would attempt simply to "begin" where he had ended, as though there could be handed to them, on a platter, the imaginative grasp of this ultimate period, which Beethoven himself earned by all that had gone before it. They tend, of course, simply to "project" his last style with efficiency into a mannerism, quite as Western borrowers of Chinese or African art tend to get the shell without the egg, or as a child will "imitate" a workman by merely making the same kind of noise.

Now, there is a crucial difference between the peace of a warrior who lays down his arms (Aeschylus wanted to be remembered, not as a poet, but as a soldier), and the peace of those who are innocent of war (innocence untried being like snow fallen in the night; let us not praise it for not melting until the sun has been full upon it). And the semantic ideal, I submit, would attempt to give us the final rewards of *Versöhnung*, of atonement, before we had ever gone through the conflicts by which alone we could properly "earn" it.

No, we are here being too thorough. Let us revise the fable in this wise: Men, out of conflict, evolve projects for atonement, *Versöhnung*, assuagement. They hand these on to others. And the heirs must either make these structures of atonement the basis of a new conflict, or be emptied. Much of the best in thought is evolved to teach us how to die well; whereupon it is studied and built upon by those who have never lived well. Either anesthesia is earned by aesthesia, or it is empty. When philosophy advances beyond the quality of Lucretius, who builds up the fear as well as the antidote, it approaches inanition.

The best thing to be said in favor of the semantic ideal is that it is a fraud: one may believe in it because it is impossible. Because poetry has been so arrantly misused, in the sophistries of the press and of political demagogues, there is apparent justification for the attempt to eliminate it. But one could with as much logic abolish printing itself, since printing has been misused. To paraphrase Mallarmé: semantics would make us Promethean inventors, minus the vulture ("*égaux de Prométhée à qui manque un vautour*").

A comprehensive vocabulary, for social purposes, will persistently outrage the norms of the semantic ideal. It will not be unweighted; rather, it will have a maximum complexity of weighting. It will strike and retreat, compliment and insult, challenge and grovel, sing, curse, and whimper, subside and recover. Repeatedly, it will throw forth observations that are as accurate, in the realistic charting of human situations, as any ideal semantic formula. Many proverbs are brilliantly so. It will "neutralize" a meaning at any desired point. But such behavior must be merely taken in its stride. And its test of a "true" meaning will be its ability to fit into a piece with all other meanings, which is something radically different from the sheer expectancy that comes with conditioned salivation at the sound of a bell. (I sometimes wonder whether all of human "progress" is to be summed up as the insertion of an "i" in the word "salvation.")

9. COMPLAINTS. *The semantic style is bad style,* except in those who violate its tenets, as Newton violated them in the resonance of the language in which he gave account of his "celestial mechanics." Charts, graphs, crop reports, "intelligence," editorial comment, low-powered description—all such is justifiable only in so far as "we gotta live," justifiable in short by the real or hoped-for "return on the investment."

Perhaps it is unfair to attack all this in the name of semantics, yet it is more legitimate to characterize it as poor semantics, than as poor poetry. Information is quite often "semantically" sound. But it is rarely resonant. The percentage of such stuff has become too high. Unawares, we have allowed ourselves to take it as the *norm,* thereby confusing a norm with an average.

Even in poetry itself, "the norm" has encroached. I wonder

how long it has been since a poet has asked himself: "What would I say if I wanted to present Miss Q with a gift, accompanied by a deft verbal compliment?—or what would I say if I wanted to knife someone *neatly*?" Or since someone told himself: "Suppose I did not simply wish to load upon the broad shoulders of the public medium, my own ungainly appetites and ambitions? Suppose that, gnarled as I am, I did not consider it enough simply to seek payment for my gnarledness, the establishment of communion through evils held in common? Suppose I would also erect a structure of encouragement, for all of us? How should I go about it, in the sequence of imagery, not merely to bring us most poignantly *into* hell, but also *out* again? Should I leave the curse of a malign spell upon us, in so far as I am able, and in so far as my audience cannot shake it off of themselves by discounting and triviality? Must there not, for every flight, be also a return, before my work can be called complete as a moral act?"

The thought suggests what must have been going on when the symphonic form was vital. The opening allegro: calm before storm. The sorrows, risks, and the ingenious struggles of movements two and three. And the final celebration, as a "way out," the bright clapping of the hands that releases the hypnotic spell (or should we say, supplants it with a daylight spell?). Then, as we move from the symphony towards the tone poem, we turn from this *rounded* aesthetic to the aesthetic of the Poe story. The one corrosive spell, leaving it for the reader's own enterprise or superficiality to shake himself free of the burden it would shift from the writer's shoulders upon his, a sacrificial goat. Alpheus without Arethusa.

Is it possible that writers are forgetting what to ask of their paragraphs? And should we think all the more on this subject, since we seem threatened with a period of political gloom ranging anywhere from a repellent aimlessness to an even more repellent aim (and if we get the latter, men will give blows with twice the fury of blows, striking the external enemy with vengeance, and making him also the recipient of their rage against the past uncertainties within themselves, a double-duty form of assertion we may fear especially in our frustrated businessmen, whose businesses have got in each other's way, and who are looking earnestly for someone to serve as vessel of their rage). We must get sturdiness from somewhere—we must seek some kind of physical muscle and its mental counterparts.

If a dismal political season is in store for us, shall we not greatly need a campaign base for personal integrity, a kind of beneath-which-not? And I wonder whether we might find this beneath-which-not in a more strenuous cult of style. This effort has been made many times in the past—and as regularly has been despised at other times, when there was no longer any need for it. Style for its own sake? Decidedly, not at all. Style solely as the *beneath-which-not* as the *admonitory and hortatory act,* as the *example* that would prod continually for its completion in all aspects of life, and so, in Eliot's phrase, "keep something alive," tiding us over a lean season. And there is all the more reason for us to attempt doing what we can by *present* imagery, since the promissory, the rewards of "postponed consumption," hold out so little of encouragement for the political future within our lifetime. So might we, rather than living wholly by a future that threatens so strongly to refute us, do rather what we can to live in a present that may in good time spread into the future?

Do not get me wrong. I am pleading for no "retreat" to anything. No literary Buchmanism, no off-by-itself, no back-to. Let our enlistments remain as they are. I am asking simply that the *temper* of our enlistment undergo a change of emphasis. That the *norm* of our tone cease to be the insulting tone that "talks down" to people. Nor would it be a presumptuous tone, that laid claim to uplift them. But rather a tone that would plead with us all, with the writer-to as well as the written-to. In it there must also be disdain, for those who have been giving the final insult to democracy, as they contrive to suggest that one almost has a moral obligation to write trivially and superficially, as though one could only show a proper love of mankind by plying the citizenry with flimsy items, "to be used once and thrown away."

The editor was late. The paper was ready for the printer, all but the columns reserved for him. Yet he knocked off his opinions on the state of the world in time to beat the deadline. Reading them, one recalled: "Yours of the twelfth inst. to hand, and have noted same. In reply would beg to state that we . . . etc." This is "the norm." By it all else is tested. It has its place. And unquestionably, the opinions of a trained opinionator, situated at a strategic point with relation to the channels of information and advice, may even thus haphazardly make better comment than could a man deprived of his advantages. The question is: have they done anything? Can they, in this form, possibly do anything? I submit that they cannot. And further, I submit that, in so far as they become "the norm," they serve to prevent the doing of anything. On the other hand, out of attempts to key up the values of style, there could emerge writers whose muscularity was a fit with the requirements of the people. As things now stand, "the norm" prevents even an attempt at such selectivity.

In keeping with this norm, bright boys are imported from the provinces, put through the mill, stamped with a method, and used hard until they are used up—whereupon other bright boys are imported to take their places, the whole being kept on its toes despite disgust and boredom by muscling in and the fear of muscling in, with financial hashish as the positive incentive.

Or imagine this hypothetical case: Imagine an investigator who confided: "I've finished collating my material; I have my findings; but I haven't been able to write them up; I can't get the right sentence to start the whole thing going." The notion seems almost impertinent. The fact is that he would say his say, without a qualm, though his sentences rattled like dice in a box. When considering the welter of minor investigations that are now taken as the normal output of the academic bureaucracy, arising from the fact that everybody is expected to codify something or other for his degree, while the disproportionate flow of incomes acts to support a vast quantity of such low-powered collations—when considering these stamp collections of an overly proliferating priesthood, I have wondered whether we might legitimately try to introduce some new kind of Occam's Razor, some new test for exclusion of the inessential. Suppose, for example, that a man were permitted only to say something that he could grow eloquent about. That is, suppose he were to place this requirement upon himself. I grant that there would be much persiflage released upon the world. But every once in a while it wouldn't be persiflage. And much that now gets "scientific immunity" by reason of its very pallor (a kind of "protection by unnoticeableness") would in its attempted keying-up expose itself the more readily to weeding-out. As things now stand, its pallor enjoys protective coloration by its close likeness to the journalistic pallor, that is "the norm."

10. CONCLUSION. It would be unfair to lay all these ills to the "semantic ideal." It might be more just to say that the semantic ideal is the *perfection* of trends which we find here in their aggravatedly *imperfect* state. At its best, it has an incisiveness, an accuracy of formulation, a nicety, that makes it itself a style. But anything short of it becomes the mere riding of a convenience. And even at its best, when isolated from the total texture of language, it is insufficient, and promotes the upbuilding of a fallacious equipment.

Above all, it fosters, sometimes explicitly, sometimes by implication, the notion that one may comprehensively discuss human and social events in a nonmoral vocabulary, and that perception itself is a nonmoral act. It is the moral impulse that motivates perception, giving it both intensity and direction, suggesting *what to look for* and *what to look out for*. Only by wanting very profoundly to make improvement, can we get a glimpse into the devious personal and impersonal factors that operate to balk improvement. Or, stating this in reverse, we could say that the structural firmness in a character like Iago is in itself an evidence of Shakespeare's moral depth. For it was in knowing what to look for that Shakespeare also knew what to look out for. We might even say that Shakespeare constructed this archdemon by making him an ominous caricature of the playwright's own methods, so that he becomes an admonishment not only to us, but to his inventor. For that peculiarly subtle variant of the "confidence game" in which Iago was an adept, inciting Othello to participate by leading him always to complete the surmises for himself, never wholly saying them, but all-but-saying them, and saying them in such a way that there is only one course for Othello to follow in building "logically" upon them, and taking double precautions to keep him in this track by constant repetition of goatish imagery—are not these Shakespeare's own profoundest wiles, here made sinister? So let the poetic ideal be sloganized as *Iago-plus-Ariel*—and let the semantic ideal be sloganized as a *neutral realm eliminating both.*

By our choice here, we should seek for neutralization *at moments,* for given purposes, and not as a blanket program for vocabulary, since the loss in *action now* (that is, in full moral asseveration) would be too great were the semantic ideal to prevail. We can understand why adepts at any given specialization might want to erect these neutralizing moments into a whole trade, asking that the whole world be seen from the perspective of their "occupational psychosis." We can understand why, through living professionally with a neutral vocabulary, they should favor the thought of its ideal extension until it has encompassed all vocabulary. But merely because they have found a way of prolonging the insight of one moment through a life-work, giving it body in documentation and routine, even that is not argument enough to make us believe that the realm of the affections can or should be expressed *ordine geometrico* (an aim that Spinoza expressed explicitly, whereas the humane attractiveness of his Ethics owes much to the fact that he implicitly violated his own program repeatedly, beginning perhaps with his first proposition, *Substantia prior est natura suis affectionibus,* for "substance" has since been shown to be a very *resonant* word).

We have, as it happens, the "neutral" word *shoe,* capable of designating equally well the shoe worn by a communist and the shoe worn by a fascist. One can imagine that we had instead only two weighted words, *bims* and *bams,* so that the same object worn by a communist *had* to be called a bim that, if worn by a fascist, could only in the pieties of poetry be called a bam. A liberal shoe manufacturer, making footwear for export, might then label his consignments to Germany bams and his consignments to Russia bims. And he would be grateful for some "neutralizer" who helped him simplify the keeping of his ledgers by inventing a purely "scientific" word, *shoe,* that would include both classes. But I have purposely imagined inventing a neutral word that we already have, to replace two weighted words we don't have, as a way of suggesting that spontaneous speech can, and repeatedly does, neutralize, where the occasion requires.

So, the poetic vocabulary, when complete, will take us into-and-out-of (the complete play with its exhilaration at the close). When incomplete, it will take us into, and seek to leave us there (the "aesthetic of the Poe story"). While the semantic vocabulary would, I think, unintentionally cheat us, by keeping us without, providing a kind of quietus in advance, never even giving the dramatic opposition a chance, avoiding the error which Lucretius made, at the sacrifice of his work as "science" and to its great gain as "poetry."

Paradoxically, however, we may also judge the semantic vocabulary as "imagery," as "secular prayer," as itself exemplifying a form of consolational dance, all in the tone of perfect peacefulness. Judged as a refuge from something, that would not permit even the mere mention of that from which it was a refuge, it becomes itself an attenuated form of poetry, with its own modes of hypnosis. Or we may consider it valuable as a *stage,* a kind of purgatorial disembodiment helpful for transition from an old poetic vocabulary whose weightings are all askew to a new poetic vocabulary whose weightings will be better fitted to the situations it would encompass. As preparation, as discipline, as itself pointing out some important things "to look for and to look out for," it can be saluted. It is only when it is considered as an ideal in itself, rather than as a preparation for new and more accurate weighting, that one need turn against it.

The ideal word is in itself an act, its value contained in its use at the moment of utterance. Its worth does not reside in its "usefulness" and promise (though that is certainly a part of it) but in its *style* as morals, as petition, in the *quality* of the petition, not in the *success* of the petition. For preparations, anything may serve, everything does serve—but preparations must not usurp the guise of fulfillments.

"The Common Language of Science"

Albert Einstein

The renowned physicist Albert Einstein was born in Ulm, Germany, on March 14, 1879. He was educated at technical schools in Munich and in Switzerland. While working as an examiner in the patent office in Berne, Einstein astounded the scientific world with his "special" theory of relativity which was published in 1905. In 1916 he published the "general" theory of relativity. For his work Einstein was awarded the Nobel Prize in physics in 1921. He came to the United States soon after Hitler's rise to power in Germany. He spent the remainder of his life at the Institute for Advanced Studies in Princeton, New Jersey. In 1953 he devised a single mathematical formula for a "unified field" theory. He died in Princeton on April 18, 1955. Some of his important works include *The Meaning of Relativity*, 1923; *The World as I See It*, 1934; *and Out of My Later Years*, 1950. This selection was a broadcast recording for the Science Conference in London, September 28, 1941. It was published in *Advancement of Science*, Volume II, number 5, and was included in *Out of My Later Years*, published by Philosophical Library in 1950.

T HE first step towards language was to link acoustically or otherwise commutable signs to sense-impressions. Most likely all sociable animals have arrived at this primitive kind of communication—at least to a certain degree. A higher development is reached when further signs are introduced and understood which establish relations between those other signs designating sense-impression. At this stage it is already possible to report somewhat complex series of impressions; we can say that language has come to existence. If language is to lead at all to understanding, there must be rules concerning the relations between the signs on the one hand and on the other hand there must be a stable correspondence between signs and impressions. In their childhood individuals connected by the same language grasp these rules and relations mainly by intuition. When man becomes conscious of the rules concerning the relations between signs the so-called grammar of language is established.

In an early stage the words may correspond directly to impressions. At a later stage this direct connection is lost insofar as some words convey relations to perceptions only if used in connection with other words (for instance such words as: "is," "or," "thing"). Then word-groups rather than single words refer to perceptions. When language becomes thus partially independent from the background of impressions a greater inner coherence is gained.

Only at this further development where frequent use is made of so-called abstract concepts, language becomes an instrument of reasoning in the true sense of the word. But it is also this development which turns language into a dangerous source of error and deception. Everything depends on the degree to which words and word-combinations correspond to the world of impression.

What it is that brings about such an intimate connection between language and thinking? Is there no thinking without the use of language, namely in concepts and concept-combinations for which words need not necessarily come to mind? Has not everyone of us struggled for words although the connection between "things" was already clear?

We might be inclined to attribute to the act of thinking complete independence from language if the individual formed or were able to form his concepts without the verbal guidance of his environment. Yet most likely the mental shape of an individual, growing up under such conditions, would be very poor. Thus we may conclude that the mental development of the individual and his way of forming concepts depend to a high degree upon language. This makes us realize to what extent the same language means the same mentality. In this sense thinking and language are linked together.

What distinguishes the language of science from language as we ordinarily understand the word? How is it that science language is international? What science strives for is an utmost acuteness and clarity of concepts as regards their mutual relation and their correspondence to sensory data. As an illustration let us take the language of Euclidian geometry and Algebra. They manipulate with a small number of independently introduced concepts, respectively symbols, such as the integral number, the straight line, the point, as well as with signs which designate the fundamental operations, that is the connections between those fundamental concepts. This is the basis for the construction, respectively definition of all other statements and concepts. The connection between concepts and statements on the one hand and the sensory data on the other hand is established through acts of counting and measuring whose performance is sufficiently well determined.

The super-national character of scientific concepts and scientific language is due to the fact that they have been set up by the best brains of all countries and all times. In solitude and yet in cooperative effort as regards the final effect they created the spiritual tools for the technical revolutions which have transformed the life of mankind in the last centuries. Their system of concepts have served as a guide in the bewildering chaos of perceptions so that we learned to grasp general truths from particular observations.

What hopes and fears does the scientific method imply for mankind? I do not think that this is the right way to put the question. Whatever this tool in the hand of man will produce depends entirely on the nature of the goals alive in this mankind. Once these goals exist, the scientific method furnishes means to realize them. Yet it cannot furnish the very goals. The scientific method itself would not have led anywhere, it would not even have been born without a passionate striving for clear understanding.

Perfections of means and confusion of goals seem—in my opinion—to characterize our age. If we desire sincerely and passionately the safety, the welfare and the free development of the talents of all men, we shall not be in want of the means to approach such a state. Even if only a small part of mankind strives for such goals, their superiority will prove itself in the long run.

"Cultural Levels and Functional Varieties

of English"

John S. Kenyon

John S. Kenyon was born in 1874. He graduated from
Hiram College in 1898. After taking an M. A. degree at the
University of Chicago, he went to Harvard where he earned
his Ph. D. in 1908. He taught English and classical languages at several midwestern universities including Western
Reserve and Hiram College. Kenyon was actively interested
in phonetic pronunciation and served as a consultant on
pronunciation for Webster's *New International Dictionary*,
1934. He is the author of *American Pronunciation*, and
co-author of the *Pronouncing Dictionary of the American
Language*. The paper included here was published in
College English in October 1948 and is reprinted with the
permission of the National Council of Teachers of English.

T HE word *level*, when used to indicate different styles of
language, is a metaphor, suggesting higher or lower position
and, like the terms *higher* and *lower*, figuratively implies 'better' or 'worse,' 'more desirable' or 'less desirable,' and similar
comparative degrees of excellence or inferiority in language.

The application of the term *level* to those different styles
of language that are not properly distinguished as better or
worse, desirable or undesirable, creates a false impression. I
confess myself guilty of this error along with some other
writers. What are frequently grouped together in one class
as different levels of language are often in reality false combinations of two distinct and incommensurable categories,
namely, *cultural levels* and *functional varieties*.

Among *cultural levels* may be included, on the lower levels, illiterate speech, narrowly local dialect, ungrammatical speech and writing, excessive and unskilful slang, slovenly and careless vocabulary and construction, exceptional pronunciation, and, on the higher level, language used generally by the cultivated, clear, grammatical writing, and pronunciations used by the cultivated over wide areas. The different cultural levels may be summarized in the two general classes *substandard* and *standard.*

Among *functional varieties* not depending on cultural levels may be mentioned colloquial language, itself existing in different degrees of familiarity or formality, as, for example, familiar conversation, private correspondence, formal conversation, familiar public address; formal platform or pulpit speech, public reading, public worship; legal, scientific, and other expository writing; prose and poetic belles-lettres. The different functional varieties may roughly be grouped together in the two classes *familiar* and *formal* writing or speaking.

The term *level,* then, does not properly belong at all to functional varieties of speech—colloquial, familiar, formal, scientific, literary language. They are equally "good" for their respective functions, and as classifications do not depend on the cultural status of the users.

The two groupings *cultural levels* and *functional varieties* are not mutually exclusive categories. They are based on entirely separate principles of classification: *culture* and *function.* Although we are here principally concerned with the functional varieties of standard English (the highest cultural level), yet substandard English likewise has its functional varieties for its different occasions and purposes. Thus the functional variety colloquial English may occur on a substandard cultural level, but the term *colloquial* does not itself indicate a cultural level. So the functional variety formal writing or speaking may occur on a lower or a higher cultural level according to the social status of writer or speaker, and sometimes of reader or audience. It follows, for instance, that the colloquial language of cultivated people is on a higher cultural level than the formal speech of the semiliterate or than some inept literary writing.

Semiliterate formal speech is sometimes heard from radio speakers. I recently heard one such speaker solemnly announce, "Sun day will be Mother's Day." Because the speaker, in his ignorance of good English, thought he was making himself plainer by using the distorted pronunciation *sun day* instead of the standard pronunciation *sundy,* he actually was misunderstood by some listeners to be saying, "Some day will be Mother's Day." About forty years ago the great English phonetician Henry Sweet used this very example to show that "we cannot make words more distinct by disguising them."[1] He was referring to the use, in this instance, of the full sound of vowels in unaccented syllables where standard English has obscure vowels. On the same page Sweet gives another example of the same blunder: "Thus in the sentence *I shall be at home from one to three* the substitution of tuw for tə [ə=the last sound in *sofa*] at once suggests a confusion between the preposition and the numeral." This was also verified on the radio. Not long ago I heard a radio speaker announce carefully, "This program will be heard again tomorrow from one two three." I have also recorded (among many others) the following such substandard forms from the radio: *presidEnt* for the standard form *president,* the days of the week ending in the full word *day* instead of the standard English syllable *-dy, ay man* for the correct man, *cahnsider* for *cənsider, tooday* for *təday, too go* for *tə go, Coalumbia for cəlumbia,* etc. This is merely one sort among many of substandard features in the formal speech of the semiliterate.[2]

To begin my strictures at home, in *American Pronunciation* (9th ed., 4th printing, p. 17), I use the page heading "Levels of Speech." This should be "Functional Varieties of Standard Speech," for the reference is solely to the different uses of speech on the one cultivated level. Similarly, in the Kenyon-Knott *Pronouncing Dictionary of American English* (p. xvi,

---

[1] Henry Sweet, *The Sounds of English* (Oxford, 1910), p. 78.
[2] See further *American Speech,* VI, No. 5 (June, 1931), 368-72.

§2), I carelessly speak of "levels of the colloquial" where I mean "styles of the colloquial," as three lines above. For though there are different cultural levels of colloquial English, the reference here is only to standard colloquial.

S. A. Leonard and H. Y. Moffett, in their study, "Current Definition of Levels in English Usage,"[3] say (p. 348): "The levels of English usage have been most clearly described in Dr. Murray's Preface ['General Explanations,' p. xvii] to the *New English Dictionary*. I have varied his diagram a little in order to illustrate better the overlapping between the categories." It appears to me that Leonard and Moffett have so varied the diagram as to obscure Murray's intention. For he is not here primarily exhibiting levels of speech but is showing the 'Anglicity,' or limits of the English vocabulary for the purposes of his dictionary.[4] The only topical divisions of his diagram that imply a cultural level are "slang" and "dialectal," and the only statement in his explanation of the diagram that could imply it is, "Slang words ascend through colloquial use." This may imply that slang is on a lower cultural level than "colloquial, literary, technical, scientific, foreign." We may also safely infer that Murray would place "Dialectal" on a lower level than colloquial and literary if he were here concerned with cultural levels. Murray's diagram rests consistently on the same basis of classification throughout ('Anglicity'), and he emphasizes that "there is absolutely no defining line in any direction [from the central nucleus of colloquial and literary]." Moreover, Murray's exposition here concerns only vocabulary, with no consideration of the other features that enter so largely into "levels" of language—grammatical form and structure, pronunciation, spelling, and meaning—of styles, in short, only so far as they are affected by vocabulary. These he treats of elsewhere but without reference to levels.

It is not quite clear just how far Leonard and Moffett in-

---

3 *English Journal*, XVI, No. 5 (May, 1927), 345-59.

4 The word *Anglicity* is a coinage of the *Oxford Dictionary*. They define it as 'English quality, as of speech or style; English idiom.'

tend their grouping "literary English," "standard, cultivated, colloquial English," and "naïf, popular, or uncultivated English" to be identical with what they call Murray's "levels," his description of which they commend. But it is clear that they call their own grouping "three levels of usage" (p. 357) and classify them together as a single descending scale (cf. "the low end of the scale," p. 358). The inevitable impression that the average reader receives from such an arrangement of the scale is: Highest level, literary English; next lower level, colloquial English; lowest level, illiterate English; whereas, in fact, the first two "levels" are functional varieties of the one cultural level standard English, while the the third ("illiterate or uncultivated," p. 358) is a cultural level.

Krapp has a chapter on "The Levels of English Speech,"[5] in which he reveals some awareness of the confusion of cultural levels with functional varieties. He says:

> Among those who pay any heed at all to convention in social relationships, a difference of degree is implicit in all use of English. This difference of degree is usually thought of in terms of higher and lower, of upper levels of speech appropriate to certain occasions of more formal character, of lower levels existing, if not necessarily appropriate, among less elevated circumstances. These popular distinctions of level may be accepted without weighting them too heavily with significance in respect of good, better, and best in speech. A disputatious person might very well raise the question whether literary English, ordinarily regarded as being on a high level, is really any better than the spoken word, is really as good as the spoken word, warm with the breath of the living moment.

At the risk of having to own the hard impeachment of being disputatious, I must express the fear that the logical fallacy in treating of levels, which Krapp rather lightly waves aside, is having a serious effect on general ideas of speech levels, and especially of the significance of colloquial English in good usage. Krapp's grouping, frankly on a scale of "levels"

[5] George Philip Krapp, *The Knowledge of English* (New York, 1927), pp. 55-76.

throughout, constitutes a descending scale from the highest, "Literary English," through "Formal Colloquial," "General Colloquial," "Popular English," to the lowest, "Vulgar English." Here the fallacy is obvious: Literary English, Formal Colloquial, and General Colloquial are not cultural levels but only functional varieties of English all on the one cultural level of standard English. The last two, Popular English and Vulgar English, belong in a different order of classification, cultural levels, without regard to function.

So in his succeeding discussion *level* sometimes means the one, sometimes the other; now a functional variety of standard English, and now a cultural level of substandard or of standard English. It is functional on page 58 ("a choice between two levels") and on page 60 ("level of general colloquial"), cultural on page 62 ("popular level" and "cultivated level") and on pages 63-64 ("popular level," "level of popular speech"), functional on page 64 ("general colloquial level"), cultural again on the same page ("popular level," "still lower level"), cultural on page 67 ("vulgar . . . level of speech," "applying the term 'vulgar' to it at certain levels"), cultural on page 68 ("its own [popular] level"), cultural and functional in the same phrase on page 68 ("speakers from the popular and the general colloquial level meet and mix"), and so on most confusingly to page 75.

The same kind of mixture of cultural levels and functional varieties is thrown into one apparently continuous scale by Kennedy: "There is the formal and dignified language of the scholarly or scientific address or paper. . . . The precision and stateliness of this uppermost level . . . is a necessary accompaniment of thinking on a high plane."[6] Next in order he mentions colloquial speech, which he refers to as "the second level, . . . generally acceptable to people of education and refinement." Clearly this is not a cultural level but a functional variety of standard English, like the "uppermost level." The third level is, however, a cultural one: "the latest slang,"

---

[6] Arthur G. Kennedy, *Current English* (Boston, 1935), pp. 15-17: "Speech Levels."

workmen's "technical slang and colloquialisms which other persons cannot comprehend," "grammatical solecisms." "The speech of this third level can fairly be ranked as lower in the social scale." His fourth level is also cultural: "At the bottom of the scale is the lingo, or cant, of criminals, hobos, and others of the lowest social level."

Finally Kennedy fixes the false mental image of a continuous and logically consistent descent from "the cold and lonely heights of formal and highly specialized scientific and scholarly language" to "the stupid and slovenly level of grammatical abuses and insane slang." In reality there is no cultural descent until we reach his third "level," since "formal and dignified language" and "colloquial speech" are only functional varieties of English on the one cultural level of standard English.

In Perrin's excellent and useful *Index*,[7] under the heading "Levels of Usage," he names "three principal levels": "Formal English (likened to formal dress), "Informal English" (described as "the typical language of an educated person going about his every day affairs"), and "Vulgate English." From his descriptions it appears clearly that Formal and Informal English are functional varieties of standard English, while Vulgate is a substandard cultural level. A similar classification appears in his table on page 365.

On page 19 Perrin uses level apparently in the sense of functional variety, not of cultural level: "Fundamentally, good English is speaking or writing in the level of English that is appropriate to the particular situation that faces the speaker or writer. It means making a right choice among the levels of usage." His advice, however, involves two choices: (1) choice of a standard cultural level and (2) choice of the appropriate functional variety of that level.

A clear instance of the inconsistent use of the term *level* is found in Robert C. Pooley's *Teaching English Usage* (New York, 1946), chapter iii, "Levels in English Usage." He names five levels: (1) the illiterate level; (2) the homely level; (3)

---

[7] Porter G. Perrin, *An Index to English* (Chicago, 1939), pp. 364-65.

standard English, informal level; (4) standard English, formal level; and (5) the literary level. In (1) and (2) *level* has an altogether different meaning from that in (3), (4), and (5). In the first two *level* plainly means 'cultural level'; in the last three it just as plainly means 'functional variety of standard English,' all three varieties being therefore on the one cultural level of standard English. So *level* in the two groups belongs to different orders of classification. All misunderstanding and wrong implication would be removed from this otherwise excellent treatment of levels if the last three groups were labeled "Standard English Level, Informal Variety"; "Standard English Level, Formal Variety"; and "Standard English Level, Literary Variety." Pooley's groups contain three cultural levels (illiterate, homely, standard) and three functional varieties of the standard cultural level (informal, formal, literary).

The misapplication to colloquial English of the term. *level*, metaphorically appropriate only to cultural gradations, is expecially misleading. We often read of English that is "on the colloquial level." For example, Krapp writes: *"Who do you mean?* . . . has passed into current spoken use and may be accepted on the colloquial level."[8] This implies that colloquial English is on a different cultural level from formal English (literary, scientific, etc.), and a too frequent assumption, owing to this and other misuses of the term *colloquial*, is that its cultural level is below that of formal English. This supposition, tacit or explicit, that colloquial style is inferior to formal or literary style, leads inescapably to the absurd conclusion that, whenever scientists or literary artists turn from their formal writing to familiar conversation with their friends, they thereby degrade themselves to a lower social status.

This misuse of *level* encourages the fallacy frequently met with of contrasting colloquial with standard English, logically as fallacious as contrasting white men with tall men. For instance, Mencken writes: " 'I have no doubt *but* that'

---

[8] A *Comprehensive Guide to Good English* (New York, 1927), p. 641.

. . . seems to be very firmly lodged in colloquial American, and even to have respectable standing in the standard speech."[9] This contrast, not always specifically stated, is often implied. For example, Kennedy writes: "Colloquial English is, properly defined, the language of conversation, and especially of familiar conversation. As such it may approximate the standard speech of the better class of English speakers, or it may drop to the level of the illiterate and careless speaker."[10] *May approximate* should be replaced by *may be on the level of.*

Similarly, on page 440: "Some measure words [are] still used colloquially without any ending in the plural . . . ; but most of these are given the *s* ending in standard English usage." Here *standard* is confused with *formal.*

Kennedy (pp. 534, 616) several times contrasts colloquial English with "standard literary English." This implies that colloquial English is not standard, while literary English is. If he means to contrast standard colloquial with standard literary, well and good; but I fear that most readers would understand the contrast to be of colloquial with standard.[11]

The term *colloquial* cannot properly designate a substandard cultural level of English. It designates a functional variety—that used chiefly in conversation—and in itself says nothing as to its cultural level, though this discussion, and the dictionary definitions, are chiefly concerned with cultivated colloquial, a functional variety of standard English. When writers of such standing as those I have mentioned

---

[9] H. L. Mencken, *The American Language* (4th ed.; New York, 1936), p. 203.

[10] Kennedy, *op. cit.*, p. 26.

[11] Greenough and Kittredge in *Words and Their Ways in English Speech* (New York, 1909), Chap. VII, only apparently treat literary English as the sole standard form: "What is the origin of standard or literary English?" (p. 80). They use *standard* in a special sense for their particular purpose, calling it "the common property of all but the absolutely illiterate," "the language which all educated users of English speak and write" (therefore including colloquial). For the usual current meaning, see the definitions of *standard* quoted in *American Pronunciation* (6th and subsequent eds.), pp. 14-15.

slip into expressions that imply lower cultural status of colloquial English, it is not surprising that some teachers fall into the error. One teacher expressed the conviction that colloquialisms should not be represented as standard American speech. But the context of the statement indicated that its author was using *colloquialism* in the sense of 'localism.' I could hardly believe how frequent this gross error is, until I heard it from a well-known American broadcaster.[12]

The best dictionaries, at least in their definitions, give no warrant for the various misuses of *colloquial, colloquially, colloquialism, colloquiality*. I urge the reader to study carefully the definitions in the *Oxford English Dictionary* with its many apt examples from standard writers, and in *Webster's New International Dictionary, Second Edition*, with its quotations from George Lyman Kittredge. Kittredge's views on the standing of colloquial English are well known. It is said that somebody once asked him about the meaning of the label "Colloq." in dictionaries. He is reported to have replied, "I myself speak 'colloke' and often write it." I cannot verify the story, but it sounds authentic.

It seems to me inevitable that the frequent grouping of so-called "levels" such as "Literary, Colloquial, Illiterate," and the like, will lead the reader to suppose that just as Illiterate is culturally below Colloquial, so Colloquial is culturally below Literary. While I can scarcely hope that my humble remonstrance will reform all future writing on "levels of English," I believe that writers who confuse the meaning of the term *level* must accept some part of the responsibility for the popular misunderstanding of the true status of colloquial English; for I cannot avoid the belief that the popular idea of colloquial English as something to be looked down upon with disfavor is due in part to the failure of writers on the subject to distinguish between *cultural levels of English* and *functional varieties of standard English*.

---

[12] Leonard and Moffett also mention the frequency of this blunder (*op. cit.*, p. 351, n. 5).

"What Is Semantics?"

Anatol Rapoport

Anatol Rapoport has, since 1955, been Professor of
Mathematical Biology at the University of Michigan. Born
in Russia, May 22, 1911, he received his Ph.D. at the University of Chicago in 1941. Earlier, in 1928, he had become
a naturalized citizen of the United States. He served on the
faculty of the Illinois Institute of Technology and of the
University of Chicago between 1946 and 1954. During the
academic year 1954-55 he served at the Center for
Advanced Study in Behavioral Sciences. He has long been
a member of the International Society for General Semantics, serving as president of the Society 1953-55. His books
include *Science and the Goals of Man*, 1950; and *Operational Philosophy*, 1953. He continues to serve as Associate
Editor of ETC., A Review of General Semantics.

"What Is Semantics?" first appeared in *American Scientist*
January 1952. We are indebted to the Board of Editors and
to Anatol Rapoport for permission to reprint this article.

THERE are two suffixes in our language (and similar ones
in other European languages) which suggest organized
knowledge. One is the venerable, academic "ology," that
reminds one of university curricula and scholarship. The
other is the energetic and somewhat mysterious "ics," which
has a connotative flavor of magic. Where "ology" suggests
academic isolation (ichthyology, philology), "ics" suggests
a method of attack on life's problems. It contains a faint
throwback to the ancient dreams of the philosopher's stone
and of "keys" to the riddles of the universe. Ancient words
ending in "ics" are mathematics and metaphysics. Of more
recent origin are economics, statistics, semantics, and cybernetics.

It is usually easy to satisfy someone's curiosity about an "ology" and quite difficult to do the same for an "ics." An "ology" can often be simply explained by translating its front part from Greek or Latin (ornithology = study of birds). But doing the same with an "ics" is nowhere as satisfactory. Mathematics comes from a Greek word for "learning," and metaphysics means "beyond physics." The same difficulty appears in translating "semantics." Semantics is derived from "meaning" or "to signify." What is wanted, however, is some information on what semanticists do.

An embryologist may do a lot of things, but looking at embryos seems a significant part of his activity, just as one would expect. By analogy, many conclude that semanticists look at or for meanings; so perhaps they have to do with dictionaries. This is not so. Dictionaries are the business of lexicographers. What, then, do semanticists do?

WHO ARE THE SEMANTICISTS?

To answer this question, let us go to the writings of those who make frequent references to semantics or to equivalent terms which have to do with the study of meaning. We find that a number of prominent thinkers have occupied themselves with this study. In England these include Whitehead, Russell, Ogden, Richards, Ayer, and others; in Austria (later scattered, fleeing from fascism), a group of writers who called themselves the Vienna Circle, which included Carnap and Frank (now in the United States), Wittgenstein (now in England), and Neurath (deceased); the United States is represented by Charles Morris, and Poland by Korzybski (deceased) and Tarski, both of whom emigrated to the United States.

The next thing to be noted is that most of these writers have confined themselves to traditional academic work; they are for the most part professors of philosophy. But Korzybski's career was an exception. By training he was an engineer; he served as an officer in the Russian army and later as a League of Nations official. He never joined a university faculty. Rather, an educational institution of a special kind was built around him. What is most remarkable is that Korzybski's work has had *direct* impact, at least in this country, on a far wider range of people than the work of the philosopher-semanticists. For one thing, it captured the fancy of a number of keen, active men who saw the practical educational implications of semantics. One of them was Stuart Chase, who had been close to Roosevelt's "brain trust"; another was S. I. Hayakawa, a student of linguistics and professor of English. Others include Irving J. Lee, whose work was in speech; Wendell Johnson, psychologist and speech specialist; Francis P. Chisholm, another professor of English. All these men were deeply interested in how people use words and how words affect those who use them. They were able to translate some of the implications of Korzybski's work (properly referred to as *general* semantics) into the language of the college freshman, the perplexed citizen, and the teacher or mother who took her work seriously.

Two of the books written by them became booming best sellers (Chase's *Tyranny of Words* and Hayakawa's *Language in Action*). Hayakawa's book, Lee's *Language Habits in Human Affairs,* and Johnson's *People in Quandaries* became standard college texts; courses in "general semantics" cropped up in colleges and universities, and even in high schools; an International Society for General Semantics has a growing membership; and the Institute of General Semantics, founded by Korzybski, has remained a going concern after his death. The Soviets have seen fit to "expose" semantics as a new low in bourgeois philosophy.[1] and there have appeared similar blasts from the "right."

In view of this widespread interest, the workers in the field owe the general public an explanation. In the writer's opinion, such an explanation has been provided in S. I. Hayakawa's article "Semantics, General Semantics, and Related Disciplines." There the history of semantics is reviewed,

---

[1] See, for example, B. Bykhovski, "The Morass of Modern Bourgeois Philosophy," *ETC.* VI (Autumn, 1948), 1-15; see also "A Soviet Account of Semantics," pp. 347-349 of the present volume.

and the particular contribution of Alfred Korzybski is evaluated in the perspective of that history. Yet among many semanticists there seems to be a sharp division of opinion on the relation of "semantics" to "general semantics." Many academic semanticists are inclined to dismiss Korzybski's work as unsound and to view his "lay following" as a cult. "What is good in Korzybski's work," they say, "is not new and what is new is not good."

On the other hand, many Korzybski-ites proclaim that Korzybski's work has nothing to do with semantics. They go so far as to say that the very term "general semantics" was an unfortunate choice; that had Korzybski known what confusion would arise between semantics and general semantics he would not have used it at all. Korzybski himself has maintained that while semantics belongs to the philosophy of language and perhaps to the theory of knowledge, *general* semantics belongs to empirical science; that it is the foundation of a science of man, the basis of the first "non-aristotelian system," which has had no predecessor and which no academic semanticist has ever achieved.

Thus, there is a resistance both among the "academicians" and among the Korzybski-ites against treating as part of the same intellectual current both the semantics of Whitehead, Russell, Tarski, Carnap, etc., on the one hand and the general semantics of Korzybski on the other. The academicians continue to associate semantics with the theory of signs and symbolic logic (written in a special sign language, which, like mathematics, only specialists can read). The extreme Korzybski-ites continue to talk of general semantics in terms of "nonverbal levels," "extensional devices," "semantic reactions," "colloidal levels," etc., and maintain that it is a far-reaching technique of psychotherapy. For the former, semantics is really an "ology"; for the latter, general semantics is definitely an "ics," with which one can finish the sentence, "It's all a matter of . . ."

This writer thinks that academicians are partly right and the Korzybski-ites are partly right. The accusations of cultism leveled against Korzybski's followers are not altogether unfounded. In the United States there is a large floating population of "truth-seekers." Many of them lack the capacity for the strenuous intellectual effort required in a fruitful pursuit of knowledge and wisdom; others lack the power of critical evaluation, which would enable them to tell the genuine from the false. Still others cannot be comfortable until they find a panacea to believe in. These people support "movements" and cults. They are as likely to "go for" Christian Science as for technocracy, for psychoanalysis as for theosophy, for the Great Books program as for dianetics. And so inevitably one finds some of them among the adherents of general semantics. Moreover, the seminars conducted by Korzybski at the Institute of General Semantics emphasized problems of personal integration, of human relations, etc., and so attracted considerable numbers of people without sufficient background to understand the philosophical implications of Korzybski's ideas. As often happens, many of these people came out of those seminars happier than when they went in. Whether they were actually helped by general semantics or by other factors cannot be determined without sufficient controls. But they went about spreading the faith, thus giving a cultist flavor to the "movement."

The accusation of dilettantism frequently leveled at Korzybski in scientific circles has a similar basis. Korzybski's aim was to place the principles of general semantics within the grasp of everyone. His was a program of "retraining nervous systems" towards greater sanity. Such a program demanded that the discipline have a primer level. Hence Korzybski's "extensional devices," which to the casual observer appear simply as eccentric punctuation habits: unrestrained use of quotation marks, hyphens, and numerical subscripts on words. Hence the "structural differential," which to many looks like a crackpot gadget. Nor was Korzybski too careful in his use of terms, which referred to various specialized branches of science in which he gave no evidence of extensive knowledge. In his major work, *Science and Sanity,* he often refers to events on the "colloidal level," to the functions of the cerebral cortex and of the thalamus, without corroborating his statements by evidence acceptable to workers in colloid chemistry or in neurophysiology. He makes a critique of the foundations of mathematics which has not impressed many mathematicians. He speaks with assurance about the power of the physico-mathematical method in science, but his work does not contain any mathematical derivations. One can understand why his book and particularly his lectures have irritated many conscientious scientists.

On the other hand, it would be a mistake not to recognize the very great importance and especially the timeliness of Korzybski's ideas. His was not a mere rehash of academic semantics with a psychiatric angle. The Korzybski-ites are right in maintaining that general semantics is considerably more than an "ology" of meaning. But in stating their case, they persist in disavowing Korzybski's intellectual debts and continue to use the characteristic Korzybskian terminology, which irritates the prejudiced academicians.

To recognize the fruitfulness of Korzybski's ideas, one must relate his work to that of the academic semanticists (over the protests of both the academic scientists and the Korzybski-ites), and one must attempt to explain it in terms other than those coined by Korzybski. This we shall attempt to do. Let us therefore first look at "ordinary" semantics and then pass to general semantics.

BASIC PRINCIPLES OF SEMANTICS

Perhaps the most important ideas in semantics (with which modern logic is intimately interlaced) are (1) the propositional function, (2) the operational definition, (3) predictive value as the criterion of truth, (4) the theory of types.

The first and last of these are largely the work of Bertrand Russell. The second and third have a long history. They emerged with the development of modern physics and are already recognizable in the work of Ernst Mach, the exponent of the "positivist" approach to physics. Rudolf Carnap (a philosopher-logician) and P. W. Bridgman (a physicist) have stated the principles of operational definition and the predictive criterion of truth in unambiguous terms.[2]

Like most great ideas, these four principles are relatively easy to grasp. One wonders how the great thinkers of past centuries missed them. But evidently it is the same with great ideas as with great inventions: they seem simple only after one has been shown how.

Let us take the propositional function first. Classical logic (whose founder was Aristotle) took it for granted that all judgments could be broken up into simple propositions, that is, statements in which something (a predicate) is asserted about something (a subject). Examples are *water is wet; grass is yellow; some Greeks are rich; no animal is rational.* It was also assumed that such propositions were either "true" or "false": *water is wet* is a true proposition; *grass is yellow* a false one. Logic was a set of rules for deriving propositions from other propositions. If *some Greeks are rich* is a true proposition, and *no Spartan is rich* is another true proposition, then *some Greeks are not Spartans* must also be a true proposition.

From the days of Aristotle to the nineteenth century hardly any important innovations were made in logic. Logic was considered largely a closed system (like euclidean geometry) and was taught in Western universities in much the same way Aristotle had taught it about 350 B.C.

The notion of the propositional function, however, was an innovation. The central idea of that notion is that one can make an assertion which *grammatically* looks like a proposition (a predicate asserted about a subject) but which cannot be said to be either true or false. An example of such a function is the statement *x is green.* One cannot tell, without knowing what x stands for, whether the statement is true or false. If x is grass, it is true, but if x is milk, it is false.

---

[2] See Carnap, *Philosophy and Logical Syntax* (London, 1935); Bridgman, *The Logic of Modern Physics* (New York, 1927).

The idea of the propositional function is obviously rooted in mathematics, where statements like $x^2 - 5x + 6 = 0$ are commonplace. It is evident that this statement is true if x stands for 2 or 3, but is false otherwise.

The propositional function is important in the theoretical development of logic, Just as arithmetic became algebra with the introduction of symbols to stand for variables (unknown quantities), so classical logic became symbolic logic with the introduction of the propositional function and of symbols to stand for propositions. Rules were developed for operating on propositions (like the rules of algebra which operate on variables), and logic became a branch of mathematics (or, one might say, mathematics was shown to be a branch of logic). And just as mathematics found wide application in science and technology, so symbolic logic is beginning to bear fruit in the design of computing machines, for example, and some theories of the structure of the nervous system.

But the notion of propositional function has another consequence more pertinent for this discussion. It showed that practically all our judgments are made not in terms of propositions but in terms of propositional functions! Consider the statement *grass is yellow,* which looks like a proposition. If by "grass" is meant the stuff that grows in Vermont in May the statement is false, but if one means the similar thing in California in July, then it is true! But then again it is not true if by "yellow" one means the color of ripe pumpkins.

Potentially, then, the question "What do you mean?" is pertinent at all times even when the "simplest" things are talked about, because the truth of statements depends on the meaning one assigns to the terms involved. This brings us to the second notion of semantics, the operational definition.

Again we must go back to Aristotle, because he made the first rules about definitions. According to Aristotle, a definition does two things. It places the thing defined in a class and then it tells how the thing is to be distinguished from other members of its class.

"Man is a featherless biped" is an aristotelian definition. It places man in a class of two-legged animals (bipeds) and distinguishes him from other members of that class such as birds (by the qualification featherless). Aside from the fact that plucked chickens and kangaroos, are also featherless bipeds (as Norbert Wiener remarks), such definitions have even more serious pitfalls. Anything can be formally defined whether it exists or not. Furthermore, the class and the distinguishing characteristics, in terms of which aristotelian definitions are made, may be no clearer than the thing defined. If the purpose of definition is to make meaning clear, then many aristotelian definitions fail to do so. If a *xyphia* is defined as a three-legged bird, and if there are no three-legged birds, then *xyphia* is just as meaningless after having been defined as before. If *worry* is defined as a species of anxiety accompanied by hypertension, the definition is useless unless "anxiety" and "hypertension" are closer to our experience than "worry."

In contrast to the aristotelian definition by "class" and "characteristic," semanticists recommended the operational definition, which is widely used in science. An operational definition tells *what to do* to experience the thing defined. Asked to define the coefficient of friction, a physicist says something like this: "If a block of some material is dragged horizontally over a surface, the force necessary to drag it will, within limits, be proportional to the weight of the block. Thus the ratio of the dragging force to the weight is a constant quantity. This quantity is the coefficient of friction between the two surfaces." The physicist defines the term by telling *how to proceed* and *what to observe*. The operational definition of a particular dish, for example, is a recipe.

From the operational definition to the operational meaning of truth is only a step. Carnap and others distinguish two kinds of truth. One is the formal kind, based only on logical consistency within itself or with certain propositions *assumed* to be true. Carnap prefers to call propositions which are true in this sense "valid." For example, *If all x are y, and all y are z, then all x are z* is a valid proposition, because of its internal consistency independently of what *x*, *y*, and *z* stand for. The propositions of euclidean geometry are valid with respect to the postulates and axioms chosen for that geometry. One may also choose other postulates with respect to which some propositions of euclidean geometry will not be valid. Validity, then, has nothing to do with observation or experience.

A true proposition, on the other hand, must be related to some kind of experience. No amount of formal proof is sufficient to establish that grass is green. The decisive criterion is looking and experiencing greenness. In a way, the criterion involves a prediction of an experience: "Look and you will see that it is green." This is not to say, however, that "seeing is believing" is always a sound criterion. No amount of "seeing" will establish the roundness of the earth or the inverse square law of gravitation. The criteria for these "facts" are indirect. They consist of certain experiments, the results of which are *predictable* if the roundness of the earth or the law of gravity is assumed true. If we assume that the earth is round, we can predict that departing ships will seem to sink into the horizon, and that the shadow on the moon during an eclipse will have a round edge, and that one can circumnavigate the earth.

Now we come to the fourth idea in semantics, the theory of types. It was known in antiquity that formal logic can be driven into a blind alley by a number of paradoxes. A typical one is the following. Consider the statement within this square.

Every
statement
in this
square
is
false.

Suppose the statement is true. Then, since it is the only statement in the square, it must be false. On the other hand, suppose it is false. Then, there must be true statements in the square. But again it is the only one; so it must be true. The example is trivial, of course, but similar paradoxes arise in mathematics and make difficulties for mathematicians. Since progress in mathematics depends on its complete internal consistency, it was necessary to re-examine the logical foundations of mathematics. One of the results of this re-examination is the theory of types. The theory rests on the principle that "a class cannot be a member of itself." That is, if you make a statement about *all* statements of a certain class, the statement you have made cannot be itself considered to be in that class. This was the principle violated in the paradox just described.

PRINCIPLES OF KORZYBSKI'S GENERAL SEMANTICS

Now let us look at Korzybski's basic principles (or the non-aristotelian postulates, as they are sometimes called), on which his "non-aristotelian system" is built: (1) the principle of non-identity, (2) the principle of non-allness, (3) the principle of self-reflexiveness.

As we shall see in a moment, logically the first principle is included in the second, so that it can be omitted. But we shall also see that, from the point of view of further development of Korzybski's system, there is a very good reason for not omitting it, and even for putting it first. However, we shall look first at the second principle. To use Korzybski's figure of speech, it says, "The map does not represent all of the territory"; that is, no matter how good a map you make, you cannot represent all of the territory in it. Translated in terms of language, it means that no matter how much you say about some "thing," "event," "quality," or what not, you cannot say *all* about it. The connection between this principle and the notion of propositional function is not hard to trace. According to the latter, *grass is green* is a propositional function, because both "grass" and "green" are variables.

Grass can refer to vegetation in Vermont, Kentucky, or California. Green can range over the color of canaries, emeralds, or gall. Therefore, even such simple propositions as "grass is green," "the earth is round," etc., can be true only within limits.

Now let us go back to the first principle, which can be stated as "The map is not the territory"; that is, the word is not the thing it represents. Clearly, if the map does not even *represent* all of the territory, it cannot *be* the territory. So logically there is no need to state the principle of non-identity in addition to that of non-allness. However, the development of Korzybski's non-aristotelian postulates implies far more than relations between language and fact. His big point is that the structure of our language affects the *functioning of our nervous systems,* and this is where his work departs radically from that of the "classical" semanticists. To say "the word is not the thing it signifies" is not just to indicate the obvious. It is to draw attention to a fundamental inadequacy of human behavior and to trace this inadequacy to the interaction of nervous systems with language.

According to Korzybski (and his idea is corroborated by numerous psychological and psychiatric findings), people do behave *as if* they identified words with things. Identified does not mean "equated verbally." Practically everyone will agree that the *word* Negro is not the same as Mr. Smith, to whom the label Negro is applied. Nevertheless many people, in judging Mr. Smith, react to the label rather than to Mr. Smith. To take another example, a man may react to some situation, say a rejected application for a particular job, by labeling the situation "I am a failure." He may then react to the *label* in ways that are far removed from an effective remedy of the situation.

The orientation recommended by Korzybski to free the individual from the tyranny of words was called by him *extensional.* Roughly speaking, to be extensional is to be aware of things, facts, and operations in the way they are related in nature instead of in the way they are talked about. The extensionally oriented person differentiates better than the

word-minded (intensionally oriented) one. He is aware of
the basic uniqueness of "things," "events," etc., and so he
is more aware of *change* than the intensionally oriented person, who mistakes the fluid, dynamic world around him for
the static, rigid world of labels, "qualities," and "categories"
in his head.

The extensional orientation of Korzybski is quite analogous to the "operationalism" of semantics. An operational
definition is essentially an extensional definition, because it
tells what to *do* (instead of what to say) to bring the thing
defined within the range of experience. Likewise the criterion of predictive value in establishing truth is basically
extensional. According to this criterion, statements, assertions, judgments, principles—in short, all kinds of talking—
are rated much as checks are rated in our economy: they
are accepted if one is reasonably sure they can be backed
by currency. For an extensionally minded person, words
that cannot be defined by operations, and statements that
do not by implication contain predictions of experience, are
like checks on nonexistent accounts.

This brings us to the third non-aristotelian postulate of
self-reflexiveness. An ideal map of a territory, says Korzybski,
would have to include a map of itself, if the map were part
of the territory. But then it would have to include the map
of the map of itself, etc., without end. This principle is illustrated on some packages, on which there is a picture of the
package itself, which in turn contains another picture of
itself, etc. To avoid this difficulty, the principle of non-
identity is intended to the more general principle of multi-
ordinality. The map is not the territory. Neither is map_2 of
the map_1 itself a map_1. A map of map_2 would then be a
map of the third order, etc., etc. In terms of language, this
means that theoretically we may have a $language_1$ about
things, a $language_2$ about $language_1$, etc. As Korzybski himself points out, this principle is an outgrowth of Russell's
theory of types. It has "counterparts" in classical semantics,
where logicians talk about languages of different order
(metalanguages). In terms of human behavior, this suggests

that one may react to the world, then react to his reaction, then to reactions of higher order, etc.

Thus, Korzybski's principles have a close relation to semantic principles. It follows that the whole Korzybskian system is an outgrowth of semantics. But the Korzybskian system goes much further. When its implications are worked out, it will be as far removed from semantics as semantics is from logic, and as logic is from grammar.

Grammar deals only with word-to-word relations. It teaches how to put words together into a sentence. It is not interested in how sentences are related to each other or how they are related to facts. Logic goes further. To a logician, sentences are assertions, and he is interested in relations between assertions (if this is true, then that is true). But for the logician words need not have any meaning except as defined by other words, and the assertions need not have any relation to the world of fact. The semanticist goes further than the logician. To him words and assertions have meaning only if they are related operationally to referents. The semanticist defines not only validity (as the logician does) but also truth. The general semanticist goes the furthest. He deals not only with words, assertions, and their referents in nature but also with their effects on human behavior. For a general semanticist, communication is not merely words in proper order properly inflected (as for the grammarian) or assertions in proper relation to each other (as for the logician) or assertions in proper relation to referents (as for the semanticist), but all these together, with the chain of "fact to nervous system to language to nervous system to action."

General semantics may indeed be considered of fundamental importance in the science of man. In Gestalt psychology, phenomenological pyschology, psychiatry, and cultural anthropology, the "neurolinguistic" factors of human behavior are assuming an ever greater importance. Human experience (according to the views developed in those disciplines) consists of *selecting* certain ones out of innumerable stimuli in the environment: and human behavior consists of *organizing* experiences along certain patterns. There is strong evidence that both the selecting and the organizing patterns bear a definite relation to the structure of language and to linguistic habits.

TOWARD AN EMPIRICAL SCIENCE OF MAN

Man's evaluative mechanisms are both causes and effects of the uniquely human trait, culture. Culture rather than the number of legs is what most clearly distinguishes man from other animals and plants. Already in an earlier work, (*Manhood of Humanity,* New York, 1921) Korzybski had developed the idea that whereas plants live by "binding energy," animals, in addition to being energy-binders are "space-binders," and man, besides being an energy-binder and a space-binder, is also a "time-binder." This is to say, animals, by moving about, are able to seek their necessities (food and mates) in space, while man, able to transmit experience by means of symbols, thereby interacts with his ancestors and descendants over periods of time, which other animals cannot do. Man thus has an extracorporeal mechanism of "heredity," culture. This "heredity" can work for better or for worse. If experience transmitted to successive generations is organized into true-to-fact orientations, man can become even more a master of his environment and of himself. If, on the other hand, experience is organized into false-to-fact orientations, man becomes a slave of his neurolinguistic reactions and a menace to himself.

All existing cultures are based partly on true-to-fact orientations and partly on false-to-fact orientations. A tribe may have highly efficient fishing and canoe-building techniques, but its notions of health and disease may be organized into a body of superstition, which renders it helpless in an epidemic. Our own culture has attained a high level of true-to-fact orientation with regard to technology and hygiene, but our social organization is such that technology threatens to blast us out of existence, and a great deal of our knowledge of health (especially mental health) cannot be applied.

Korzybski examined these discrepancies in the light of language behavior. He found that this behavior has a broad range in our culture. At the one extreme is the language behavior of scientists and engineers at work. This behavior is highly effective. Its tasks are to explain the world and to learn to control it whenever possible so as to satisfy specific needs. At the other extreme is the language behavior of psychotics and of people under the spell of superstition and of demagogy. Korzybski finds that the language behavior of scientists at work is in harmony with his non-aristotelian principles: scientists at work are aware of the limitations of language; they constantly put their notions and judgments to operational tests of meaningfulness and predictive value. They are aware of different orders of abstraction. The linguistic behavior of psychotics, or rigid "believers," of demagogues and of victims of demagogy, on the other hand, violates semantic principles. These individuals confuse words with things; they mix orders of abstraction, etc. The shaman of a prescientifically oriented tribe and the demagogue of the modern national state both hold their power because people react to words as if they were facts. Both word magic and demagogy aim to channelize the reactions of people to symbols, so as to make responses automatic, uncritical, immediate (what Korzybski calls "signal reactions"). Such reactions make possible gigantic sales volumes unrelated to the quality of the product; they make for persistent hostilities among groups; they make wars inevitable.

Korzybski set for himself the task of analyzing the structure of language (ranging from the language of the insane to that of the methematical physicist) and of relating that structure to human behavior, to a theory of culture and of history. This task was a means to an end. Korzybski's ultimate goal was to construct a program of retraining human nervous systems toward more hygienic neurolinguistic habits (i.e., toward greater sanity). A description of this program can be found in *Science and Sanity* (Lancaster, Pa., 1933) and in various books which have utilized certain aspects of the program for various educational tasks.

As already stated, Korzybski preferred to think of general semantics as an "empirical science." Perhaps this emphasis on empiricism was called forth by Korzybski's displeasure at having his work confused with the purely linguistic aspects of semantics. As we have seen, there is a great deal more to general semantics than a "theory of meaning." An impartial examination of Korzybski's actual output, however, fails to reveal anything like a systematized empirical science. Doubtless Korzybski has made extensive observations, and he must have read an enormous amount. But conclusions and conjectures based on observations stretched over a half a lifetime and on what various thinkers have written do not constitute an empirical science. This does not, of course, detract from the importance of Korzybski's work. For that matter, neither was Freud's approach to behavior and personality an empirical science. Freud's work contains brilliant conjectures, fruitful generalizations, signposts for future workers; and, in the opinion of this writer, so does the work of Korzybski.

If Korzybski cannot be said to have established an empirical science, what then has he done? He has pointed a way toward the establishment of such a science. He was a precursor of an intellectual revolution which is just now beginning and which promises to match that of the Renaissance. If Korzybski is seen in this role, then the question of his originality or erudition is not important. He might have had something of the dilettante in him. He might have pretended to have more specialized knowledge than he actually had. Great portions of his outlook might be found in the works of more modest and more meticulous workers. That is not important. He was a man of vision and an apostle. Such men are all too rare in our age of specialization.

There is evidence that his vision (an empirical science of man formulated in a structural language, like that of mathematical physics) is already in the making. An attack on the problem of constructing such a science has been launched from two directions. On the one hand, the rise of automaton technology (servomechanisms, "mechanical brains," etc.)

made necessary the development of a structural theory of that technology. Norbert Wiener, a leading theoretician in this field, called the theory *cybernetics*. He has pointed out that in view of the striking analogies between the behavior of automata and the seemingly "purposeful" behavior of organisms, one might well try to apply cybernetics to a theory of behavior controlled by the homeostatic functions of the nervous system. On the other hand, the new hybrid science of mathematical biology, developed largely by Nicolas Rashevsky and his associates at the University of Chicago, has made the methods of mathematical physics available in the development of a unified theory of the living organism.

It might be noted that this work has gone on independently of Korzybski, and perhaps many workers in those fields might even resent the implication of Korzybski's intellectual paternity. But one must not confine oneself to Korzybski's intellectual progeny in estimating the influence of his ideas. One must also count his "nephews," and "cousins," yes, and even his "stepchildren," whom he has repudiated and who have repudiated him. That is to say, in our culture based on a tremendously dense communication net, it is a hopeless task to trace the ancestry of the "legitimacy" of ideas. Ideas simply diffuse through our culture. They are in the air and are often picked up unconsciously and then propagated in modified form. This is why questions of priority should not in our day be taken seriously. *Relations* between ideas, however, are important. What we have attempted here is to show, not who learned what from whom, but rather what relation some leading intellectual movements of our time have to each other.

"Semantic Therapy"

Francesco Barone

Francesco Barone is professor of theoretical philosophy at the University of Pisa. Among his publications are *L'ontologia di Nicolai Hartmann* (Turin, 1948); *Il neopositivismo logico* (Turin, 1953); *Studi hartmanniani* (Turin, 1954); *Logica formale e logica transcendentale—I: Da Leibniz a Kant* (Turin, 1957); as well as numerous essays, published in Italian journals, on the development of formal logic and in the philosophy of language. His contribution to *ETC*. was published under the title, "General Semantics: an Italian Philosopher's View" (15, 255-266); it was a translation of "La semantica generale" in *Archivio di Filosofia* (Rome, 1955). The present selection is a chapter, "La terapia semantica," from *Il pensiero americano contemporaneo* (Milan: Edizioni di Comunità, 1958), and is used by permission of Francesco Barone. The translation is by Walter E. Stuermann, professor of philosophy at the University of Tulsa and is used by his permission.

I N the development of civilization, one of man's most profound and ancient interests has been the study of language. This is because reflection on language is connected closely to reflection on the possibility of and justification for human culture. It is in language that the human creature expresses his penetration and understanding of the structure of that reality which he senses both within himself and around him. By language man communicates the multiple expressions of this penetration and interpretation of the real, which, when integrated and reconciled with one another, produce the social context called "culture."

One's disposition before the problems of language is, therefore, a revelation of his orientation to human "culture" in general. In any epoch, one can confront the historical cultural situation with either of two attitudes: a confident acceptance of it and a celebration of the energy at work in it, or a critical suspension of the acceptance and an insistence upon a revision of the basic principles upon which the situation rests. There clearly result, then, two limiting positions, which are really never perfectly realized (since historically they mutually condition one another and intermingle), but which nevertheless have a value in so far as the relative prevalence of one of them gives to an age a characteristic "tone." They tell us something about language and, therefore, about the cultural situation. In the first case, attention is focused upon the positive constructive, utilitarian, or instrumental functions of language. In the second case, it is placed precisely on the problems of such functionalization and on the necessity of ascertaining first of all the conditions and limits of all such constructive ventures.

This latter tendency in the study of language is a typical mark of ages of "crisis." The accent falls light or heavy on the mark in proportion to the degree to which the crisis, as it finds expression here or there, takes up within itself both the problems and results of the multifarious scientific principles and procedures, and the values which have been codified in a highly diverse group of institutions and movements.

Specific examples of this situation are immediately evident in the whole course of Western culture. But perhaps never before, as in the first half of our century, has the "cultural crisis" moved so clearly in such a direction. It has provoked in contemporary society a restlessness which still agitates it. The crisis in our time concerns not only social, moral, religious, and esthetic values but also those domains which heretofore seemed most firm and secure. It has, for example, exhibited itself in issues related to the "foundations" of mathematics and in the "revolution" achieved by the overthrow of classical physics in contemporary inquiries.

It is significant that this orientation of contemporary culture is characterized by an unprecedented interest in language and in the problem of its functional clarification. Many currents of contemporary philosophy are engaged in these studies, pursuing their inquiries in the fields of logic, epistemology, psychology, sociology, and axiology. With these activities are connected the names of Russell, Moore, Richards, Wittgenstein, Carnap, Morris, and Tarski. Nevertheless, in the midst of the different inquiries and specific problems there is a common element and a constant conviction. It is that the difficulties of the diverse problems— which make the prevailing cultural situation unacceptable —are strictly related to their linguistic formulations. The resolutions of the difficulties are dependent on the analysis of the capacities and limitations of the symbolic structure of the linguistic expressions.

Among the characteristic representatives of this orientation of contemporary culture we discover an American movement which goes by the name "general semantics." The origin and the name of the movement are to be traced to Alfred Korzybski (1879-1950), who published in 1933 the book, *Science and Sanity: An Introduction to Non-Aristotelian Systems and General Semantics*. The second edition of this work was published at Lancaster, Pennsylvania, in 1941. The fundamental thesis was that the complex of linguistic-symbolic instruments on which the communications and institutions of human society are based is inadequate to the development of science. Furthermore, their infantilisms are the immediate causes of the hardships and of the pathological abnormalities which disturb the contemporary world. Korzybski described the linguistic instruments with which we are furnished as a legacy from a primitive worldview, which is, of course, to be contrasted to the structure of reality as revealed by contemporary science. This legacy is like a diaphragm which blocks access to a realm in which words would have their meanings determined by facts disclosed through scientific inquiry ("extensional" orientation). While that diaphragm remains in place unbroken, we find ourselves operating all too often in a world of words, as contrasted to facts ("intensional" orientation).

Our all-too-prevalent and inadequate "intensional" orientation is the result chiefly of the dominance of Aristotelian logic. Its sovereignty in the human situation can only be eliminated by establishing a clear distinction between the symbol (for example, a word) and the symbolized (for example, a spatio-temporal event). The propositional form "x is y" (which was the sole consideration of classical logic) led not only to the identification of subject and predicate but also to the identification of symbol and symbolized, of word and thing. The transition to an "extensional" orientation is, therefore, connected with the development of an anti-Aristotelian position. The anti-Aristotelianism of general semantics has a purely polemic function and is not based on a historical and philosophical exegesis of the works of the Stagirite. A recognition of the inadequacy of the traditional logical and linguistic instruments for formulating the results achieved by contemporary science is most significant. Science provides us, it is contended, with an "extensional" orientation and shows to us, with its electronic theory of the composition of matter, the "real" structure of the world in its extra-symbolic consistency. The essential purpose of general semantics is to formulate, on such a scientific basis, a theory of language which is capable of a neurological explanation of symbolic activity. The meanings of words and of signs in general are found in responses of the nervous system ("semantic reactions"). The signs act as stimuli, and the mechanism of nervous response determines the fundamental characteristics of the whole symbolism. According to Korzybski, semantic reactions are typically "abstractions." The stimuli to which the nervous system responds arise in the "real" world, in the "scientific objects" with their extra-symbolic, electronic structure. The response of the brain to such stimuli is to make a selection from the multiplicity of elements in the "real" structure of an event. Thus the world of common-sense objects is an "abstraction" with respect to the "real" events of the microscopic level. The process of abstraction continues, according to him, as we pass from the common-sense object to its name, and from that to the name of the species, et cetera, proceeding indefinitely in successive steps in which we symbolize symbols. Consequently, language is a complex stratification of abstractions of different orders. In the case of any abstraction, however, the meaning is to be discovered by back-tracking to the pre-symbolic level of "scientific" reality. A knowledge of the abstract character of semantic reactions guarantees adherence to the extensional orientation and a blocking of the habit of identification, which leads to a confusion of the "real" world with the products of the nervous system. The theory of general semantics thus becomes an efficient therapeutic technique for rectifying the abnormalities which vitiate human communication and the social institutions founded on it.

The work of Korzybski has secured a very great response in the United States, particularly in terms of the therapeutic functions it proposes. The offer of a method of linguistic therapy for the individual and for culture cannot fail to be received with enthusiasm in an age like ours—one in which propaganda has achieved an unprecedented efficacy through new means of communication, in which ideological contests lie at the base of political and social tensions, and in which the individual so often finds himself at a loss before the complex conditions of modern life. The "scientific" character of general semantics, the fusion of modern physics and neurology in fixing the central concept of "semantic reaction," and the synthesizing of the results and motives of specialized types of research, with an elaboration in terms of practical applications, are all features of the movement which give it great popularity in a cultural environment in which people have a great faith in scientific methods and where—due to brilliant results in the technical organization of industrial and commercial power—they have an optimistic confidence in their ability to improve human life in general and to achieve a rationally founded, free society.

The scientific enthusiasm which favors the diffusion of general semantics is the very factor which disposes the American academic community to accept and to elaborate the suggestions of neopositivism, which is after all of European origin. General semantics has some affinity with neopositivism—not so much in terms of specific doctrines, but in terms of its general outlook and aspirations. As for semantics, it is nevertheless convenient to remark that its diffusion and efficiency have gone beyond the academic world with a spread of broad popular interest.[1] There is now a rich bibliography of "semantic" studies, in which the doctrines of Korzybski are elaborated, integrated with related ideas in linguistic analysis, and carried to the level of practical application. Two associations have been formed to represent the interests of general semantics: The Institute of General Semantics and The International Society for General Semantics. Since 1943 the official organ of the latter has been the journal, *ETC: A Review of General Semantics*. The activities of the International Society include congresses and conferences and the sponsoring of chapters or representative groups in educational institutions of all orders and grades. As the general semantics movement developed, a strong accent was placed on the "therapeutic" functions, on putting its doctrines into action in the most various fields. In some

---

[1] The representatives of the American "academic culture" have often looked with suspicion upon the general semantics movement. It has exhibited some of the marks of a religious reformation movement or of a cult from time to time (Cf., for example, A. Rapoport's "What Is Semantics?" in this volume). There has been a recognition, however, that in general semantics we find reflected certain fundamental themes of contemporary thought. Notice, for example, the words of Wilbur Marshal Urban in his *Language and Reality: The Philosophy of Language and the Principles of Symbolism* (New York: Macmillan Co., 1939), p. 51:

"The theme of the evil ideology of language has even become grotesque in messianic hands. Count Alfred Korzybski, in his latest panacea, semantics (as developed in *Science and Sanity*, 1934), has apparently found not only the source of all evils in natural language and the subject-predicate logic, but also a cure for these evils, individual and social, in a true semantics based upon science. Wrong identification of words with things may, because of false evaluations, ruin human life, science, or the entire social system. True identifications will cure insanity, create right social relationships, and eliminate from science the evil ideology which, in this case, is the survival of Aristotelianism. It would not be just to make too much of these extreme developments, but it is only fair to say that it is in principle the same theme which, in a more moderate form, underlies a large part of recent philosophic thought."

representatives of the movement, one senses the conviction of possessing in semantics a magical key for the solution of all difficulties. In general, however, a seriousness of intent and a proper balance have been preserved, so that the instruments semantics proposes for the interpretation of experience merit our considerate attention.

General semantics is a significant expression of an orientation which is characteristic of the culture and civilization of America and which preserves in a measure the freshness and vigor of youth. It has not been content to crystallize into a contemplation of theory, but has insisted on pushing forward to practical applications by drawing all the possible consequences of its doctrines for the common life. Now to attend to theory in action is one effective means for testing the consistency of theory, and it is a method also for avoiding fallacies which are likely to appear in the mists of abstraction. An evaluation of the theory of language proposed by general semantics can, then, perhaps best be formulated by examining some "semantic" writings in which the central doctrines of Korzybski are presented in close connection with their therapeutic uses. A direct comparison of "theory" and "therapy" can throw into bold relief the difficulty which arises when linguistic problems are met with a preconceived doctrine of the nature of language. On the other hand, the therapeutic usefulness of the theses may be enriched through the modifications and amplifications of theory that are found necessary. The comparison we wish to make here is one which will proceed by analyzing two now "classic" works in the field of general semantics: *The Tyranny of Words* by Stuart Chase (New York: Harcourt, Brace and Co., 1938) and *Language in Thought and Action* by S. I. Hayakawa (New York: Harcourt, Brace and Co., 1949). The latter is a second revised edition of the 1941 volume, *Language in Action*.[2]

---

[2] Besides other works by Chase and Hayakawa, one can profitably consult the contributions of other representatives of the semantic perspective: Irving J. Lee, *Language Habits in Human Affairs* (New York, 1941); *Customs and Crises in Communication* (New York, 1954); Francis P.

II

The fundamental doctrine of Stuart Chase results from a coordination of Korzybski's neurological theory of meaning with the causal theory maintained by C. K. Ogden and I. A. Richards in *The Meaning of Meaning*. For the latter theory, the problem of meaning—of any linguistic meaning whatsoever—can be reduced to a situation in which a stimulus, proceeding from a physical event, becomes interpreted as a "sign" of another event. Repeated experience by an "interpreter" (a man or an animal) in which a spatio-temporal event R (for example, the striking of a match) is always followed by a spatio-temporal event S (for example, the appearance of a flame) modifies the brain of the interpreter in such a way that the event R, when it appears again, is interpreted as a "sign" of S, in so far as it gives rise to the expectation of S. The cerebral process at the base of this transaction is designated as the "reference" (the idea, the thought) and the expected event is named the "referent." This process, which is common to man and the higher animals, finds its fullest expression in the verbalization of the "reference" by a word, a phrase, or in general a "symbol."

The mechanism described gives a fixed order to linguistic phenomena—"referent," "reference," and "symbol." For Chase it is the key to the problem of meaning and to the distinction between meaningful language and meaningless language.

We cannot escape from concrete referents by using abstract language. If we try to dodge the difficulty, our

Chisholm, *Introductory Lectures on General Semantics* (Chicago, 1944); Wendell Johnson, *People in Quandaries: The Semantics of Personal Adjustment* (New York, 1946); Anatol Rapoport, *Science and the Goals of Man: A Study in Semantic Orientation* (New York, 1950); *Operational Philosophy: Integrating Thought and Action* (New York, 1953); Kenneth S. Keyes, *How To Develop Your Thinking Ability* (New York, 1950).

An interesting selection of the better articles in the journal, *ETC.: A Review of General Semantics,* in the first decade of its activity (1943-1953) was published, with Hayakawa as editor, under the title, *Language, Meaning and Maturity* (New York, 1954). Of particular importance for orienting one to general semantics are A. Rapoport's "What Is Semantics?" and Hayakawa's "Semantics, General Semantics and Related Disciplines."

words become meaningless. . . . To make a statement is to symbolize a reference, to give a label to a thought. But a reference without a referent hangs in mid-air. No cat would be guilty of such nonsense. . . . The point of every discussion is to *find the referent*. When it is found, emotional factors dissolve in mutual understanding. The participants are then starting from a similar foundation, talking about similar things. (*Op cit.*, pp. 100-1).

Such a univocal theory of meaning fits very comfortably into the framework of Korzybski's ideas. If the meaning of a symbol (and, therefore, of a thought) is found in a causal relation between a physical event and a cerebral process, then the Korzybskian theory seems to offer a satisfactory picture with its presentation of the "scientific" structure of the two-termed relation: on the one side is the physical event (in its extra-symbolic status) as an electronic structure; on the other side is the cerebral process as an activity of abstraction. Although Chase does not explicitly say so, it is perhaps not inappropriate to credit him with an attempt to express the difference between human symbolism and the semantic reactions of other animals. But the common ground of symbolism and of all semantic reactions is found by him in survival behavior. (p. 19) Is the simple verbalization of the "reference" a sufficient condition for the explanation of the specific characteristics of human behavior? We doubt it.

Now Chase repeatedly emphasizes with much feeling the nature of the cat's behavior.

He [the cat] will remain a realist all his life, interpreting real things on the macroscopic level with appropriate responses, and having no traffic with philosophy or formal logic. It is highly improbable that he will ever suffer from a nervous breakdown. He is certainly able to think after a fashion, interpreting signs in the light of past experience, deliberately deciding his course of action, the survival value of which is high. (p. 49)

Just as frequently, by consequence, he seems to espouse an ideal human language in which the symbolic mechanism is quite as "realistic" and as distant "from philosophy and from formal logic" as that of the cat. What falls under that evil use of abstract language is, therefore, a negative factor in survival behavior and employs terms weighted with a magical significance. Characteristic (though not original) is the example which is used in the attempt to throw a little light on the origin and growth of language. On a deserted island, John and Louis, an Englishman and a Frenchman, each speaking only his own tongue, must communicate with each other, if there is to be any probability of success in the struggle to survive. For certain tasks, communication by means of gesture must be supplemented by communication with words. Those words can be any sounds whatever, provided their meanings are fixed by demonstrative definitions, that is, by the indication of the "referents."

> In due time, Louis becomes lonely and wants to talk to John about his soul. But after a hurricane of French, he finds nothing to point to. He has to get along without abstractions as best he can. But with the new language, essential tasks are done, and whenever Louis and John do not clearly understand one another, they have but to point, first to the nameless thing or act, and then to a word on the pad. Happy pair—they have no words for "communism" and so cannot get into an argument about it! (p. 72)

Whoever admires, as does Chase, such an ideal situation cannot, however, refuse to recognize the fact that the survival behavior of man—indisputably superior to the cat's behavior in many respects—is really based on "abstractions," not only of the type in which the "reference" is verbalized, but also of those higher types in which symbols are symbolized. The whole process of acquiring scientific knowledge seems, for example, to require these types of abstractions. To such a thesis Chase responds, offering Korzybski's theory as a satisfactory reply. The stimuli from the "real" world prompt in the human nervous system a whole series of "abstractions." The world of common sense is itself already the result of a process of the filtration of the stimuli of the electronic structure, which is the only extra-symbolic reality.

[Tr.: The human nervous system is also of that degree of sensitivity and complexity as to allow man to use verbal and other symbols and even to produce and use symbols of symbols. These human achievements take man's behavior beyond the cat's, but, according to Korzybski's theories, they rest on a refinement of a neurological mechanism which is operative also in the cat in a more primitive form.] The conception of cerebral mechanisms of abstraction in the step from submicroscopic objects to macroscopic objects is such as permit a reduction of all the diverse levels of "abstraction" to the same semantic theory. "The chief difference between the brain of a man and the brain of an ape is not in apparatus but in association paths, which are more numerous and more complex in man." (p. 42)

Abstracting being thus understood, the possibility of the existence of science becomes clear. Furthermore, according to Chase, it is to be taken as a model for all meaningful language. The "operational" method, delineated by P. W. Bridgman as a typical process of experimental science for the definition of its own concepts, is considered by Chase as a characteristic example of returning to the "referent," of the sole semantic relation in which there is no place for emotion and passion. Through the combination of the operational method with the devices of mathematics, science can speak in a clear and exemplary manner. "If we wish to understand the world and ourselves, it follows that we should use a language whose structure corresponds to physical structure." For Chase as for Korzybski, mathematics "is a language with structural similarity to the human nervous system and to the world outside." (pp. 80 and 162) Mathematics functions wonderfully in establishing orders and relations—but it does not speak of *things* between which such orders and relations are fixed. It is purely abstract. Consequently, on the basis of Chase's interpretation, it would be just as illusory as ordinary language when the connection with "referents" fails.

Facts are the central exhibit of the scientific method. Around the fact the fakers throw their verbal smoke. But ultimately the fog lifts. It must lift. We are creatures of a world of stubborn and unyielding facts. On their recognition and correct interpretation depends our existence as a species. We cannot live on lies, fantasies, and propaganda. (p. 171)

The theoretical considerations thus appointed by Chase must, however, be put into practice in order to acquire the efficacy of a semantic discipline: this application consists in asking the interlocutors for the meaning of their assertions. Chase's doctrines constitute therefore an "Occam's razor," appointed to cut away linguistic fantasies and for building a sober, healthy interpretation of our common life. The field in which the razor operates is, for Chase, that of *principles,* that is, of assertions which provide

standard rules for judgment and for conduct. . . . A principle is a judgment involving high-order abstractions, normally without referents, difficult to test by experiment or operation revered for itself as such. If . . . a principle . . . fits the facts, it may be a useful timesaver. If it is based on facts of a bygone age, its application to new facts and new conditions may be ridiculous or disastrous. . . . The trouble is that, after adoption, people begin to regard them as eternal, good for any situation, anywhere, at any time. Perhaps a collection of fictions is inevitable. But I confess I look forward to the day when we shall dispense with concepts not derived from careful observation and from the necessities of survival and well-being *under the conditions of this earth.* Nothing else can we know surely, and nothing else should be bowed down to. Or so it seems to me. (pp. 109, III, 115)

The abstract principles against which the implacable savagery of the razor is directed are those of philosophy and logic, since they are typical examples, according to Chase, of fields where formulations lack "referents." In philosophy, one goes from reference to symbol and back to reference again in a circle of "word, thought, word" which leaves the basic semantic reactions to the side; and formal logic, with its pretense of attending to formal relations, is discovered an opponent of scientific method, which "is flexible and frequently changes its deductions and 'laws' as more facts come in." (pp. 208, 233) The semantic discipline is not restricted to the destructive function exercised in the two areas just mentioned. In the field of social affairs, the destructive function is supplemented by a constructive one. Here the introduction of a "good language" (one in which the abstractions are related to their spatio-temporal "referents") "will help us to communicate with one another about the realities of environment, where now we speak darkly, in alien tongues." (p. 361) The last chapter of *The Tyranny of Words,* which are the most original of the whole work, develop a semantic examination of economic, legal, and political arguments, on the basis of the rule that "any study where students cannot agree upon what they are talking about is outside the scientific discipline." (p. 240) In such fields, it is necessary to flee from the "tumult of emotions" and, in a search for a scientific approach to the problems, to "divest our minds of immutable principles and march after tangible results." (p. 304) What is pertinent here are not judgments of "right" and "wrong," but the adoption of methods which give promise of an advance. "An advance to what? To making Adam, and his family more comfortable and more secure."

The theoretic foundations of semantic therapy proposed by Chase exhibit numerous difficulties and therefore do not completely satisfy a reader that the exactness of the diagnosis of linguistics recognizes the many problems of modern man and sympathetically looks to the proper end of therapy. A number of these difficulties have already been treated in numerous critical works on the Korzybskian sources.[3] They are perhaps even more aggravated in the

---

[3] Cf., M. Black, "Korzybski's General Semantics," in *Language and Philosophy: Studies in Method* (Ithaca, N.Y., 1949) and F. Barone, "General Semantics: An Italian Philosopher's View," *ETC.: A Review of General Semantics,* XV, 4, pp. 255-266.

form in which they appear in Chase. It is sufficient at this point simply to present several examples: the relation of "reality" to "abstractions," and the conception of mathematics.

The characterization of the cerebral process as one of abstracting—this is the pivot on which Chase's synthesis of the causal theory of meaning with the Korzybskian doctrines turns—does not have the clarity which is desirable in a hypothesis directed to the cure of the individual and social confusions provoked by the equivocations of language. Using the semanticist's interpretation of abstraction as a key to the explanation of the typical symbolism of man, one ought to be able to assign to the various degrees of abstraction an identical fundamental meaning. This does not seem to be achieved by Korzybski and Chase, as may clearly be seen by comparing two kinds of "abstraction" treated by them. One is that kind which occurs when from the extra-symbolic reality (the electronic structure) the nervous system selects and produces the world of common-sense objects. The second is that type which is operative when names are applied to objects and groups of objects. In the first case, "abstraction" signifies the abandoning of the multiplicity of particular characteristics of the real world (this "abandoning" has, indeed, an extremely metaphorical sense, for it does not explain the rise of the qualities of common sense). In the second case, it is completely incomprehensible to assert that the "name" arises from an abandoning of sensory qualities. Consider a "common name," which is a word or phrase that denotes a class by calling attention to some quality or qualities possessed by all the individuals in a set, while neglecting the peculiar characteristics of the individuals themselves. It is obvious that the simple neglecting of some characteristics of the individuals is not a sufficient condition for definition of the class or meaning of the class name; it is just as necessary to present and to conserve in the definition the common characteristics of the individuals in the set. This implies a comparison of the individuals and therefore a dimension of meaning in "abstraction" which is not found in the Korzybskian interpretation of the process. What "referent" can there be for the assertion of a "comparison" of elements of the electronic structure for the purpose of drawing out the common characteristics?

Chase's insistence on a "realistic" orientation ("extensional") in the process of abstraction and his negative attitude in the face of abstractions (clearer in his work than in Korzybski's) rest on a very slippery argument. He requires that human symbolism be assessed in terms of an appeal to the level of real, extra-symbolic objects, that is, the level of the electronic structure of the world. But such a structure seems, upon examination, to be far from that unspeakable, objective level which Chase needs as the original and secure foundation of language. The determination and description of it require the use of a complex symbolic structure (both mathematical and non-mathematical) which belongs to a very high degree of abstraction. The "real" foundation of "abstract" language turns out, then, to be a matrix of high abstractions. Consequently, Chase is either entangled in a vicious circle, which is unbreakable on his criteria, or he must renounce the all-too-simple contention that abstractions find their justification solely as "indications" of "real objects."

The situation is not greatly improved when we consider the conception of mathematics which Chase, following in the footsteps of Korzybski, holds. In the first place, it is surprising to discover that simultaneously mathematics is made an essential element of scientific method and formal logic is anathematized as anti-scientific. Putting aside a consideration of their historical connection, it is sufficient to point out that both logic and mathematics do business in "forms" and in searching for the deductive connections between forms. This requires in both cases a rigorous determination of the rules for the constitution and the transformation of forms. Now the "flexibility" of scientific methor permits the adoption of different formal systems from that of traditional logic, but it does not imply the abandonment of the criteria of exactness, deductive rigor, and attention to form in the mathematical and logical tools it employs. An empirical interpretation of mathematics is one which does not take account properly of the formal structures intrinsic to it and founds the validity of mathematical propositions on correspondence with the "real" structure of the world. It is to such a position that Chase alludes when he speaks of mathematical language as an "abstract" language and, at the same time asserts its "structural similarity to the human nervous system and to the world outside." In other words, mathematical language would be "abstract" as regards the "rules of formation" for its own terms (which do not correspond to any unspeakable entities that may be indicated), but it would have a "real" foundation as regards the "rules of transformation," which should reflect nervous and physical structures. Such a reflection of empirical structures is, however, precisely what is called into question by the most serious and careful of contemporary mathematical methodologies. Emphasis is placed very strongly on the "conventional" character of the rules of transformation and of the deductive structure. The postulation of rules is not bound necessarily to useful physical "interpretations" and much less is it conditioned upon an observation or description of specific nervous processes. To connect mathematical structure with nervous structure is gratuitous, if indeed it has a sense. Whoever affirms such a connection shoulders the burden of bringing forward some example of an original language which is purely mathematical and also reflects some structure of the nervous system. He has the additional job of explaining the rise of the semantic illusions of every-day language as departures from the natural, mathematical functioning of such a system.

The set of difficulties we have cited seem to gravitate around a common center, namely, the conception of "semantic reaction," which results from the synthesis achieved by Chase from the doctrines of Korzybski and those of Ogden and Richards. The position held by Chase can have some useful applications and it confirms in certain ways experiments in the laboratory (for example, those dedicated to the study of conditioned reflex and to the fixing of habits). Nevertheless, it becomes extremely inadequate and over-simplified when a general application of it is attempted. In such a case, it calls to mind the illusion operative in the field of epistemology from time to time—that there is such a thing as a pure "datum," free of all interpretation, and that it is the one sure ground on which the whole structure of knowledge is to be constructed. The theory exhibits its insufficiency even with respect to the "operational" method. How can Chase conclude the characterization of this method—on which he insists so rightly—for blockading the drive toward absolutism in our conceptual structures, by means of which reality is interpreted, with the affirmation that the "interpretation depends on past experience"? (p. 96) To accept in science only concepts whose meaning can be determined by means of physical or experimental operations does not mean that such concepts are the cumulative result of stimuli and nervous reactions. The elimination of the prejudice of absoluteness in the case of certain interpretative structures would not be possible, if the symbolic structure arises only from the above-mentioned mechanism of stimuli and reactions. A good many new turns in science occur without the appearance of new physical data or contexts in which, to new stimuli, there arise new semantic reactions. On the contrary, many take place through the appearance of new and original conceptual frameworks into which already repeated past experience is cast. The occurrence of such conceptual novelties is precisely the sort of thing which falls outside the scope of explanation of the theory adopted by Chase.

The greatest weakness of his semantic doctrines is revealed, however, when Chase attempts to use them, for therapeutic purposes, that is, when he launches into discussions of economic, social, and political "principles." The really effective aspect of the "therapy" is the polemic against idolizing these principles and against their absolute indifference to the context of experience. Chase's discussion of the principles of classical economics and those of Marxism and of the dogmatic absolutism at work among adherents of these positions possesses an uncommon liveliness and interest. A similar thing may be said for his historical analyses of the context in which the American Constitution was elaborated, analyses in which Chase opposes the verbal illusions that are hidden in talking of the "inviolability" and "intangibility" of the Constitution. There is, for example, a deep sense of the human character of legal constructions in the affirmations that, "from the semantic point of view, we cannot expect the meaning of written constitutions to survive extensive changes in culture" and that "this is one reason why the unwritten British constitution provides a more flexible and practical instrument than the American." (p. 316) But the "semantic viewpoint" from which Chase's considerations arise does not depend upon the theory of "semantic reactions." It is rather an extension to other areas of human activity of the critical spirit of the operational method, warring against the absolutizing of conceptions. The attempt to relate the symbolism of "principles" to the semantic system is wrecked on rocks which are quite evident. As Chase attempts to apply in economics and politics the canons of scientific discourse corresponding to the semantic scheme and attempts to eliminate the "tumult of emotions" and the world of "fictions," the language he uses in bringing forward his arguments reveals insuppressible aspects of a distinctly human kind of symbolism. A "realistic" orientation in the field of economics and politics cannot be circumscribed by "careful observation" and by "the necessity of survival," since adherence to the facts must be correlated with a use of them in a certain direction. This is what is suggested by Chase when, for example, he uses the phrase, "to make Adam$_1$, and his family more comfortable and more secure." The determination of directions or of goals implies the constitution of new symbolic contexts, since the symbols representing the "facts" must be coordinated in a framework which expresses, at least, the "emotional reactions" which I, Adam₂, have in face of Adam₁, and all the other Adams. Those facts will have to be coordinated in other frameworks also, ones which take account of other inescapable, normal aspects of human behavior. The polemic by Chase against "principles" in the name of the unilateral scheme of "semantic reactions" thus exhibits inconsistencies. A rigorous application of the scheme would render senseless the result of the "realistic" arguments presented by him in economics and politics. The evaluative and normative meanings of the "principles" which are inextricably bound up with distinctly human behavior do not bring forward that kind of unspeakable "referent" which is laid down as the indispensable condition for a meaningful semantic reaction. We come thus to situations where the very theoretical basis of semantics blocks effective therapy.

III

The central difficulty of general semantics now has become somewhat clear. The continuing development of techniques for the improvement of linguistic communication throws stronger and stronger light on the limitations of certain initial assumptions. The work of the International Society for General Semantics and its organ, *ETC-: A Review of General Semantics*, edited by S. I. Hayakawa, has placed great emphasis on the practical therapeutic aspects of semantics. A comparison of the work of Chase with that of Hayakawa's *Language in Thought and Action* is sufficient to convince one of the shift in perspective. Hayakawa recognizes that his volume is much more than a second revised edition of the *Language in Action* of 1941: "So much has been changed and so much has been added that more than half the material in the present volume is new." (p. iii)

The Korzybskian themes are certainly not abandoned and, in an explicit manner, they still constitute the basis of reference in theory. The second part of the volume—"Language and Thought"—rests the theory of language clearly on the doctrine of levels of "abstraction" which rise from the "real" level of events on which the nervous system operates, "automatically *abstracting*" or "selecting." (p. 167) Consequently, the basic intent of semantics is purely and simply that of producing an "extensional" orientation, that is, a knowledge of the process of abstraction and a habit of responding to determinate semantic stimuli with "delayed reactions." (p. 192) This orientation insures against confusing symbols with things and against confusing the various levels of abstraction in the symbolic structure.

The references to theory nevertheless remain frequently in the background and do not often hamper the analysis of linguistic use, forcing it in a predetermined direction. The direct connection we have seen in Chase's work between the neurological explanation of meaning and the phenomenological scheme, "sign—'referent'—'referent'—symbol," is not to be found in Hayakawa. Some traces of such a scheme remain in the distinction Hayakawa introduces between the "extensional meaning" and the "intensional meaning" of a verbal symbol, defined respectively as that which the symbol "*points to* or denotes in the extensional world" and that which is suggested by it "inside one's head." (p. 58)

> An easy way to remember this is to put your hand over your mouth and point whenever you are asked to give an extensional meaning. . . . When utterances have extensional meanings, discussion can be ended and agreement reached; when utterances have intensional meanings only and no extensional meanings, arguments may, and often do, go on indefinitely. Arguments of this kind may be termed "non-sense arguments," because they are based on utterances about which no sense data can be collected. (pp. 58-60)

In these affirmations there is still present the conviction of the privileged position of spatio-temporal "facts" in the determination of meaningful language and, by consequence, an aversion of scientific cast for the discussion of the clarification of meanings in a context where demonstrative definitions cannot be given. Hayakawa's perspective does not, however, remain locked within such limits. In the pages in which the nature of "extensional" meaning is treated, there are repeated affirmations of the necessity of attending to the "context" in fixing the meanings of terms. "Words do not have a single 'correct meaning'; they apply to *groups* of similar situations, which might be called areas of *meaning*." (p. 65) The verbal context runs back always to the "physical and social context." This is presented by Hayakawa, not as a matrix of unspeakable "objects," but as the "result of actual situations in life." (p. 57) From this point of view, "extensionality" is not quite as narrow and harsh a thing as when the criteria are derived from the privileged semantic scheme, and it represents an insistence that symbolism draw its meanings from life experiences in all the multiplicity of their forms, it is not to degenerate into autonomous chatter. What prevents the complete liberation of the criterion of extensionality and makes the idea of meaning as physical ostensibility reappear is the persistence of certain Korzybskian theoretical themes; for example, the doctrine of "semantic reactions" in terms of a hierarchy of levels of abstraction of "decreasing value"[4] as one departs more and more from the "real" level of electronic structure has a tendency to attribute to spatio-temporal facts of privileged position.

One symptom of a promising future development for general semantics is the fact that in the work of Hayakawa the theory of "abstractions" loses some of the rigidity which it had in Chase's work.

The fact that the symbolic process makes complicated follies possible is no reason for wanting to return to a cat-and-dog existence. A better solution is to understand the symbolic process so that instead of being its slaves we become, to some degree at least, its masters. (p. 26) It is to be regretted, although it is understandable, that there

---

[4] Cf., A Korzybski, *Science and Sanity* (2nd ed.), p. 406.

exists a tendency in our times to speak contemptu-
ously of "mere abstractions." The ability to climb
to higher and higher levels of abstraction is a distinctively human trait, without which none of our
philosophical or scientific insights would be possible. High level abstractions acquire a bad reputation, because they are so often used, consciously or
unconsciously, to confuse and befuddle people . . . ,
but *all we know is abstractions*. (pp. 175-176)

What is important is not the high degree of the abstraction, but the ability to permit levels of abstractions to intermingle and to fertilize one another without reducing all
of them to some "dead level."

It is obvious, then, that interesting speech and
interesting writing, as well as clear thinking and
consequent psychological adjustment, require the
constant interplay of higher and lower level
abstractions, and the constant interplay of the
verbal levels with the nonverbal ("object") levels.
(p. 179)

In these statements there is still a tension between the
doctrinal scheme of "abstractions" and the considerations
of the effective use of linguistic symbolism. The interplay
of levels of abstraction can have this sense: it is an inter-
mingling and cross-fertilization of the diverse forms in
which the interpretations of experience come to be symbolized. Equivocation arises, however, when one pretends
to stabilize the "higher" and "lower" levels with respect
to some presupposed "ground level." How is this possible, if
"all that we know are abstractions"? If abstractions$_1$, abstrac-
tion$_2$, et cetera, refer back to something which is, in effect,
abstraction$_3$, there is nothing from which to abstract and
nothing which may be abstracted. Furthermore, to introduce the abstracting and selecting of the nervous system
in the analysis of symbolism is to promote a game of prestige
which outstrips the capacity of the most expert illusionist,

who is not able, for example, simultaneously to extract the rabbit from the hat and the hat from the rabbit (for he cannot dispense with either the hat or the rabbit).

The theory of abstractions suffers another blow at the hands of Hayakawa through his recognition of the non-empirical character of mathematics.

> It must not be overlooked that our highest ratiocinative and imaginative powers are derived from the fact that symbols are independent of things symbolized, so that we are free not only to go quickly from low to extremely high levels of abstraction . . . and to manipulate symbols even when the things they stand for cannot be so manipulated . . . but we are also free to manufacture symbols at will even if they stand only for abstractions made from other abstractions and not for anything in the extensional world. Mathematicians, for example, often play with symbols that have no extensional content, just to find out what can be done with them. (p. 174)

At this point we are far from the empiricism of Chase, but Hayakawa's expressions still require a semantic clarification. What is intended by the "independence" of symbols from the things symbolized? Hayakawa returns often to the imagery of Korzybski for indicating the abstract character of semantic reactions: "the map is not the territory" (cf., for example, Chapters 2 and 10), that is, the symbol is not the thing symbolized, since it is the result of a selective nervous process. Yet "this verbal world ought to stand in relation to the extensional world as a *map* does to the *territory* it is supposed to represent." (p. 32) It appears that the "independence" of the symbol can only mean non-identity with the symbolized. The symbol remains bound, however, to an extra-symbolic entity by virtue of the relation of representing it. It is, then, a moot question as to how it is that we are able—as in mathematics—"to construct symbols at will," without any "extensional content."

It is not a sufficient explanation that "we can by abstractions make other abstractions," since according to the semantic doctrine those other abstractions ought in the last analysis to rest on the "reality"—the extensional world. The freedom of postulation is thus precluded. A recognition of the operative liberty in mathematical symbolism requires, therefore, a diligent revision of the presumed mechanics of abstraction by semantic reactions. This must be done to take account, for example, of the possibility of constructing geographical maps to ever more refined scales and of the possibility of the invention of symbolic structures which, in their context, have the status of territories.

One of the most original features of Hayakawa's presentation of general semantics is the broad phenomenological description of linguistic usages beyond the informative function, whose most adequate expression is scientific language. He insists, of course, on taking advantage of the opportunity given in the latter type of language for avoiding the confusion of "informative" sentences ("protocol" sentences) with "judgmental" sentences, that is, *"expressions of the writer's approval or disapproval of the occurrences, persons, or objects he is describing."* (p. 42) But he does not succumb to that scientistic attitude which we encounter in Chase and which expresses itself in a general disdain for the "tumult of emotions" and an attempt to dismiss as senseless anything which does not fit into the scheme for informative symbolism.

Alongside the informative function of language, Hayakawa explicitly sets forth "affective" and "directive" functions with treatments of their meanings.

> The language of science is instrumental in getting done the work necessary for life, but it does not tell us anything about what life feels like in the living. We can communicate scientific facts to each other without knowing or caring about each other's feelings; but before love, friendship, and community can be established among men so that

we *want* to cooperate and become a society, there must be, as we have seen, a flow of sympathy between one man and another. This flow of sympathy is established, of course, by means of the effective uses of language. (p. 117)

Hayakawa devotes many interesting pages to the examination of the affective significance of semantic instruments—metaphor, simile, allusion, rhythm, et cetera—which the literary arts, *"the most exact expression of feelings"* (p. 132), prize and among which poetry is *"the language of expression at its highest degree of efficiency."* Efficiency is the criterion he repeatedly proposes for assessing the validity of the affective significance of literature and of art. It is efficiency from a biological point of view, in which affective language functions as a "relaxation of the nervous tension in the organism."

Both the enjoyment and the production of poetry and literature, then, being human symbolic devices employed in the day-to-day process of maintaining adjustment and equipping ourselves for living, appear to be extensions of our adjustment mechanism beyond those provided for us by that part of our biological equipment which we have in common with lower animals. (p. 148)

From this point of view, affective language has, in a social context, a biological function directed to the survival of the species. The same can be said for the "directive" use of language, which is the attempt "to control, direct, or influence the future actions of fellow human beings with words." (p. 101) The directive and affective functions are often united, because of the hortatory and persuasive character of the latter. Simple examples of directive expressions are "Come here" and "Open the window," but under the same semantic category fall the various forms of law on which society is based, since such laws are assertions *"about future events which we are supposed, with our own efforts, to bring about"* (p. 105) and *"prac-*

tically all directive utterances say something about the future." "They are 'maps', either explicitly or by implication, of *'territories' that are to be."* (p. 103)

It becomes clear that in Hayakawa's version of general semantics we have a presentation which overcomes the narrowness and rigidity of Chase's interpretation, under which arguments in the economic and political field are vitiated, for example, by an impoverished concept of semantic "referent." Nevertheless, we observe that some parts of Hayakawa's work have not been liberated completely from certain theoretical themes of Korzybski. In particular, we refer to the biological foundation for symbolism and to the interpretation of it as an extension of the mechanism for survival. These are a direct consequence of Korzybski's conception of the neurological nature of abstraction and selection in "semantic reactions." It is not that we deny the importance of research on the relations between symbolic behavior and biological factors. The question is whether the situation is quite as simple as Korzybski pictures it. Furthermore, there seems to be a tendency to let the matter stand where Korzybski places it, conceiving it to be "scientifically certain." When he suggests that in the mechanisms of survival we discover a key which unlocks all doors, a question immediately arises: can the distinctly human forms of symbolism be demonstrated as tools for survival, or can they be shown to be illusory with respect to the organic mechanisms of the lower animals so greatly admired by Chase as "realistic"? If linguistic symbolism is purely an expression of a biological "mechanism" directed to survival, how is the very purpose of general semantics (to make "semantic reactions" "delayed" reactions) possible? Indeed, the mechanism ought to function automatically, unhampered by any "delay." We can only conclude that it is necessary to renounce the position by which symbolic processes are classified as such mechanisms.

Hayakawa's analysis of the affective and directive functions of language rests on the prejudicial generalization about the biological functioning of symbolism. In interpreting the language of art as affective and in placing it thus in dependence upon the biological transaction of the "relaxing of nervous tension," we have a point of view in which it becomes very difficult to distinguish the immediate and violent expressions of the animal state from artistic expressions. It becomes even more difficult to understand the character of theoretical detachment which a careful phenomenological analysis finds in artistic creation or in esthetic delight. Similarly, in the analysis of directive language, the characterization of it as a map for a territory which is to be realized in the future reflects the exclusive attention directed to those types of prescriptions which aim at the realization of the conditions for survival. It is very hard to see how we can insert into Hayakawa's interpretation of directive language "moral" prescriptions, which are not maps for territories which are to be, but maps for territories which ought to be, without any temporal restrictions and without any reference to effective existence, present, past, or future. The most singular thing is that Hayakawa, at the end of his book, gives this judgment: "that widespread intraspecific co-operation through the use of language is the fundamental mechanism of human survival" is "an ethical judgment on which the argument has been based throughout." (p. 307) If that is an "ethical" judgment—and therefore not a map for a future territory, since otherwise it would be a scientific prediction—then it does not seem to fall under any of the linguistic uses proposed by Hayakawa.

In concluding this rapid survey of some of the themes and of the development of general semantics, I wish to make it clear that the discussion is a frank confession of my recognition of the importance of a clarification of linguistic problems. My own critical motives against the semanticist's theses are inspired by the same requirement of knowledge in the use of language as we find expressed in those theses. I must contend, however, that such knowledge can better be achieved by a greater phenomenological fidelity to the actual forms of linguistic symbolism and by a greater vigilance against the temptation to adopt a unilateral scheme of interpretation.